I0709743

ABOUT HOXTON MINI PRESS

Hello. Hoxton Mini Press is a small publisher from east London. We want to bring unusual photography to a wide audience; arty books should be beautiful (but they needn't be big or expensive). Books are no longer just about information. They are objects in their own right: things to collect and own and inspire. Thank you for supporting us.

www.hoxtonminipress.com

PHOTOGRAPHS 1900–1980

A VERY VINTAGE
CHRISTMAS

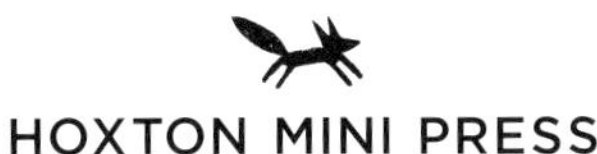

HOXTON MINI PRESS

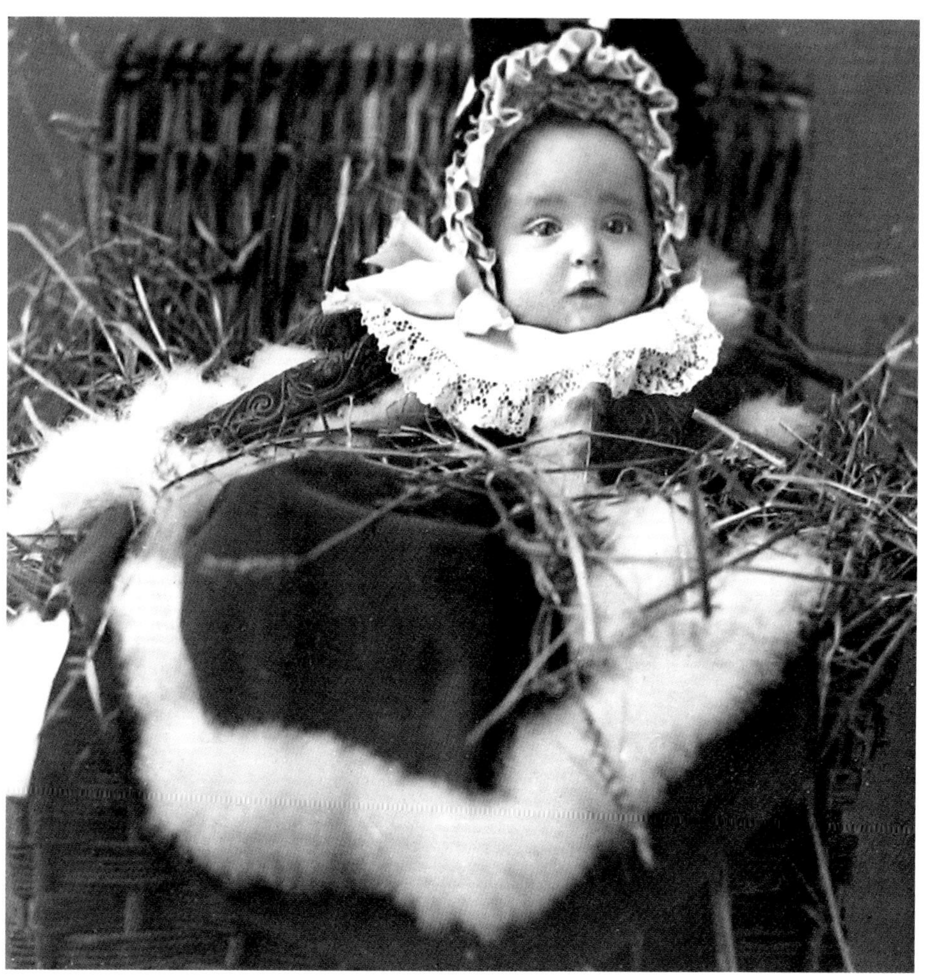

INTRODUCTION

Cut-paper snowflakes, icicles glinting in the eaves, the smell of woodsmoke on a freezing morning – what is Christmas but a collection of memories, strung together lovingly from year to year?

'Tis the season for French hens and five gold rings, for tinsel halos and no room at the inn, for walnuts and marzipan, mince pies and 'Little Donkey', for *Home Alone* ('Kevin, you're such a disease') and the sticky, dusty bottles at the back of the drinks cabinet.

You do it this way because, a long time ago, someone did it that way for you. You add your own flourishes and refinements, of course, but the day's sacred breviary – from Stockings to Tree Presents, Feasting and Charades – remains solidly the same; a ritual that is as reassuring as a warm bath or a favourite pair of pyjamas. It's constancy in a world that, on every other day of the year, spins obstinately and disinterestedly on.

Christmas changes its shape as you get older, though. For children, it's defined by anticipation: the lists and advent calendars, the shop windows, the glitter and the paper chains. It's marked by the arrival of Santa Claus, and the whisky he will toss back as he and his reindeer pass through. Later in life come office parties and the last posting days, the end of the Sellotape and not enough room in the fridge. Those precious, butter-stained recipes in a grandparent's handwriting that you dig out from the drawer, carols are sung that resemble silk unspooling in the cathedral dark – the words to which you still remember, despite forgetting where you hid the contents of child two's stocking.

But though the demented excitement of the

season wore off long ago, we never really lose the sense that Christmas is somehow magic. There's a mysterious, folklorish side to midwinter, a time when flying snowmen and nutcrackers come to life and a trio of spirits impels an old man's redemption.

Some of that feeling might be in our pagan bones – Christmas comes within days of the winter solstice, after all, when the Earth begins its slow tilt towards the light. Both festivals offer a spark of warmth and welcome in the deep midwinter, gladness in the bruising cold.

Christmas became especially precious in the Victorian age, when the pleasures and virtues of home, hearth and family became a major theme. Advancements in technology and industry ushered in mass-produced toys, decorations and cards – plus a new, wealthy middle class eager to buy them.

Stories and pictures were key to nourishing Christmas traditions. Pretty illustrated gift books with contributions from the likes of Mary Shelley and Charles Dickens that were published each December; sentimental engravings in *The Illustrated London News*; and photographs of course: the moment the handheld box camera came to market in 1888 it was co-opted to the Christmas cause and has been a staple ever since.

Some of these photos remind us of that time, a long-gone era of blur and blinks, of sailor collars and breeches, of smoking indoors, shampoo and sets and the curly parsley garnish. Even so, their rubric is timeless: the tumble of family, the oiled turkey centrepiece, the hands clutching new cowboy hats and holsters, train sets and dolls under the tree. Christmas, say these pictures, is not meant to be tasteful; it's meant to be merry and bright. So, deck the halls, drink the Baileys – it's what the angel Gabriel would have wanted.

Lucy Davies
London, 2024

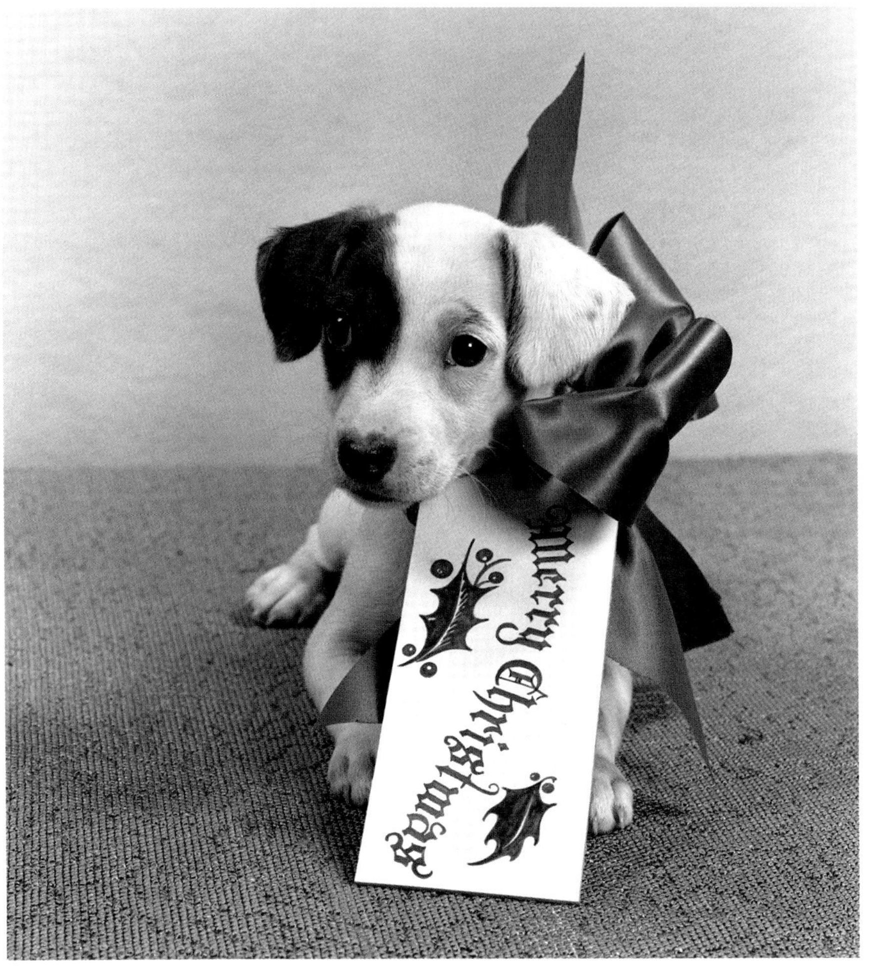
Merry Christmas

Carrying a Christmas tree home,
Funäsdalen, Sweden, 1950s

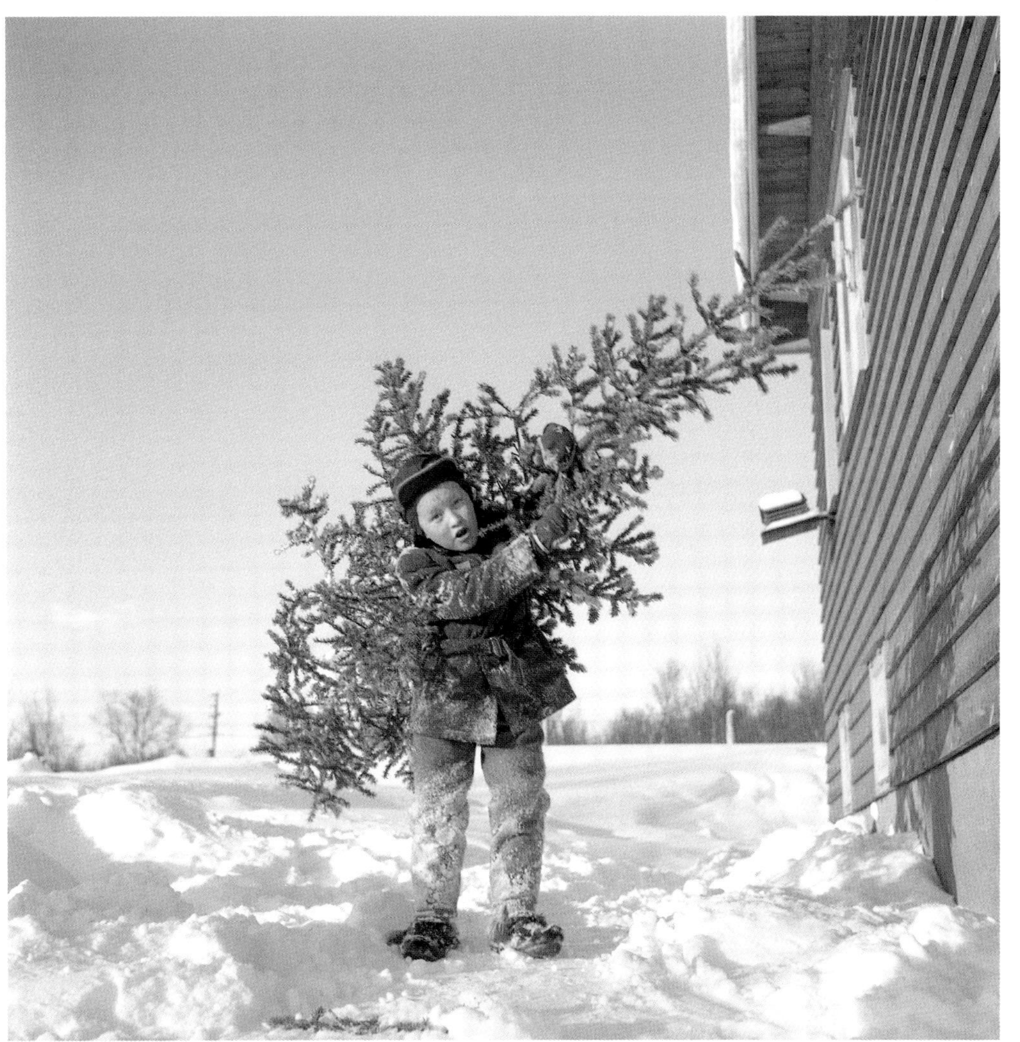

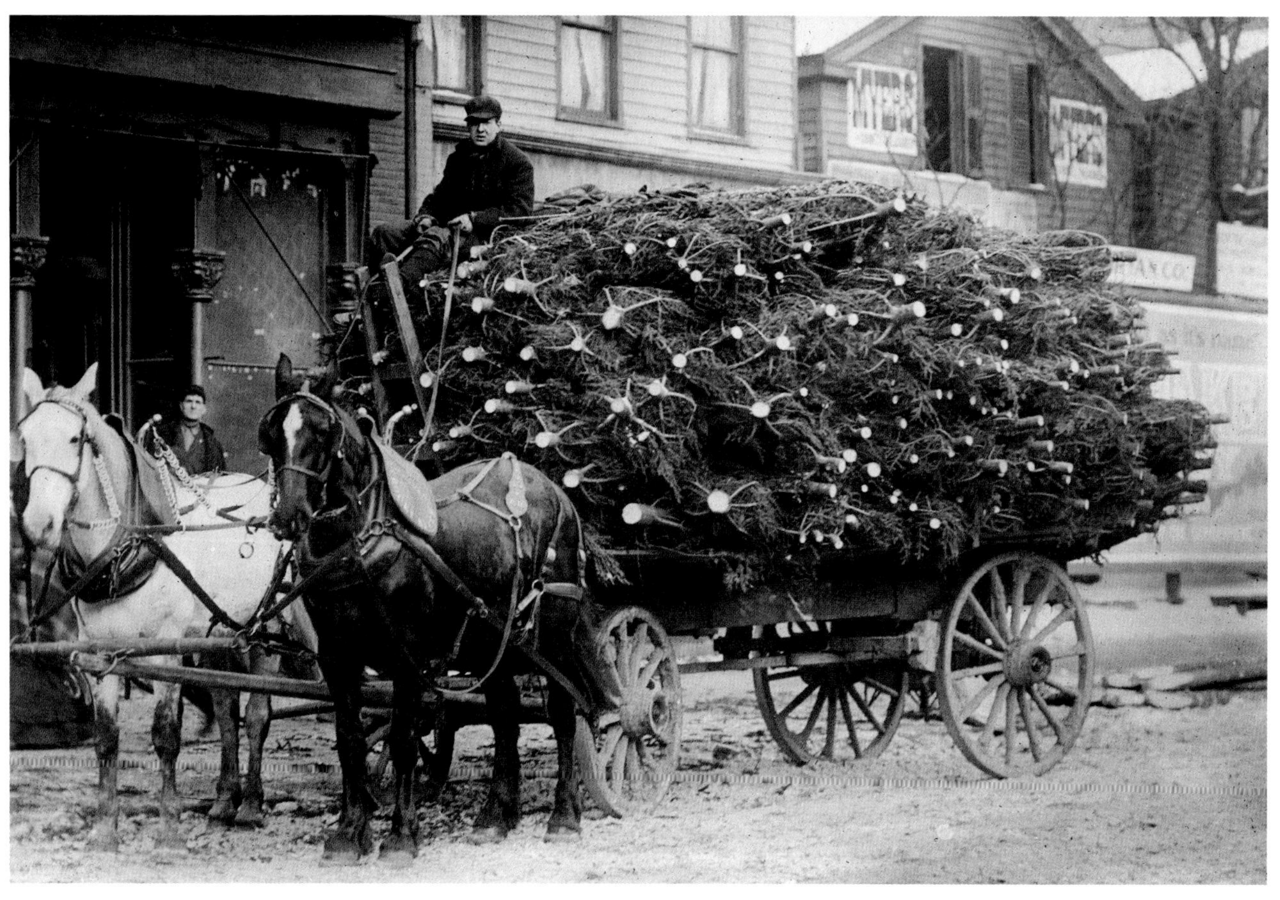

Laden with Christmas trees,
New York, New York, USA, 1910s

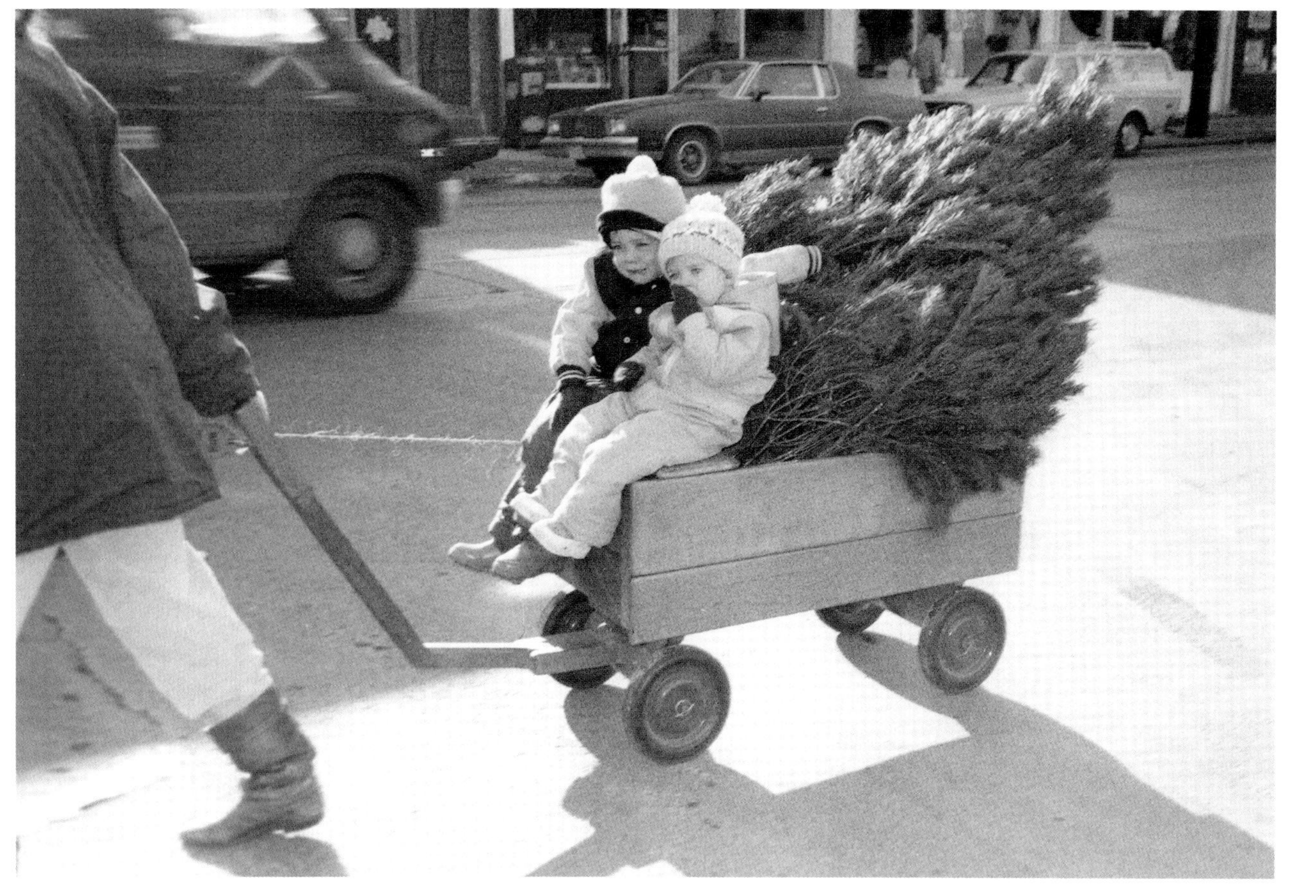

Picking up the tree on Christmas morning,
Canada, 1986

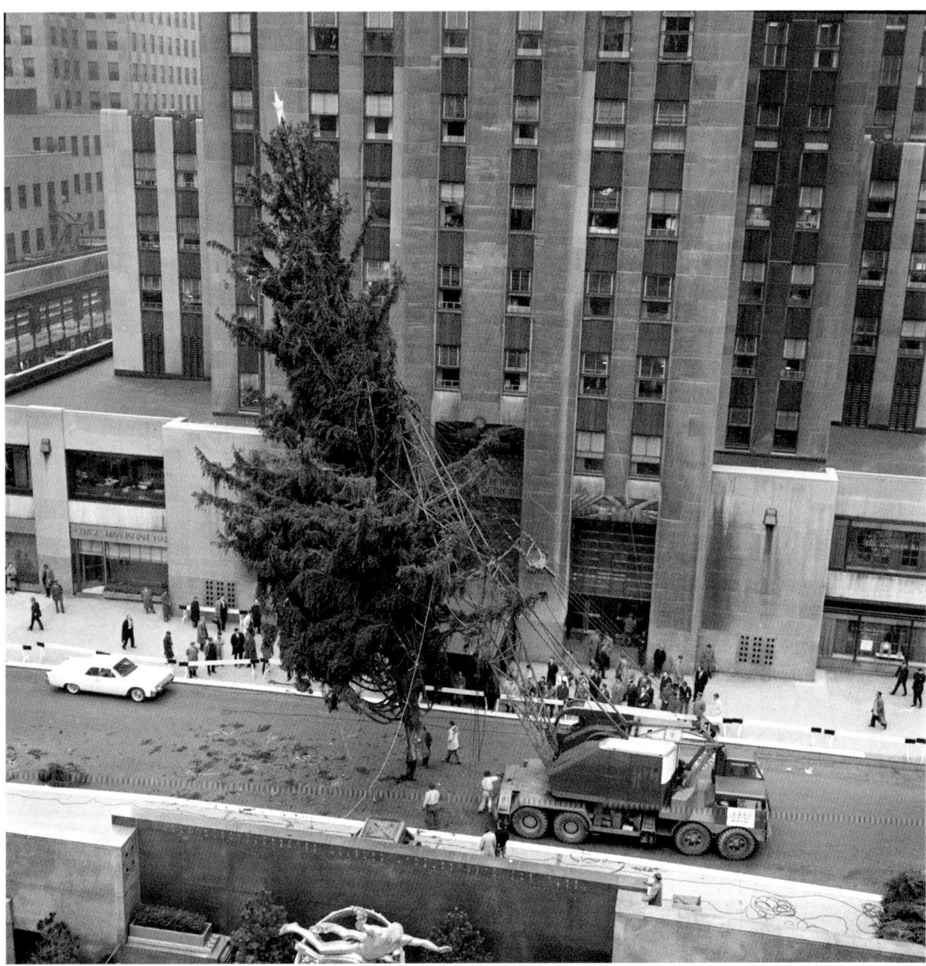

An 85-foot Norway spruce at Rockefeller Center Plaza,
New York, New York, USA, 1961

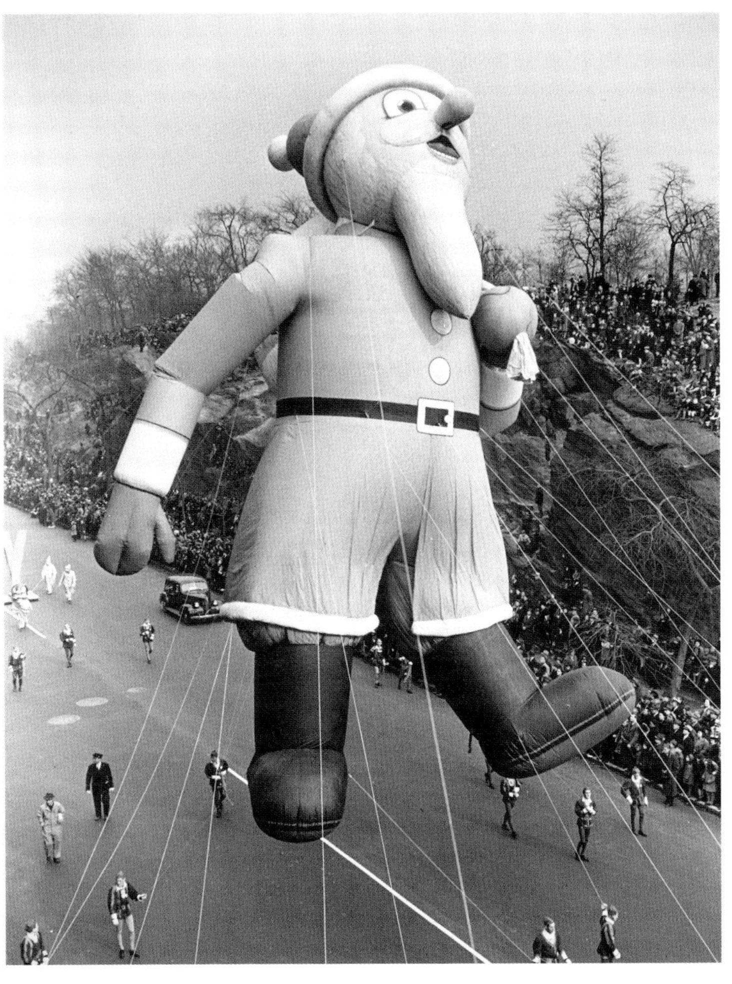

The Santa float at the Macy's Thanksgiving Day Parade,
New York, New York, USA, 1971

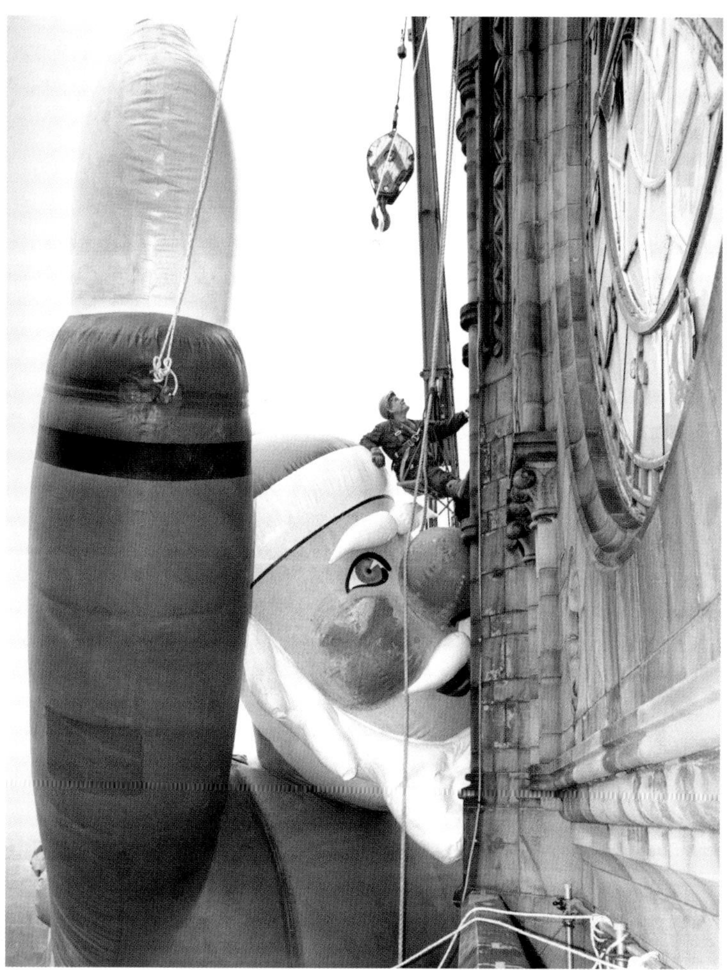

Inflatable Santa at Town Hall,
Manchester, UK

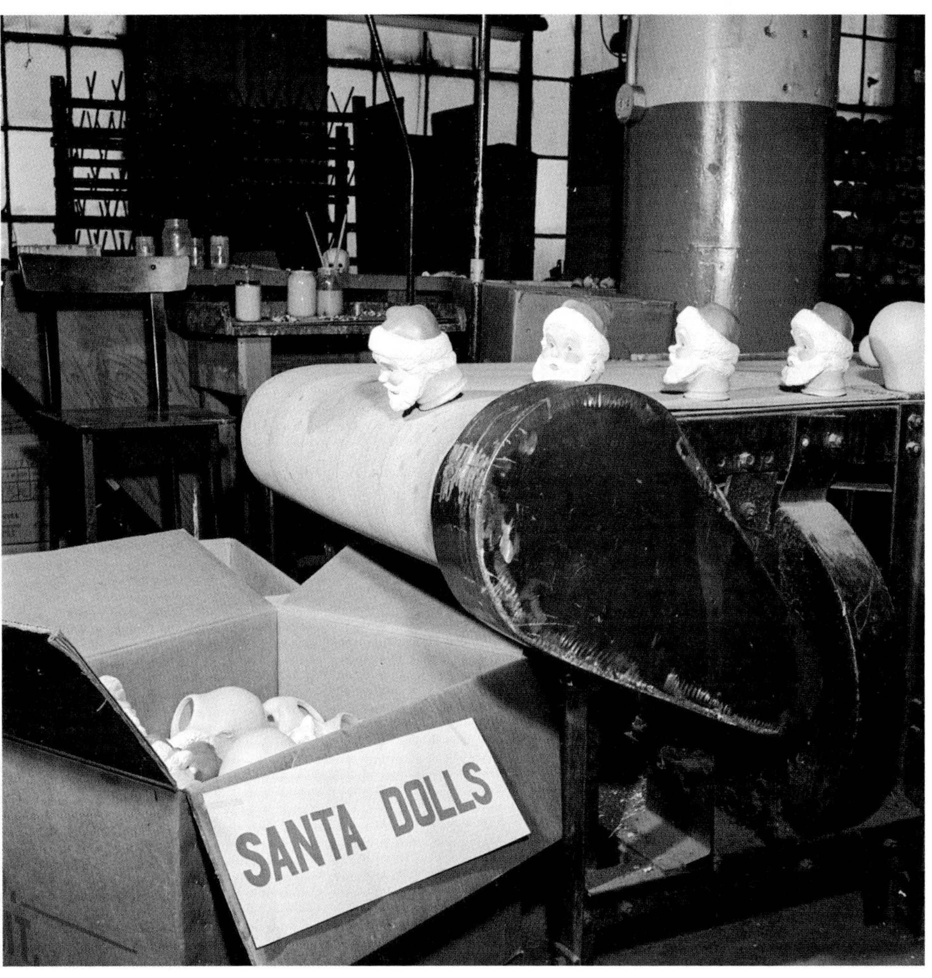

Santa Claus doll heads on the conveyor belt at
Ideal Toy Corporation, Hollis, New York, USA, 1955

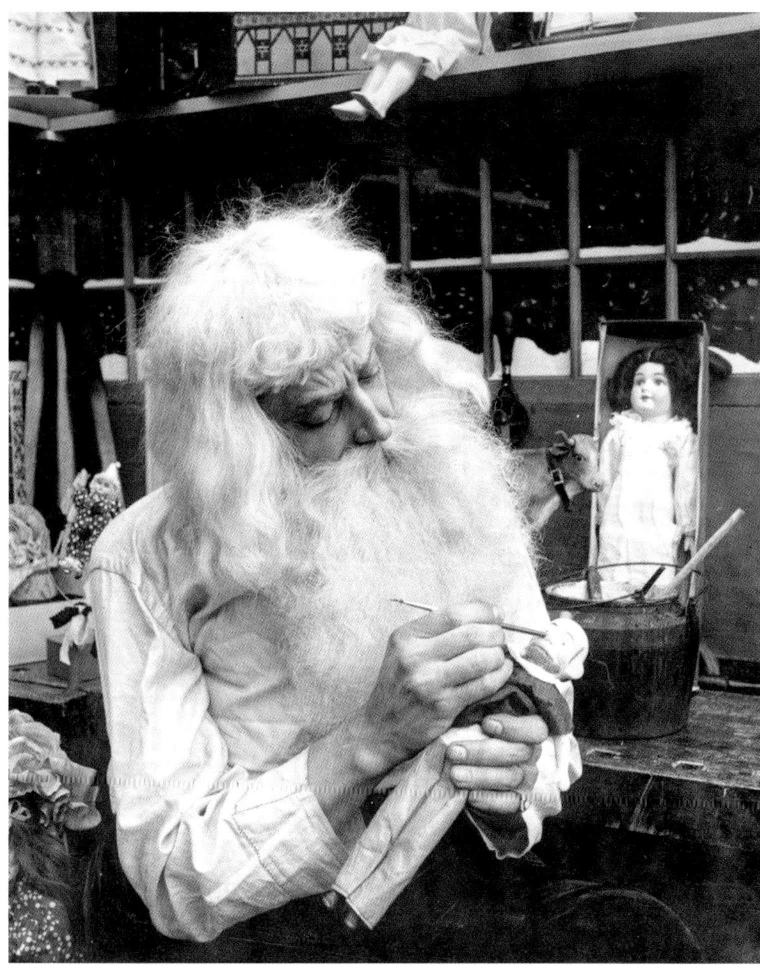

Santa Claus at work,
USA, 1970

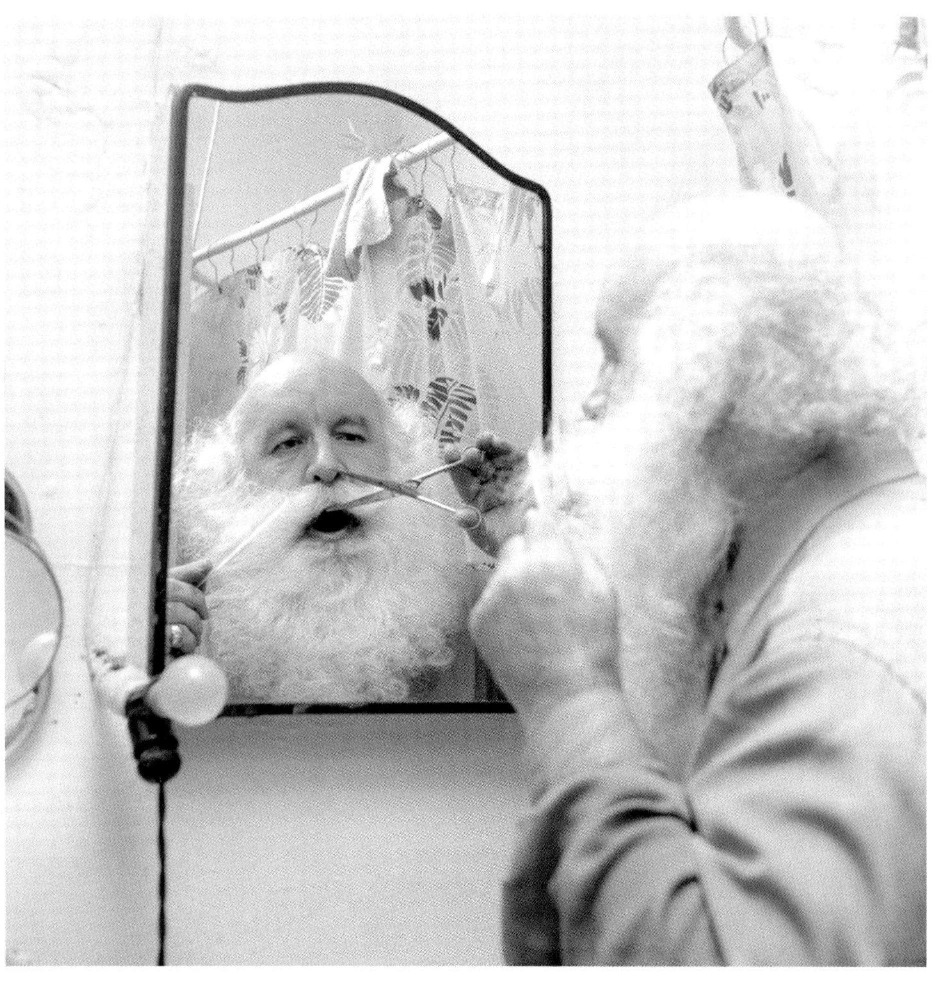

Famous Santa impersonator Lucky Squire tidies his beard as
the Christmas season begins, New York, New York, USA, 1955

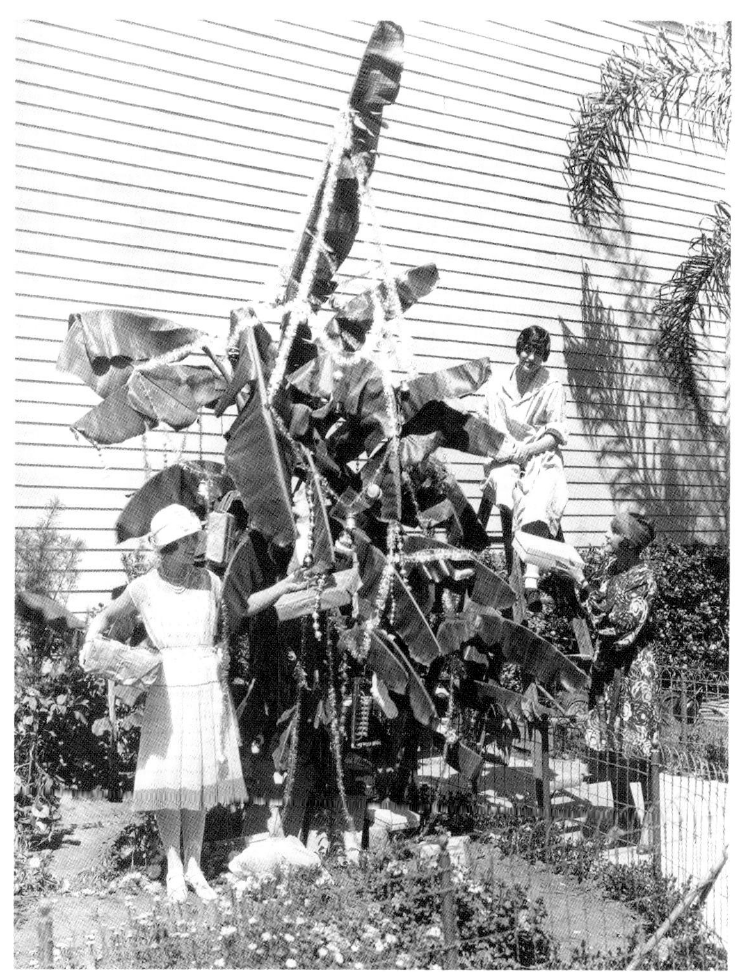

Three women decorate a banana tree
for Christmas, 1940s

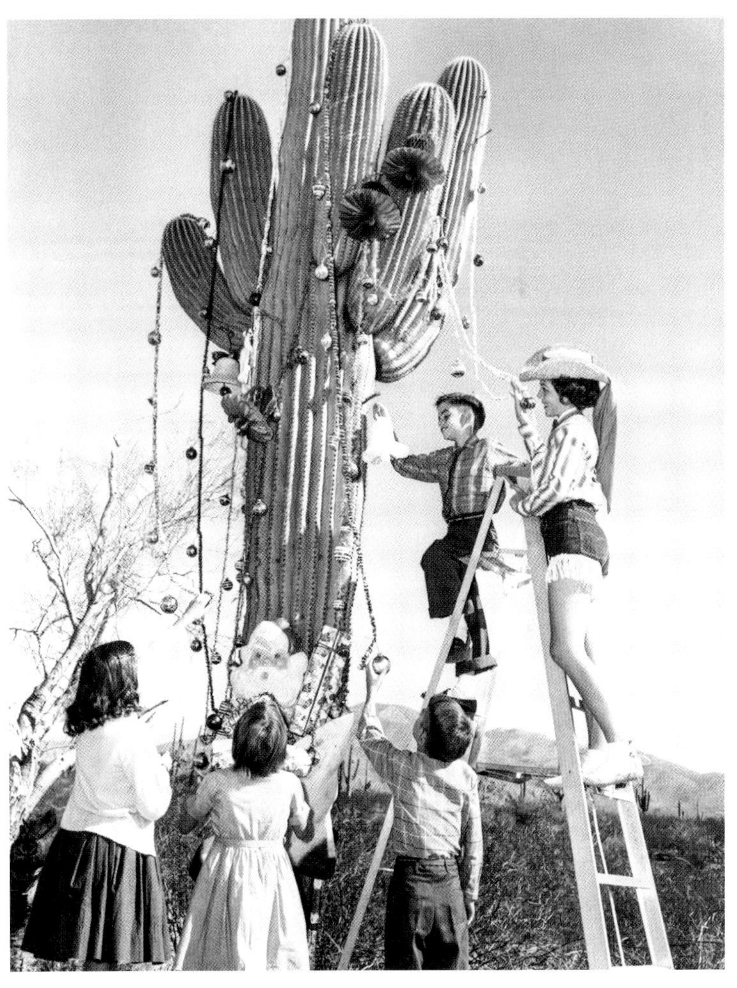

Children decorate a towering saguaro
Christmas cactus, Tucson, Arizona, USA, 1959

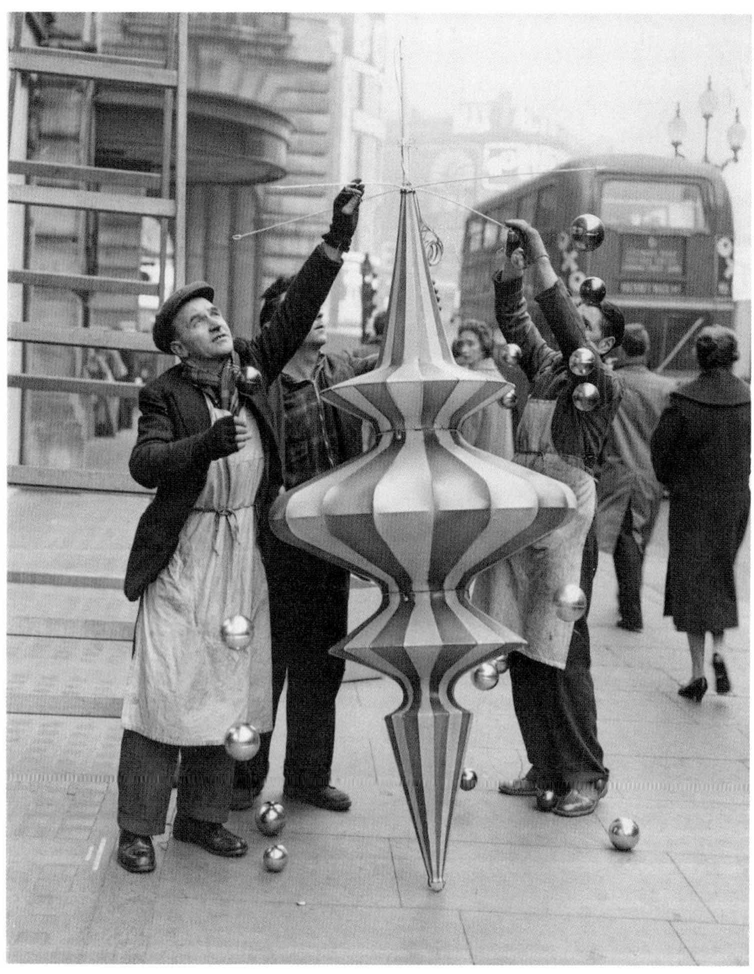

Preparing seven-foot Christmas decorations
for Regent Street, London, UK, 1956

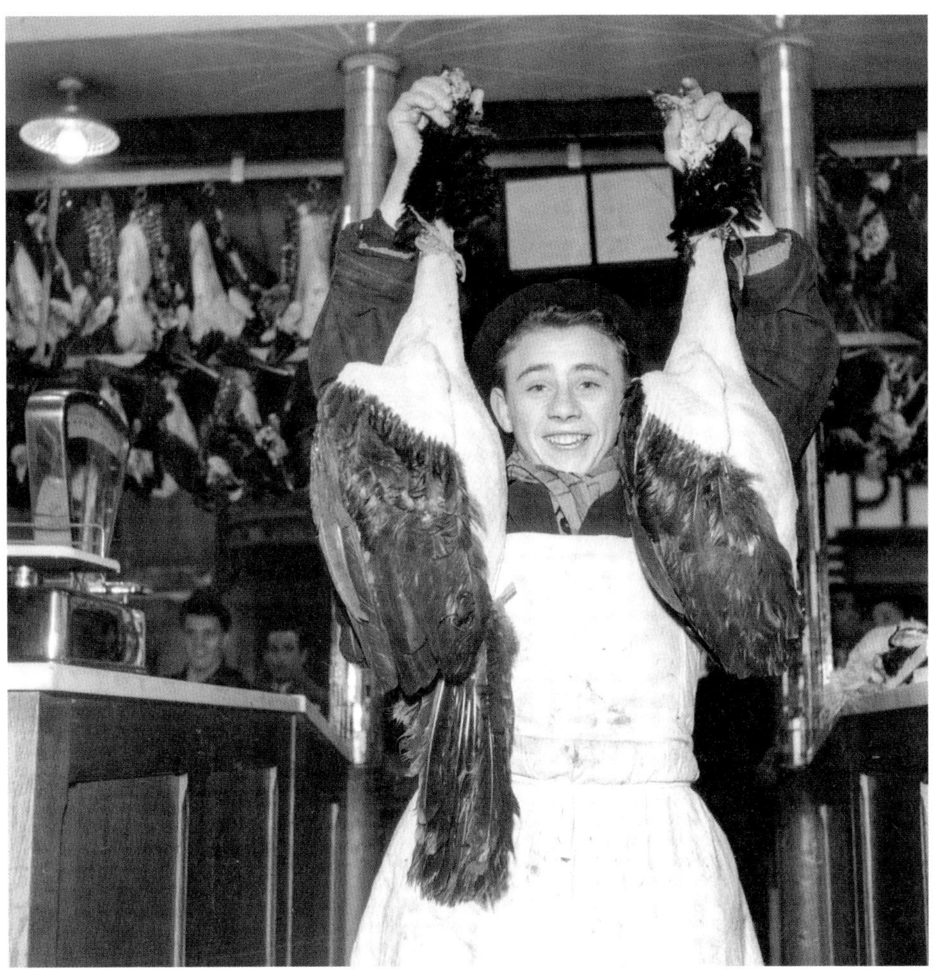

Proudly displaying the
Christmas turkeys, 1954

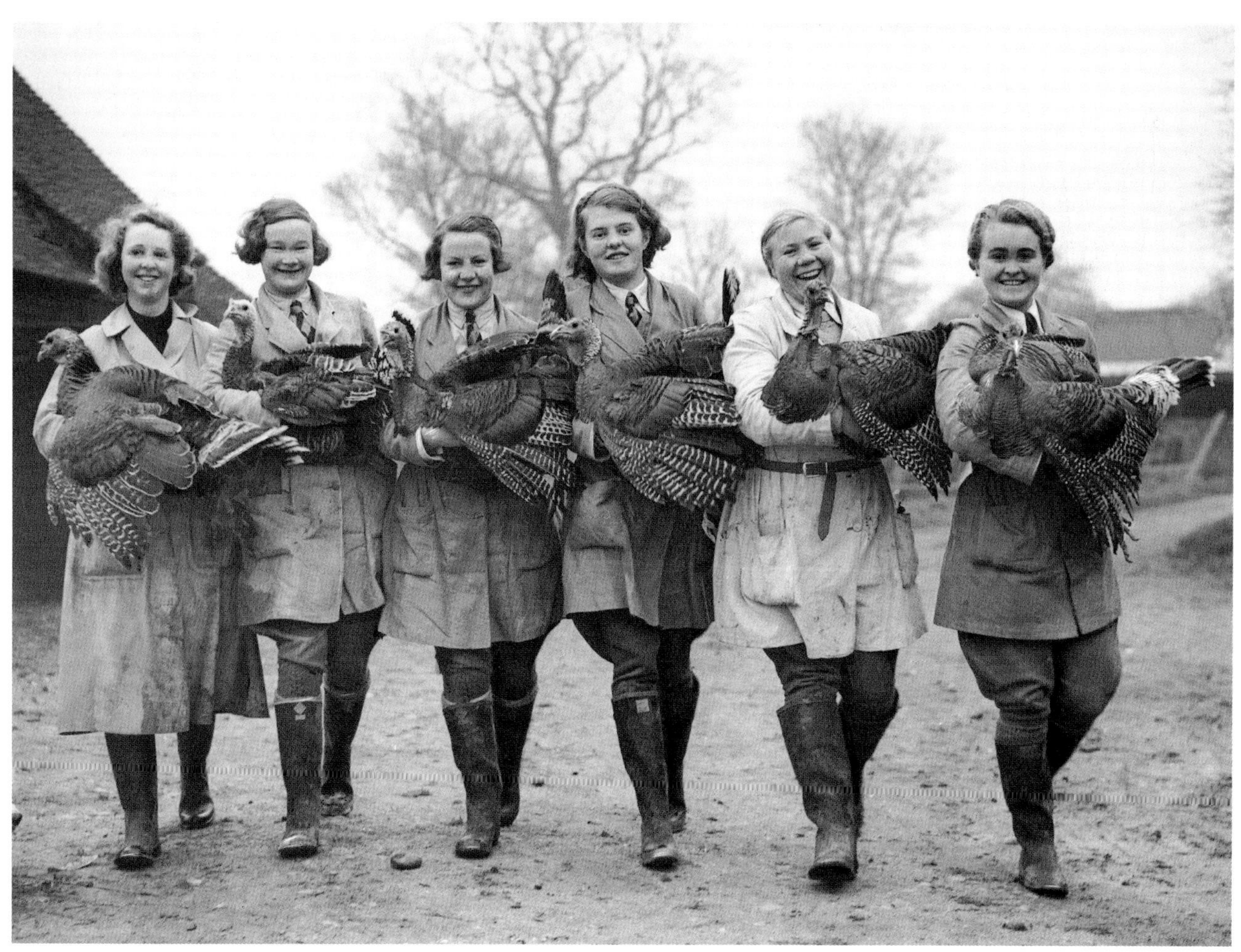

Turkeys for Christmas dinner at
Harrison Bell's farm in Welwyn, UK, 1930s

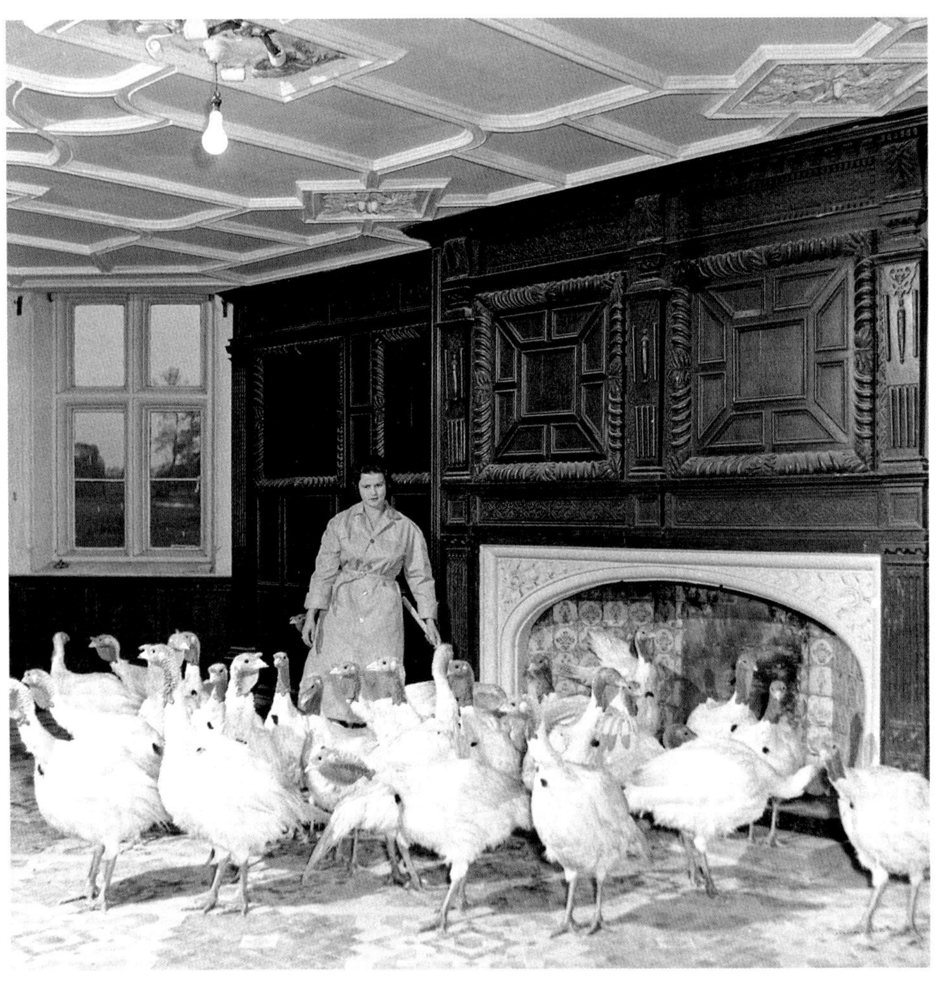

A group of turkeys inside the vacant front room
of a mansion at a Norfolk Turkey farm, 1955

Christmas preparations,
Paris, France, 1951

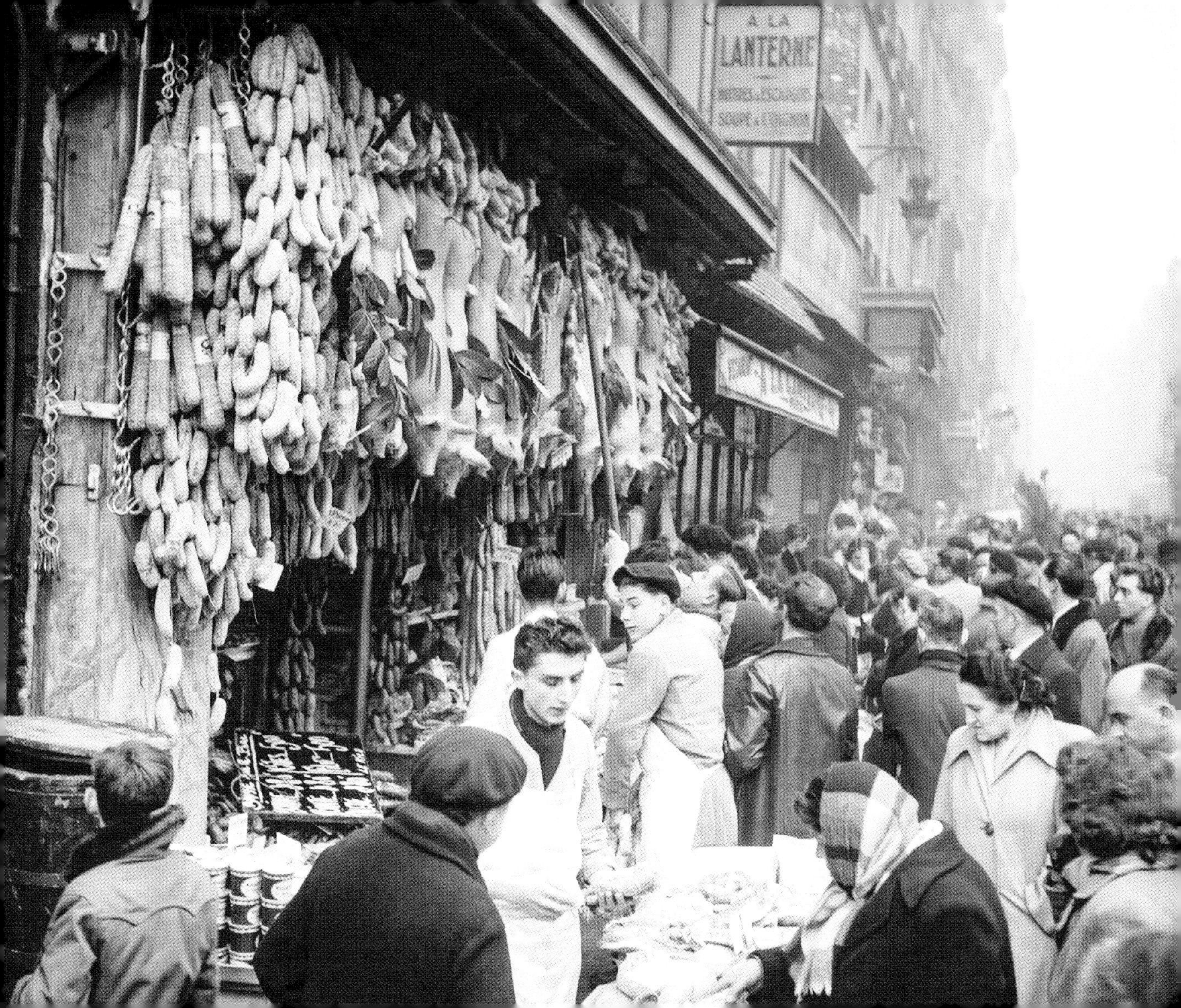

A LA
LANTERNE
HUITRES & ESCARGOTS
SOUPE A L'OIGNON

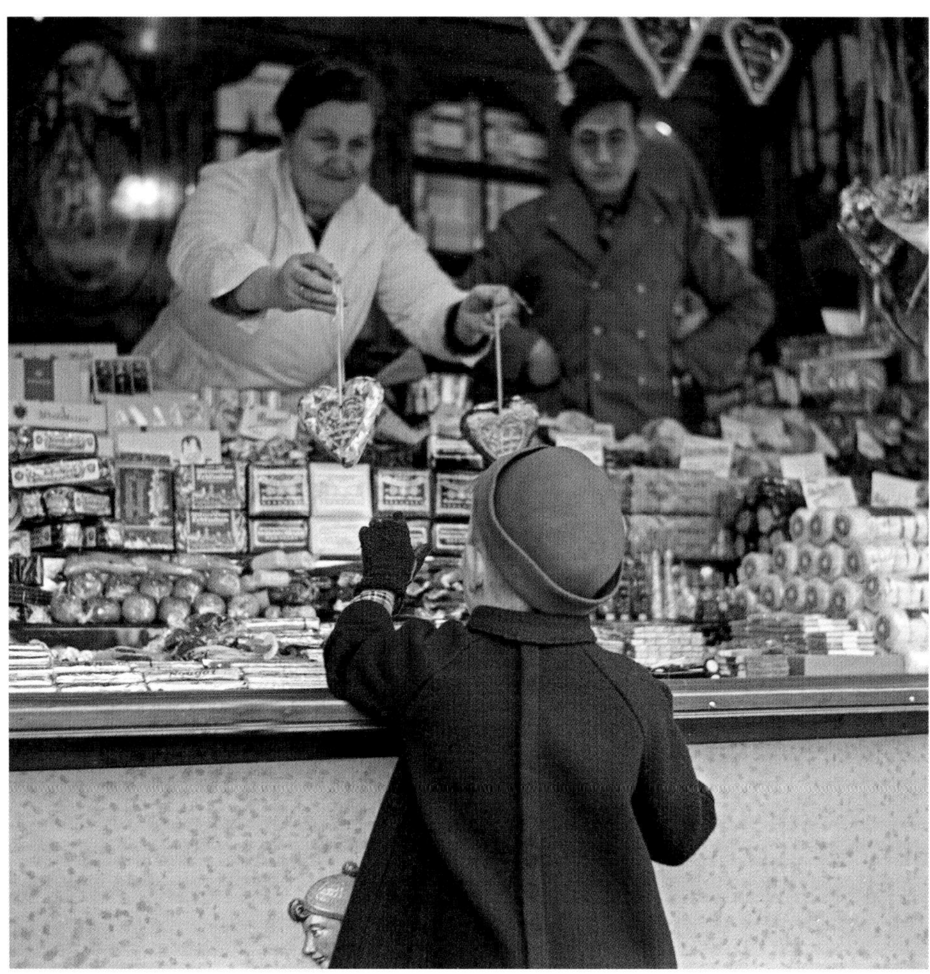

Christmas sweets,
Germany, 1930s

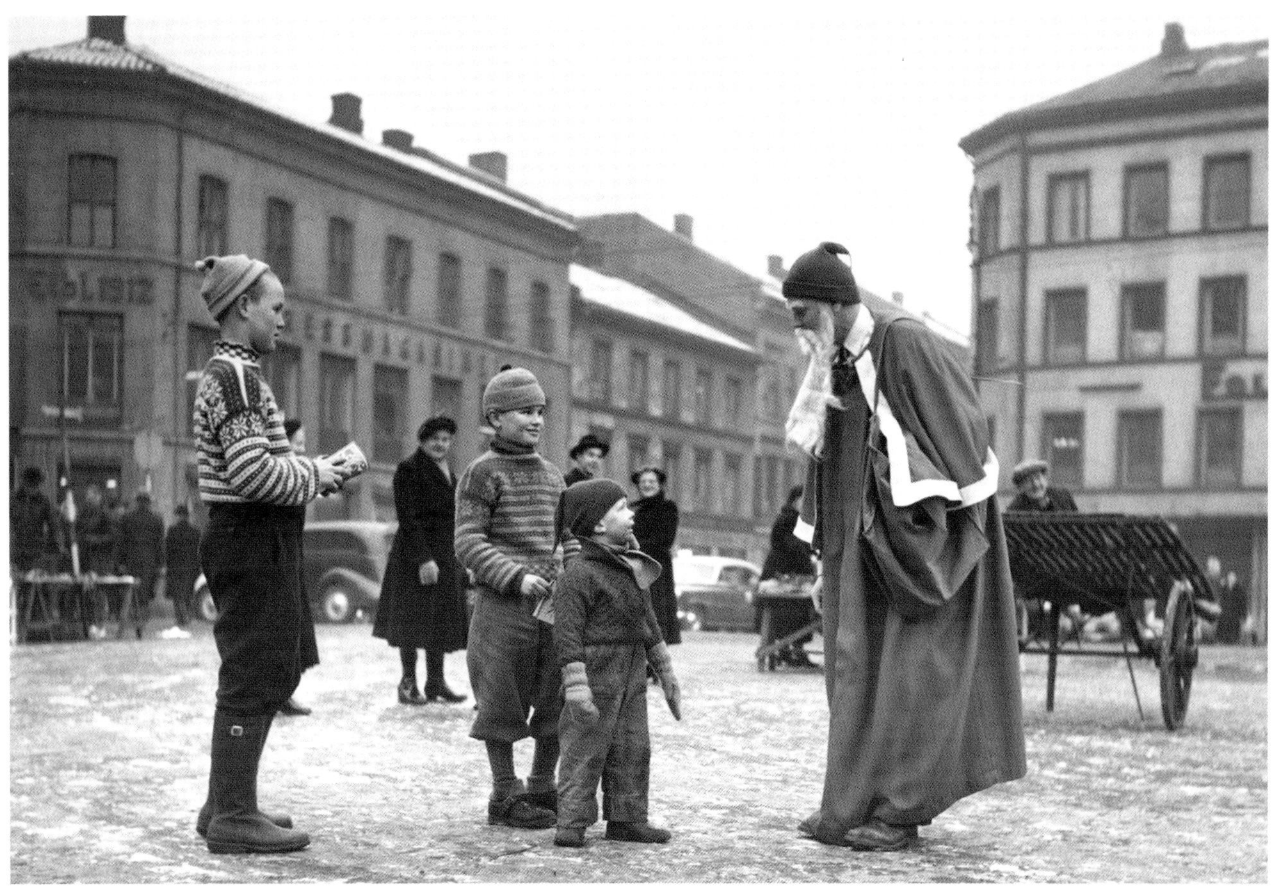

Meeting Santa Claus,
Oslo, Norway, 1954

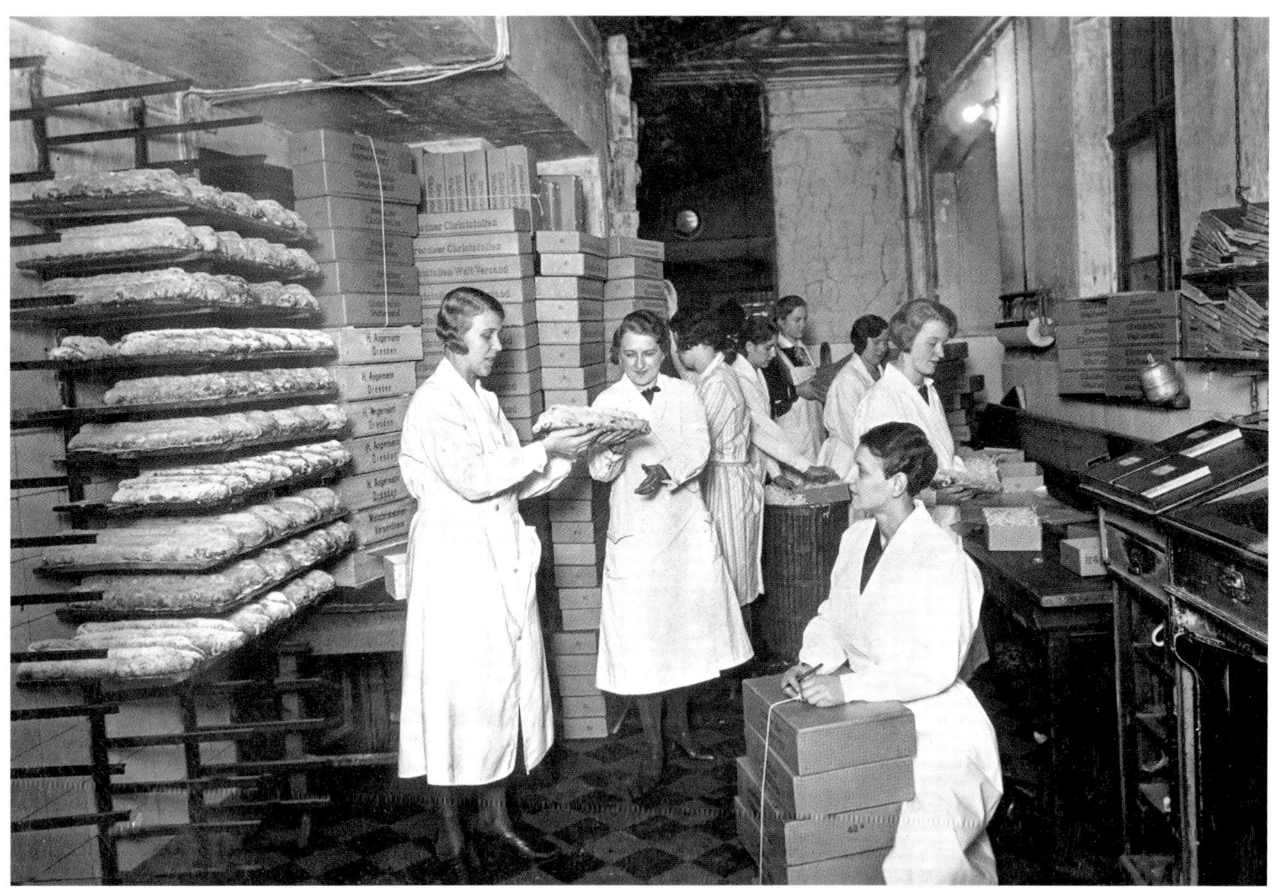

Wrapping Christstollen loaves,
Dresden, Germany, 1928

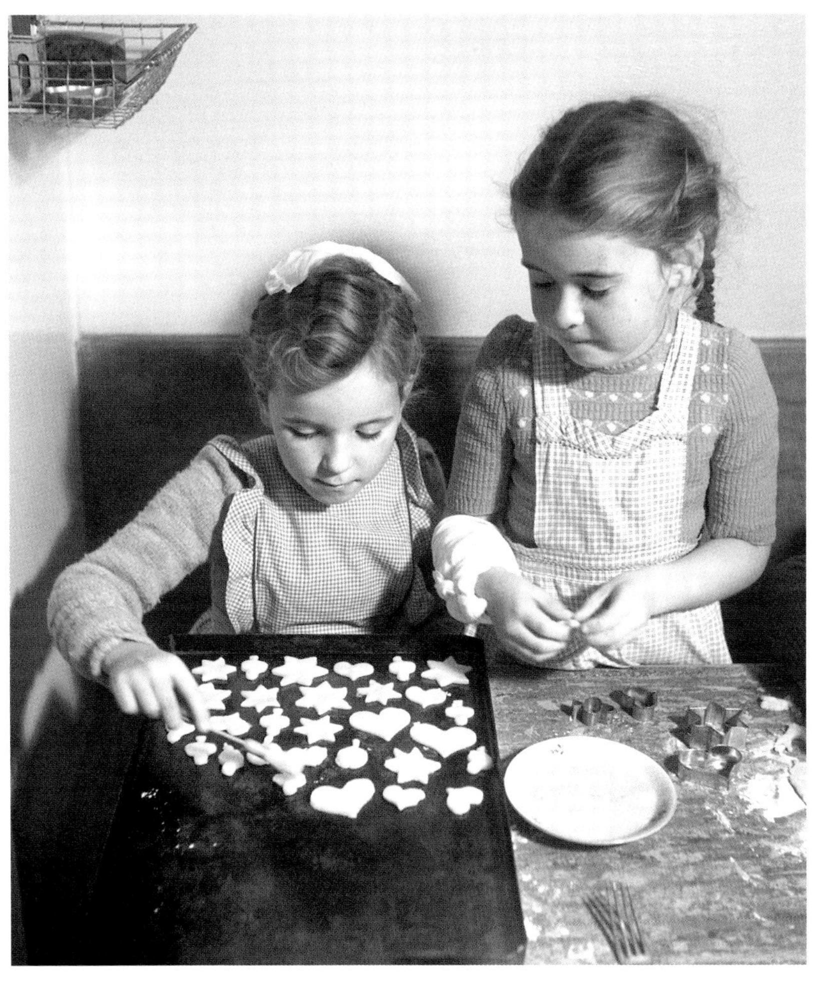

Baking Christmas biscuits,
Switzerland, 1950

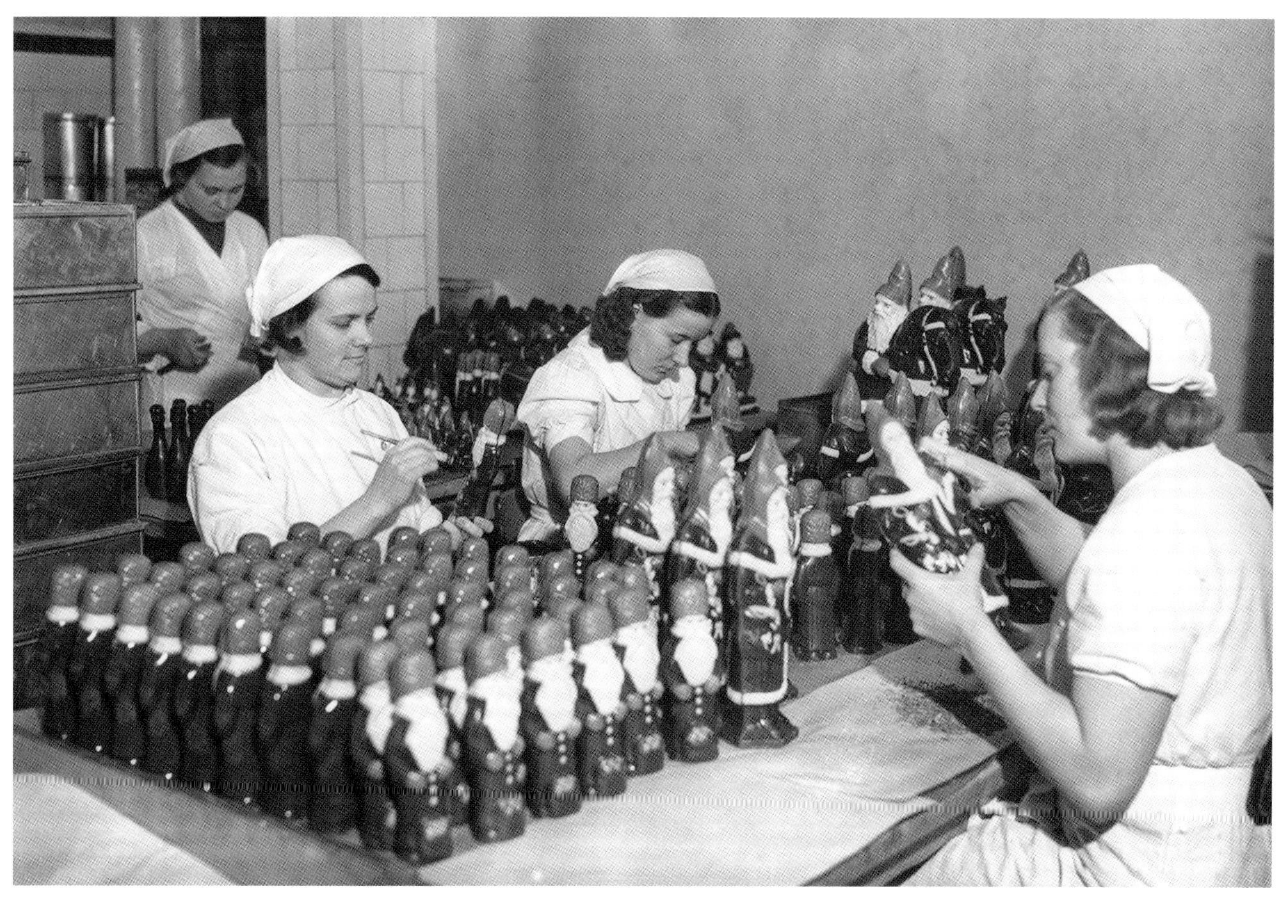

Employees at Cloetta, a pioneer in industrial
chocolate production, Sweden, 1940s

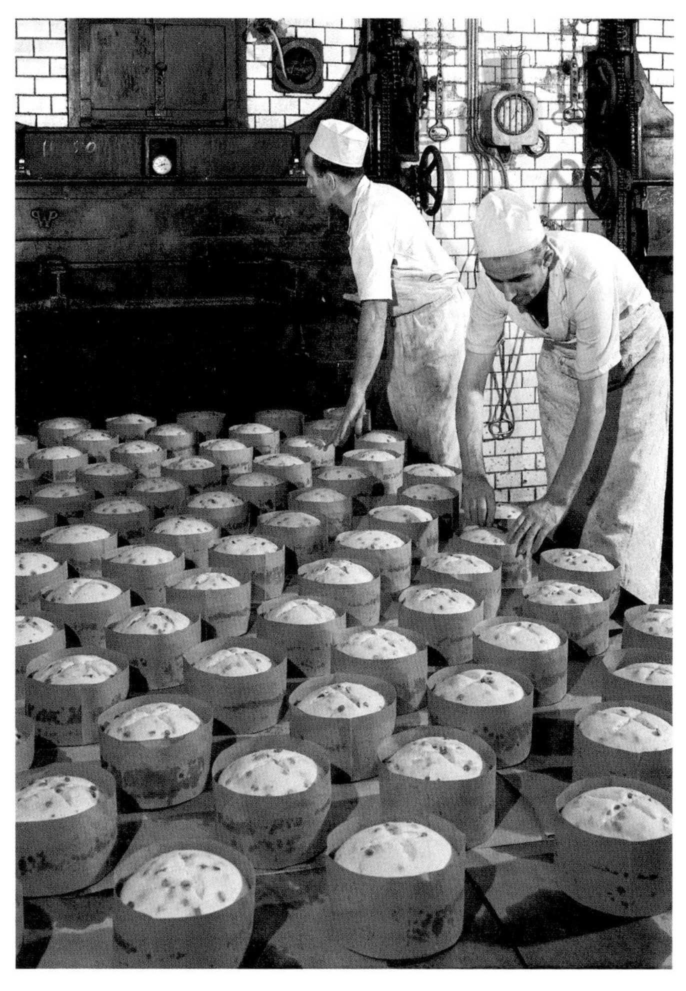

Panettones lined up and ready for baking
at the Motta factory, Milan, Italy, 1950

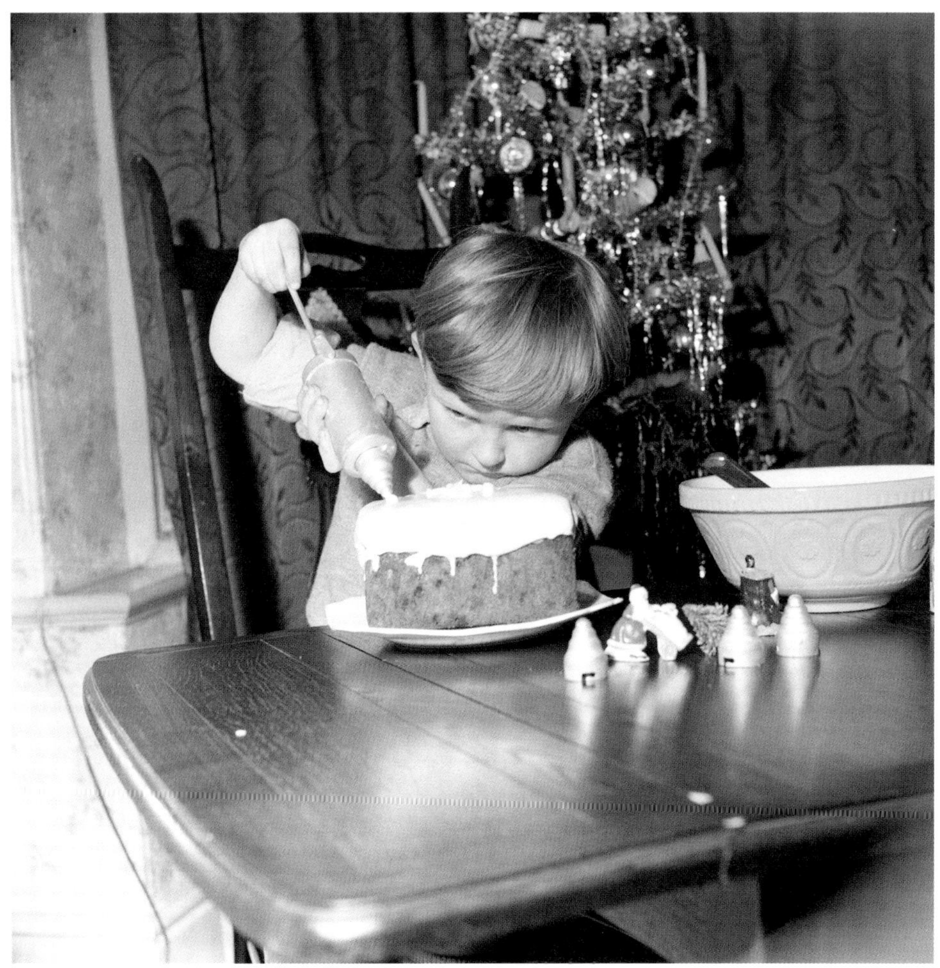

A five-year-old boy carefully icing a
Christmas cake, Manchester, UK, 1954

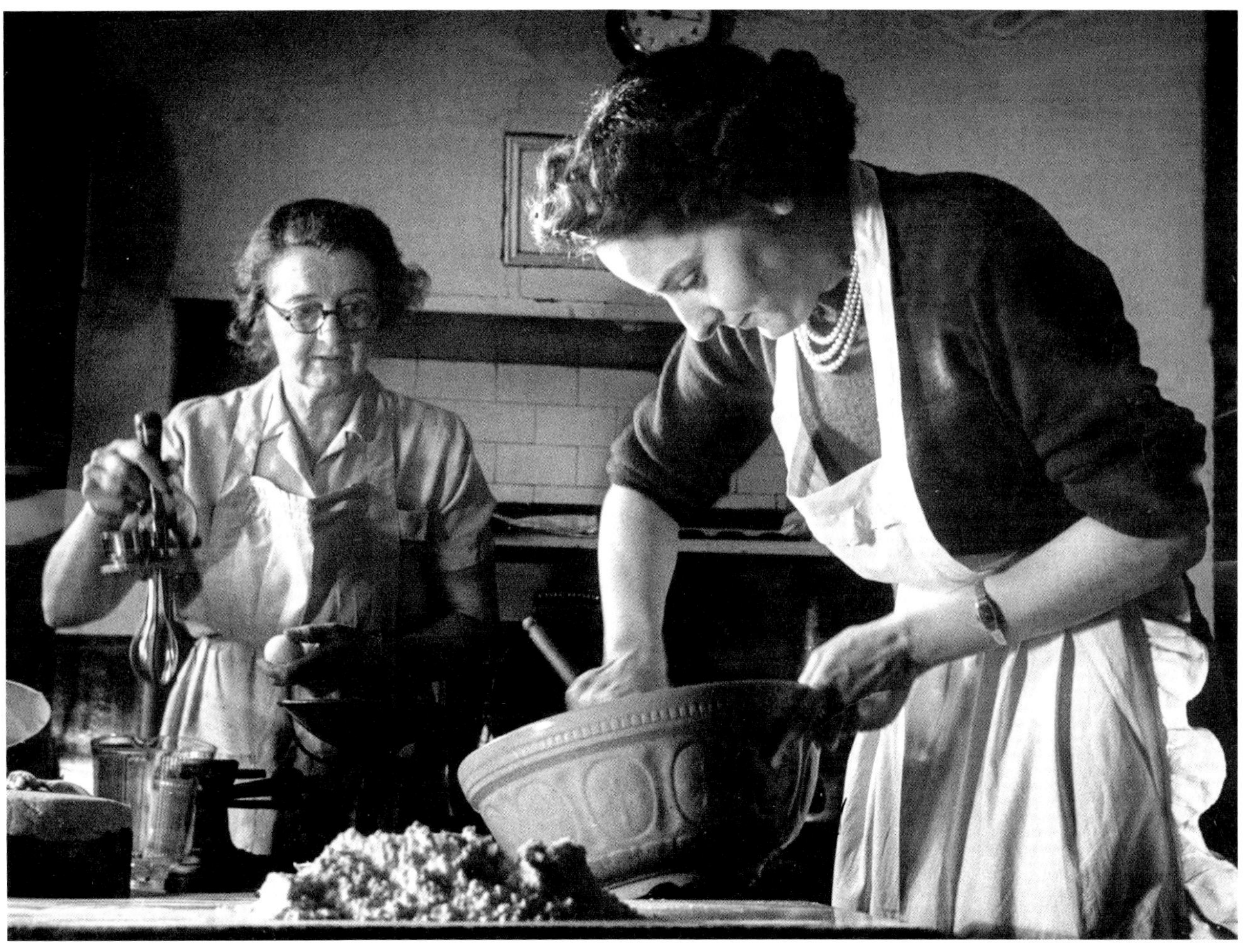

An expert cook instructing a young housewife
on preparing Christmas dinner, UK, 1951

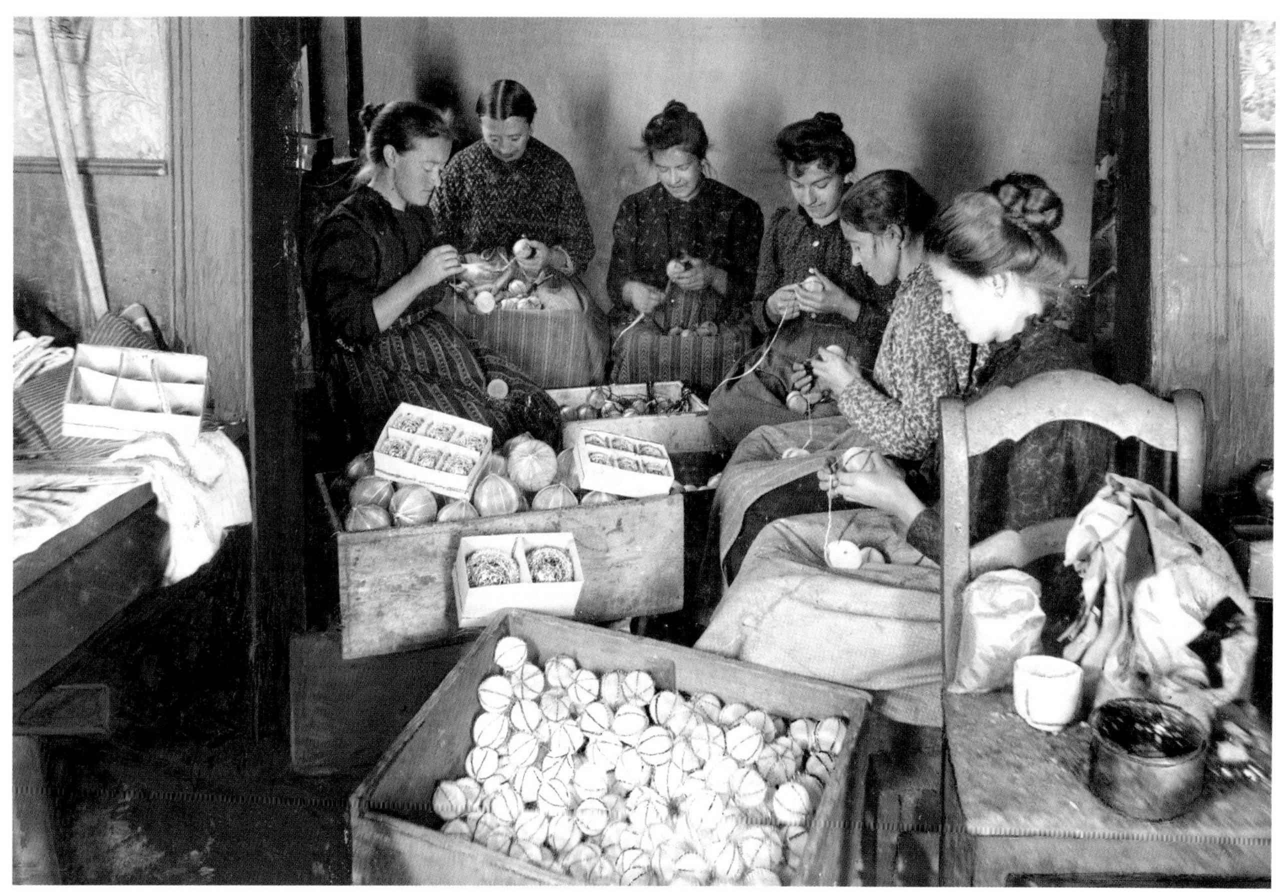

Workers adorn Christmas baubles with gold
thread and spun glass, Germany, 1890s

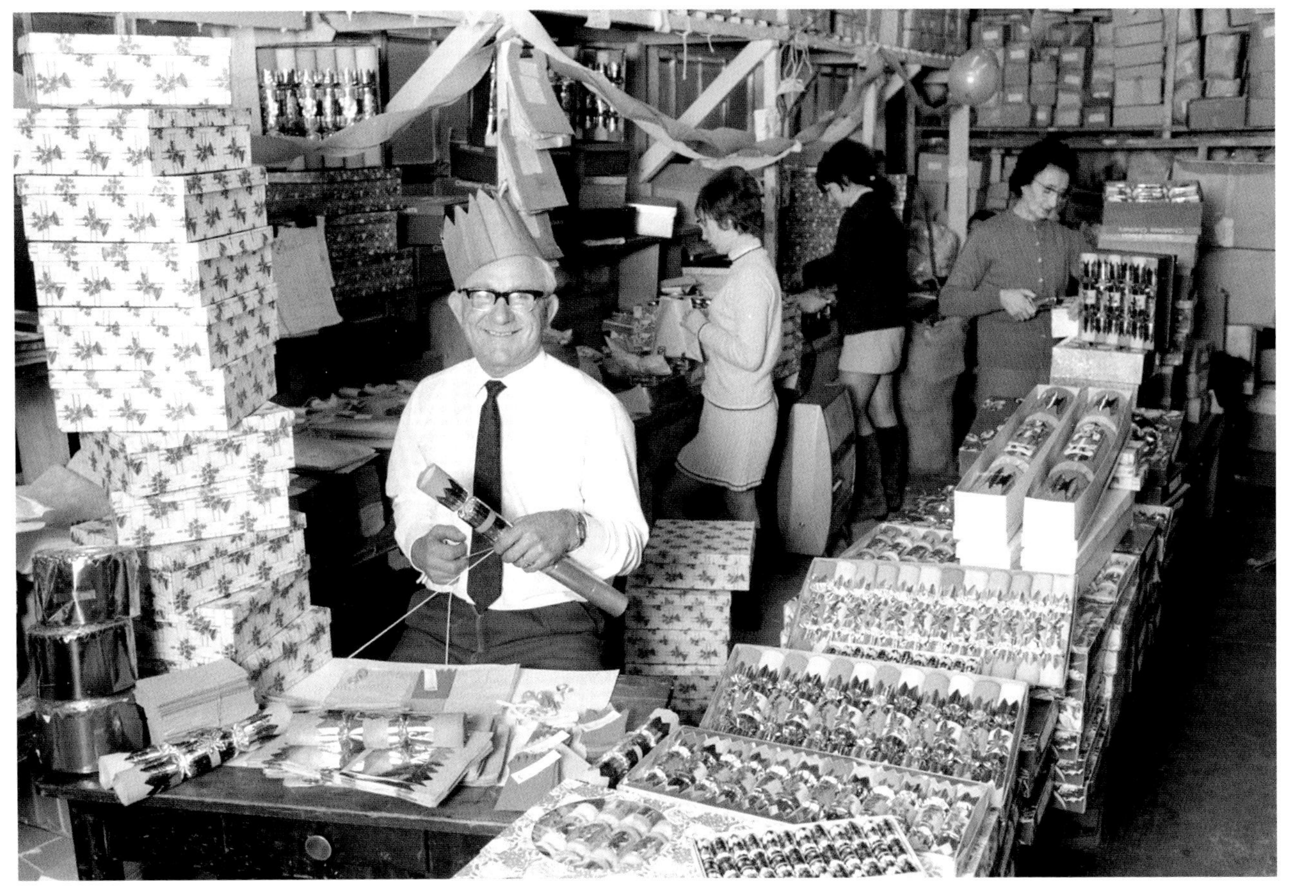

Workers at Napier Novelty Company producing boxes
of Christmas crackers, Rickmansworth, UK, 1969

Selling Christmas crackers at Caledonian Market,
Islington, London, UK, 1936

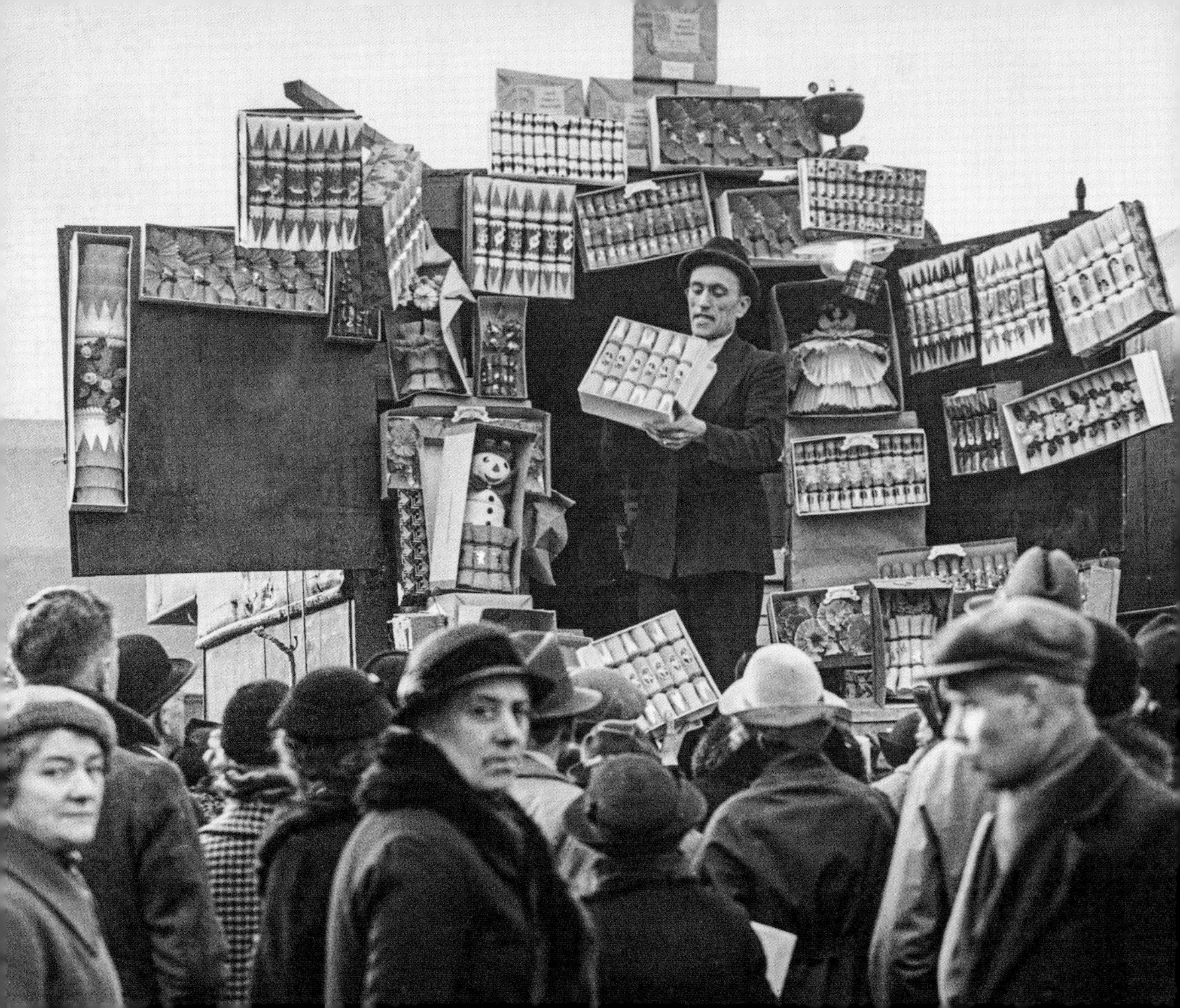

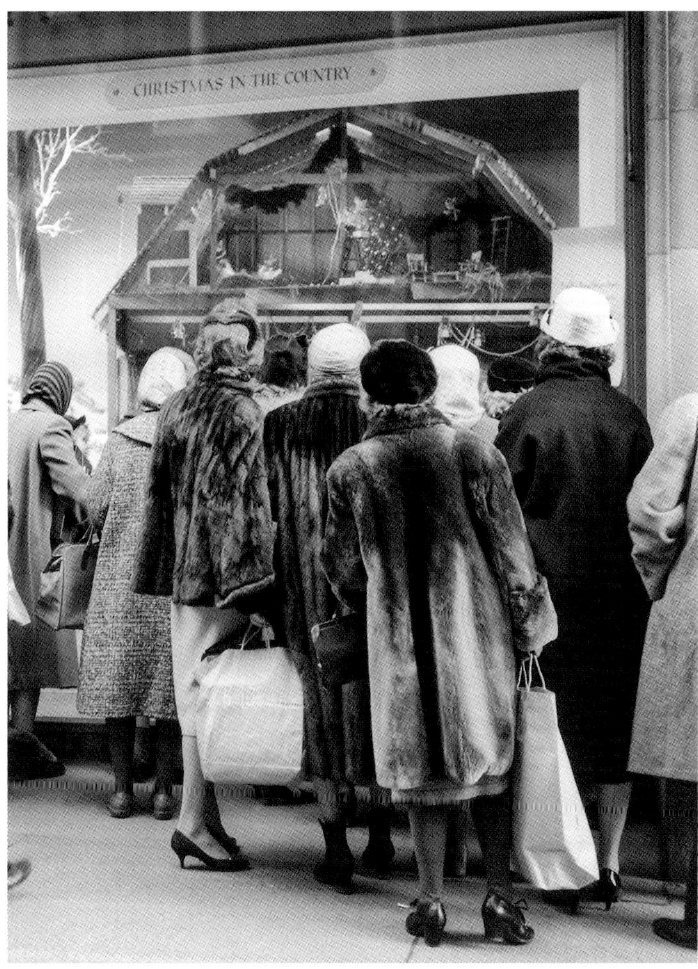

Christmas window shopping

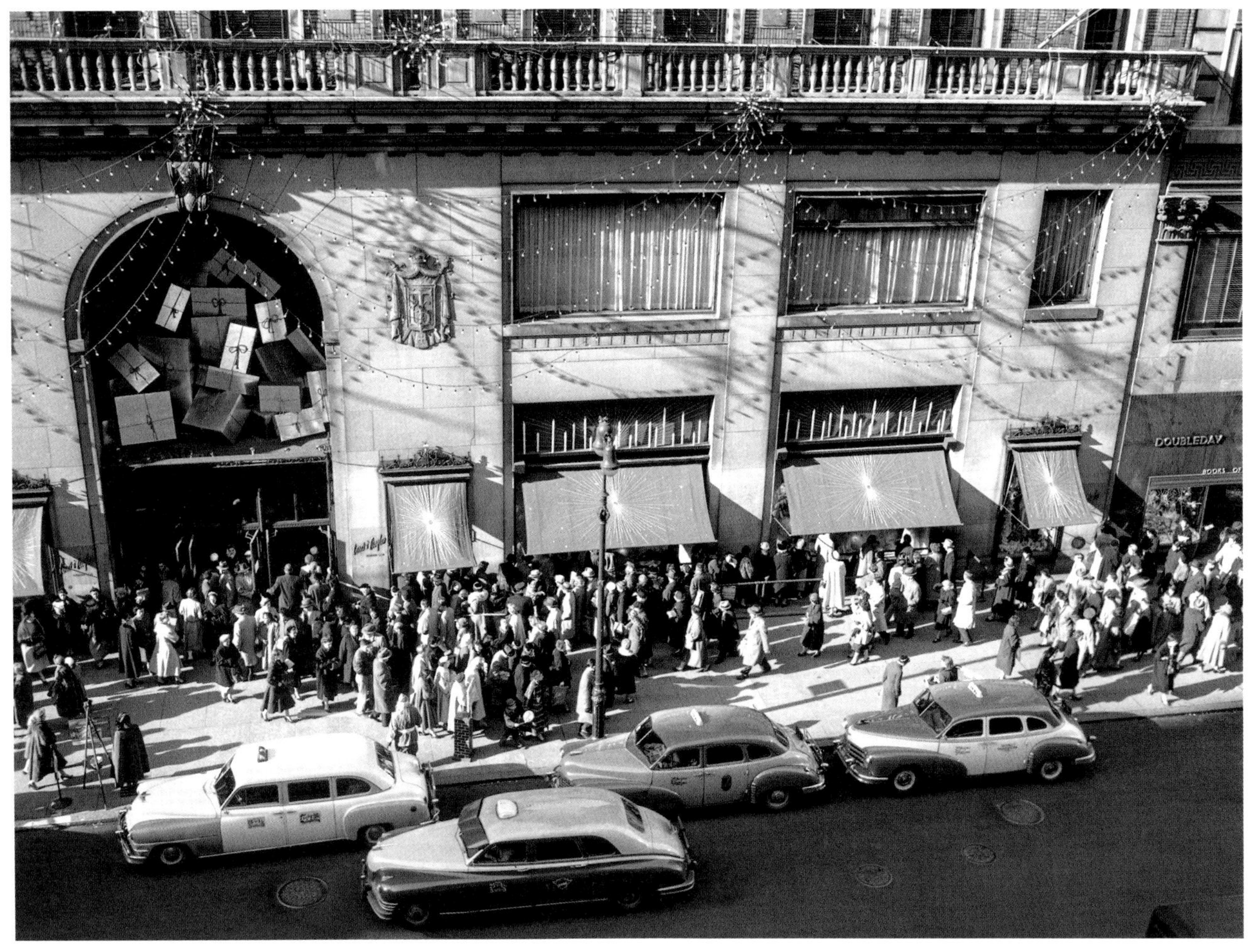

Lord & Taylor department store at Christmas,
New York, New York, USA

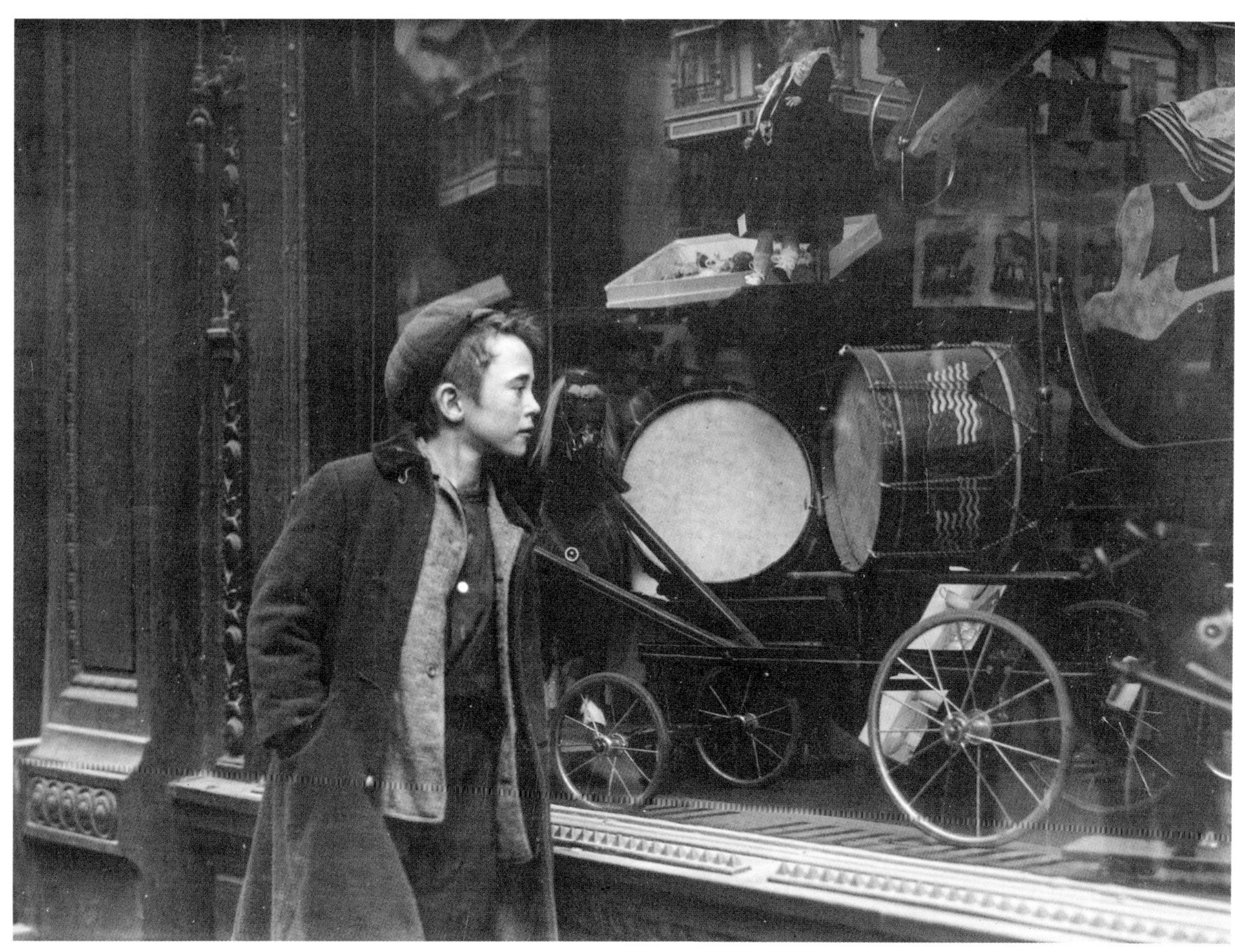

Admiring Christmas toys,
New York, New York, USA, 1910

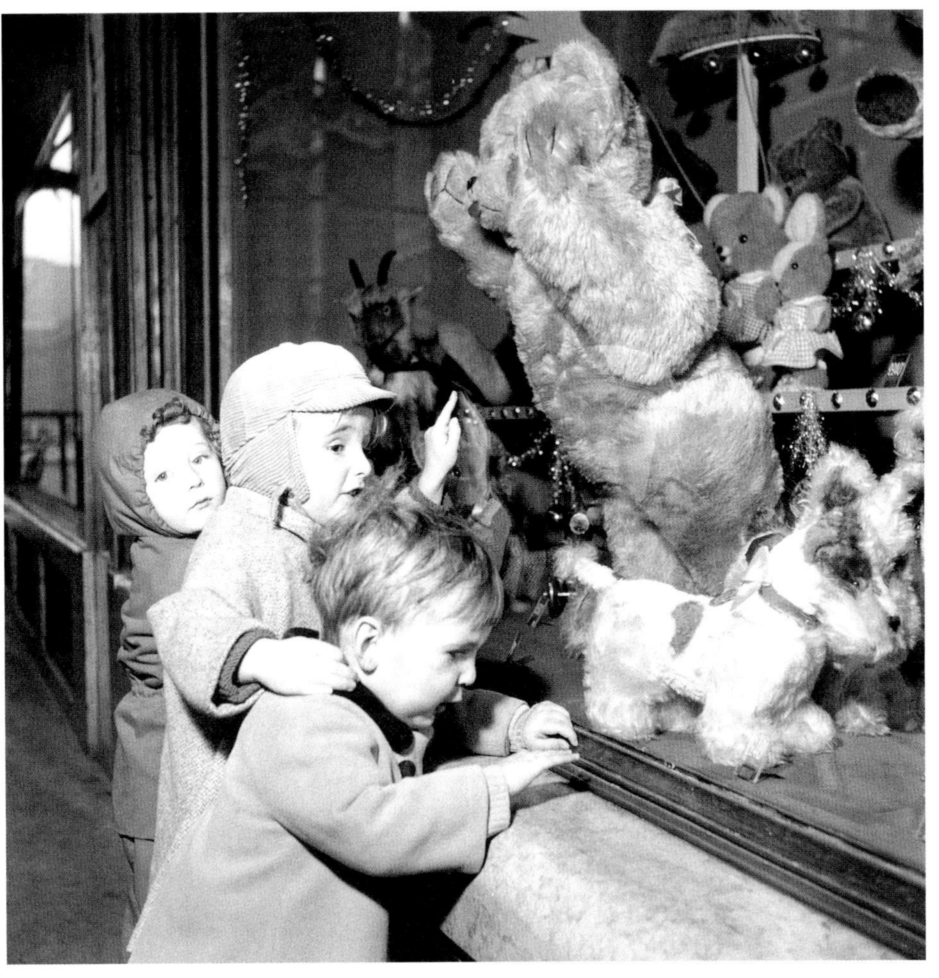

Captivated by the Christmas
window displays, 1951

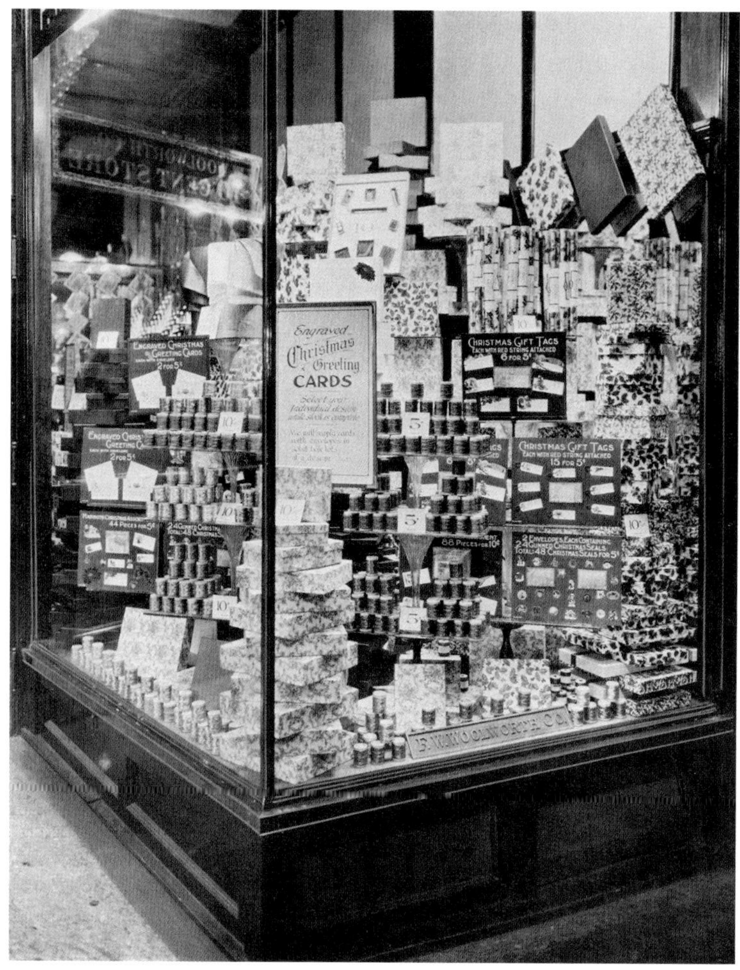

Festive window displays, USA

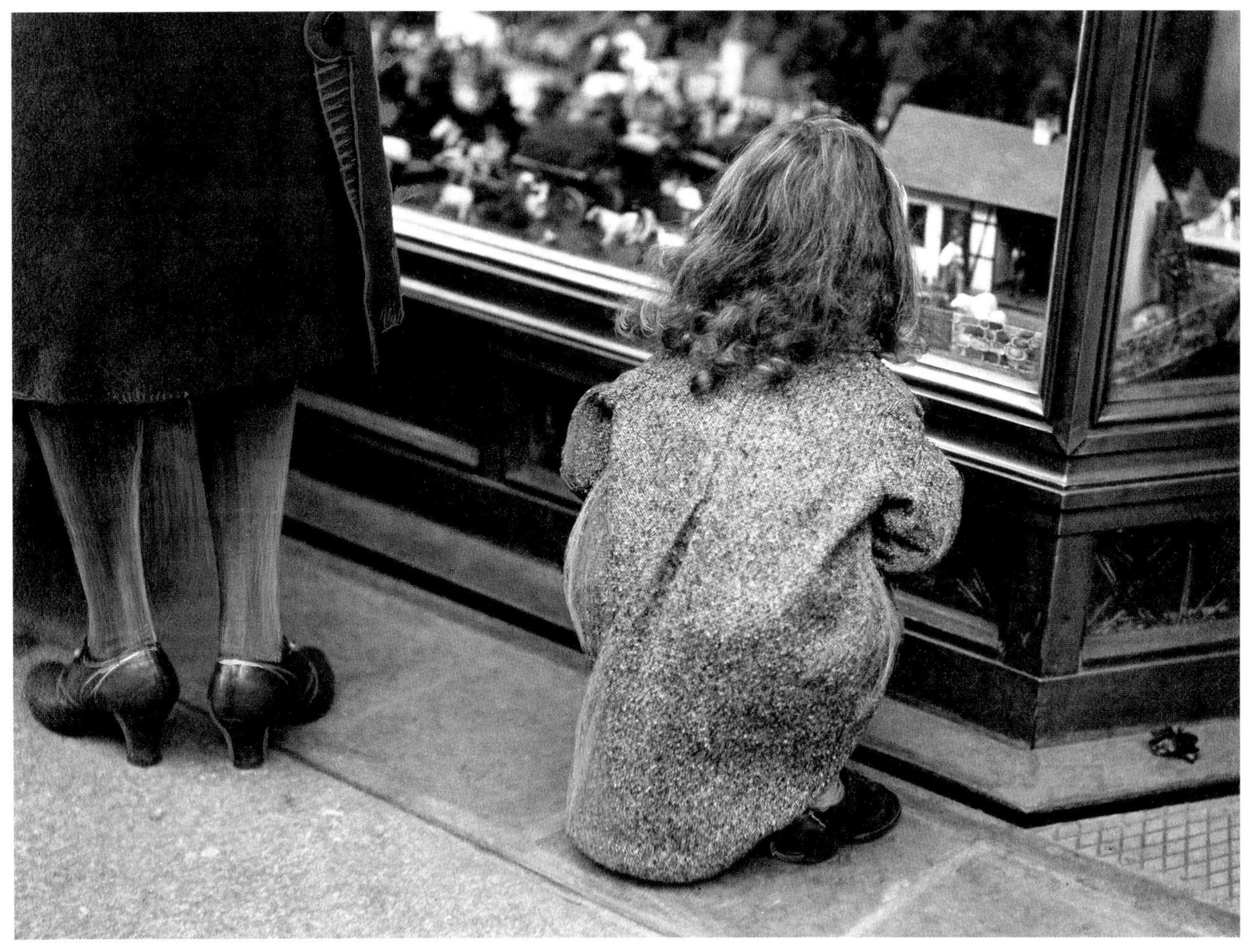

Kneeling to look at a doll's house,
Germany, 1930

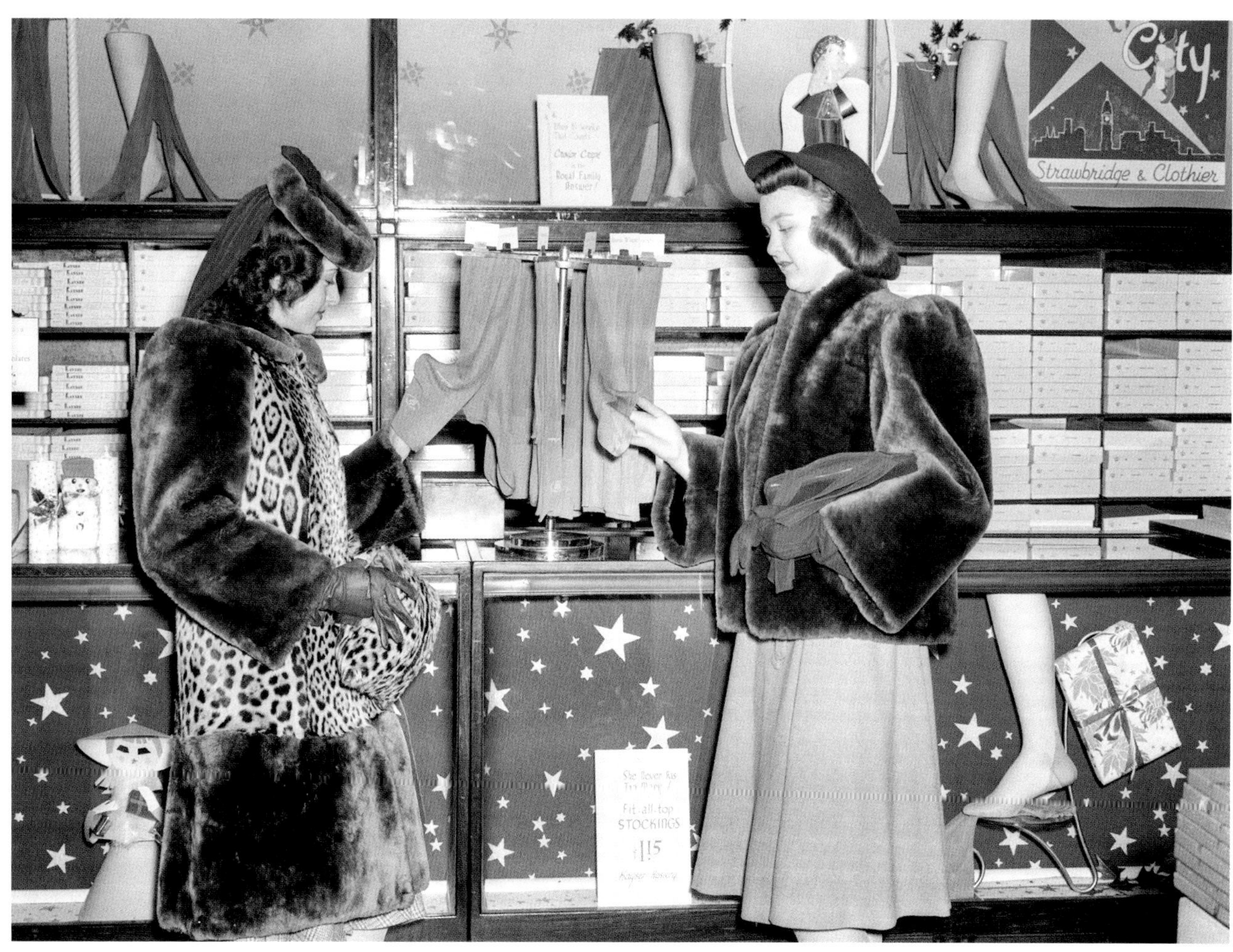

Department store shopping,
Philadelphia, Pennsylvania, USA, 1940s

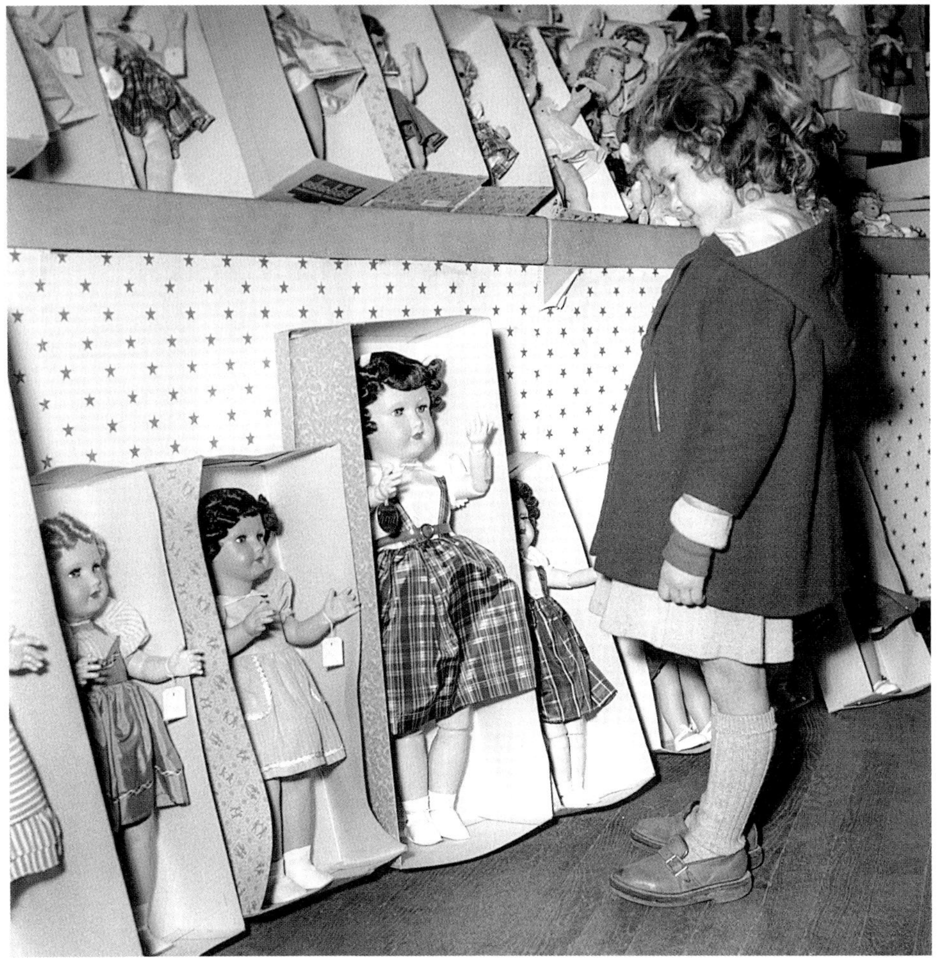

Christmas dolls, 1954

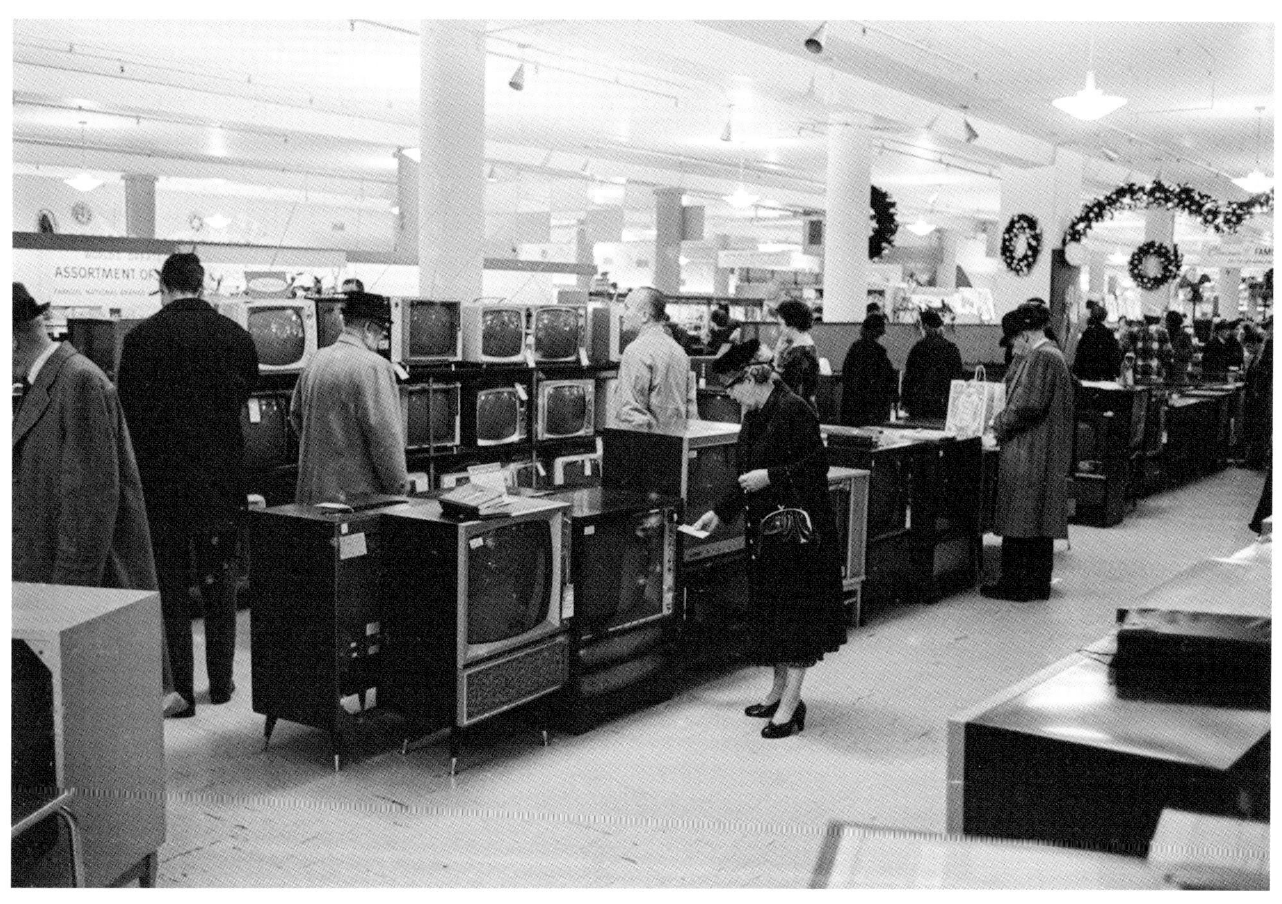

Televisions in Macy's deprtment store,
New York, New York, USA, 1960

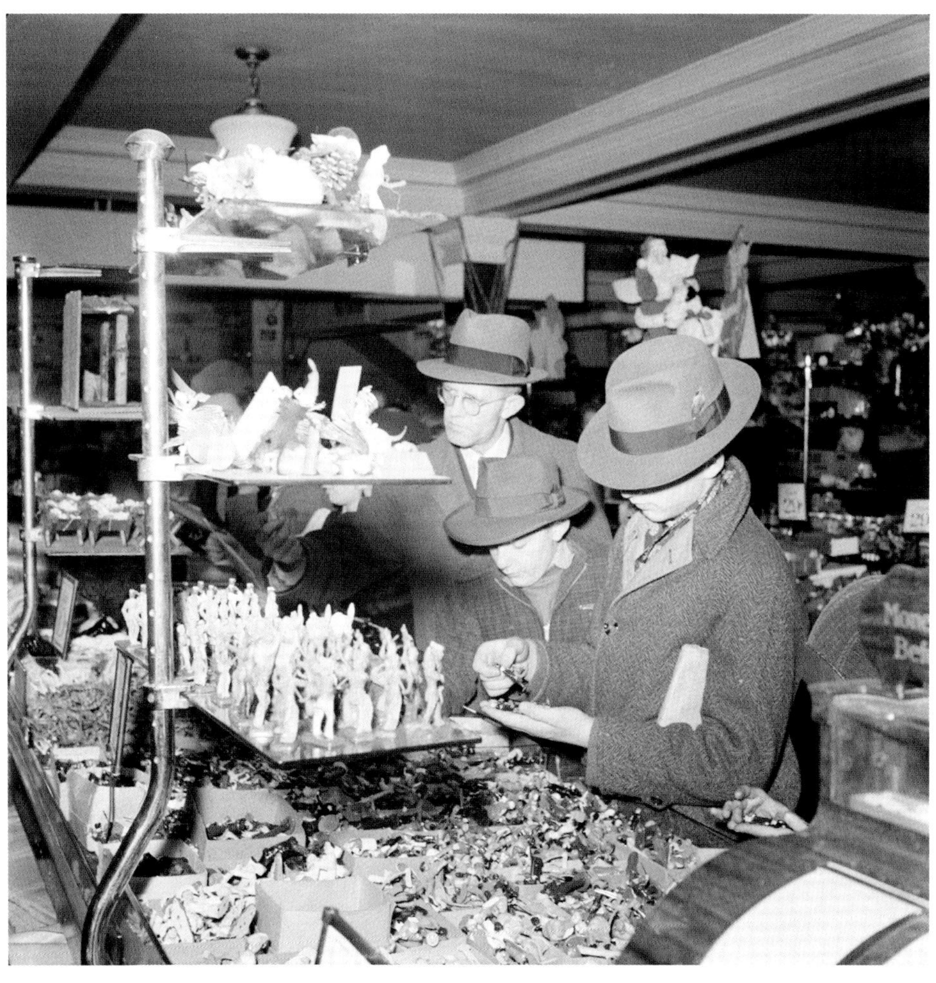

Christmas shopping in Woolworth's
five-and-dime store, Washington, D.C., USA 1941

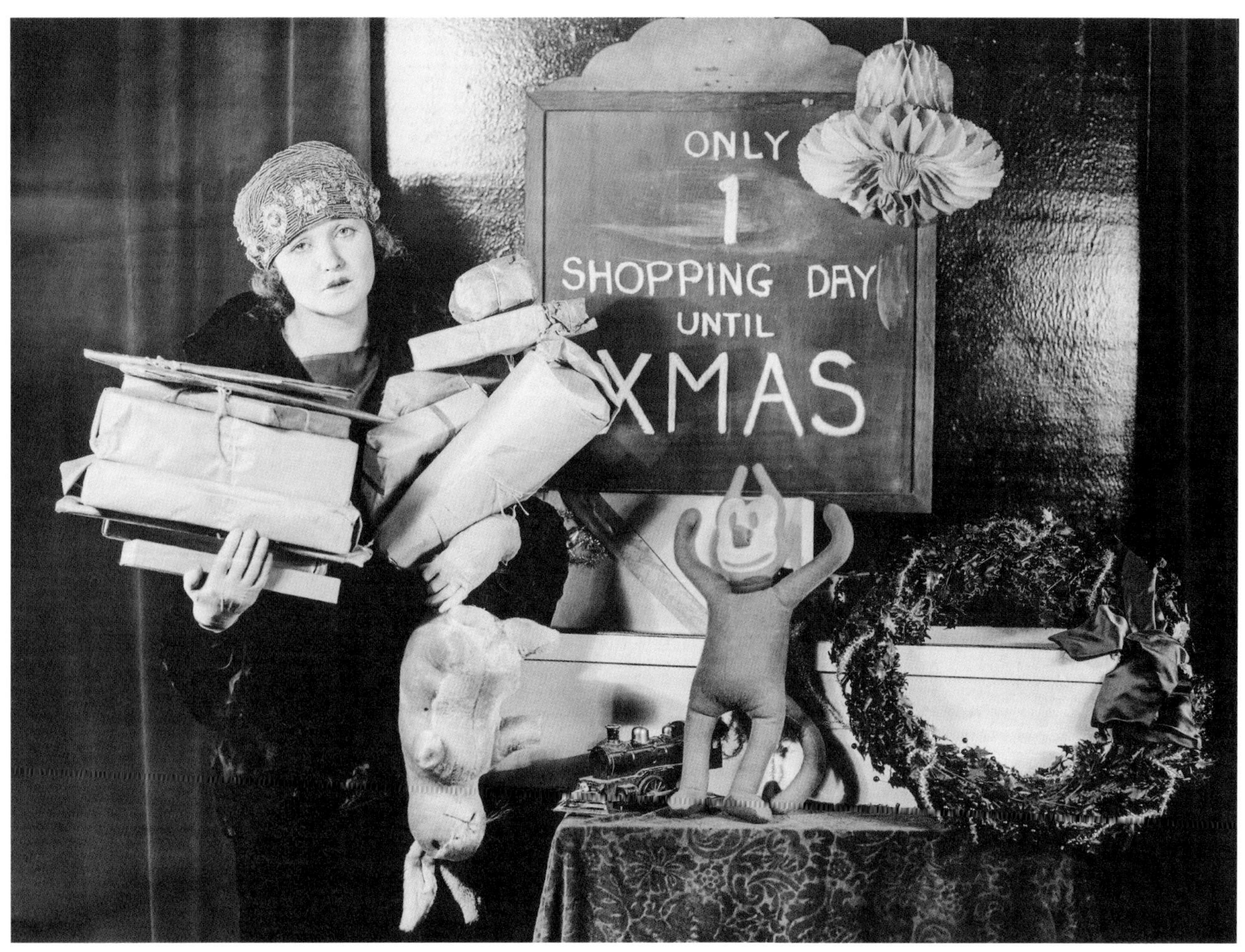

Last posting day reminder
for Christmas presents

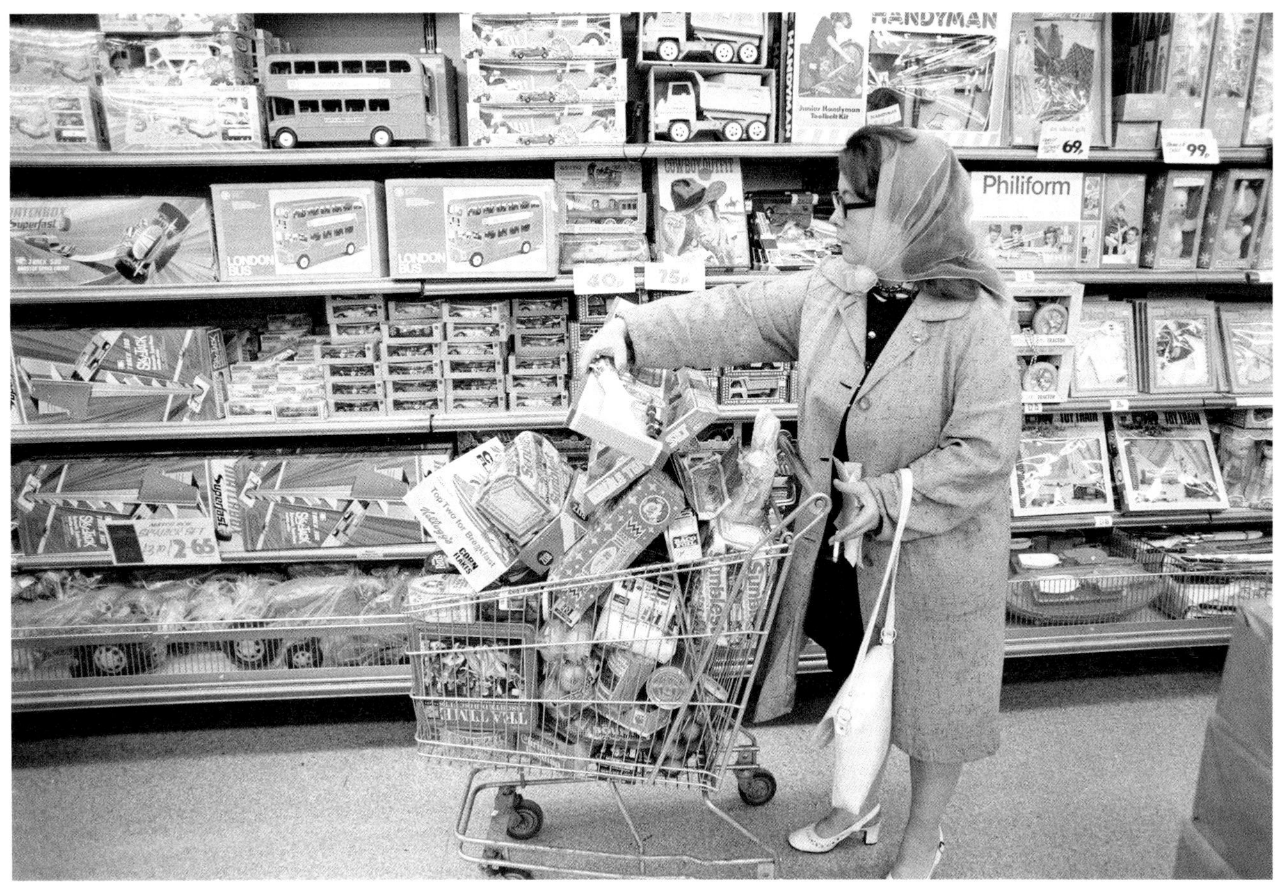

Christmas shopping at Tesco
in Brixton, London, UK, 1972

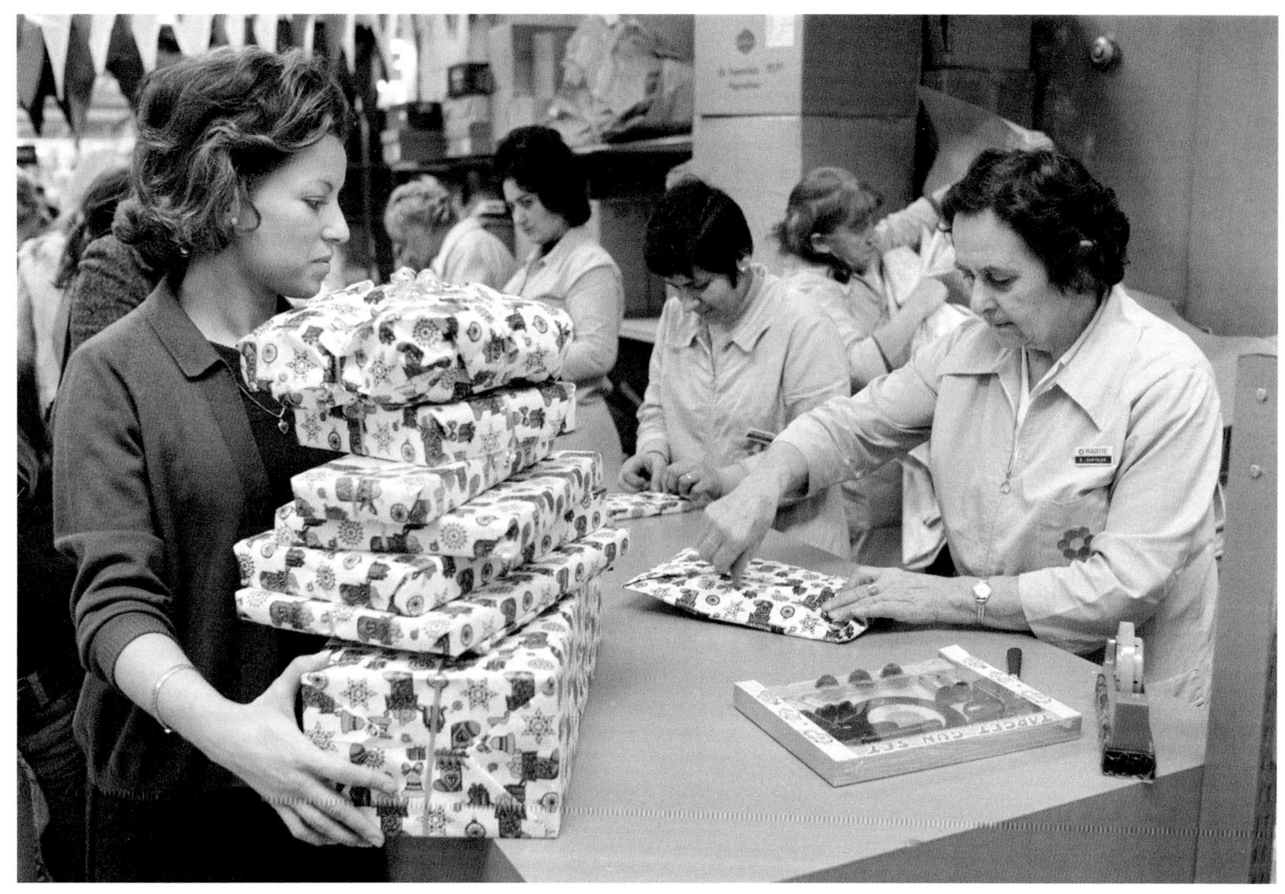

Sales assistants at work,
Geneva, Switzerland, 1971

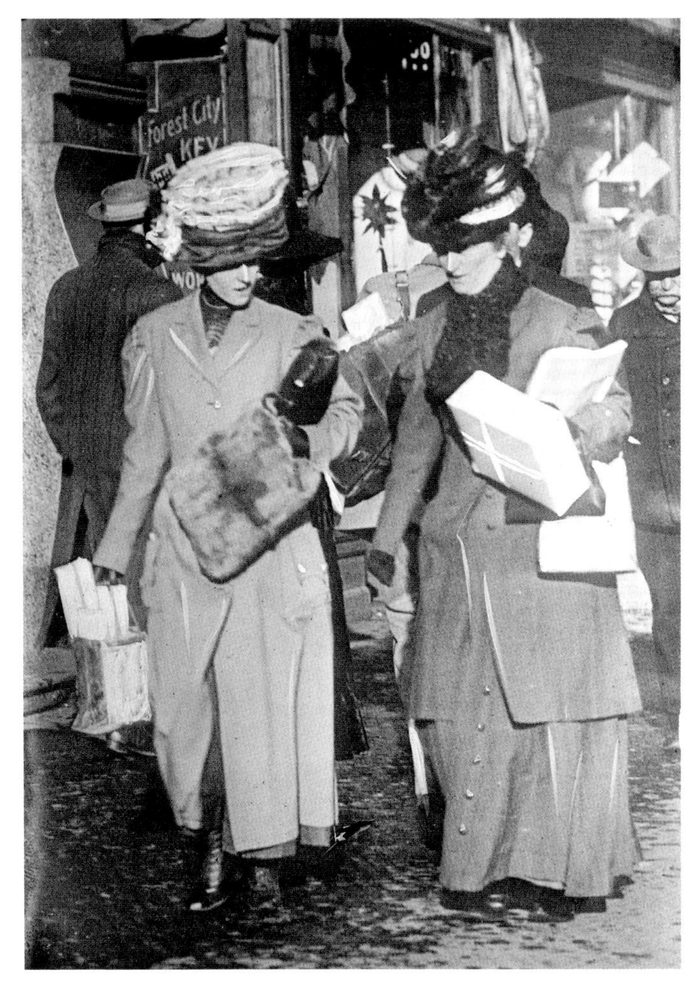

Carrying Christmas shopping,
New York, New York, USA, 1910

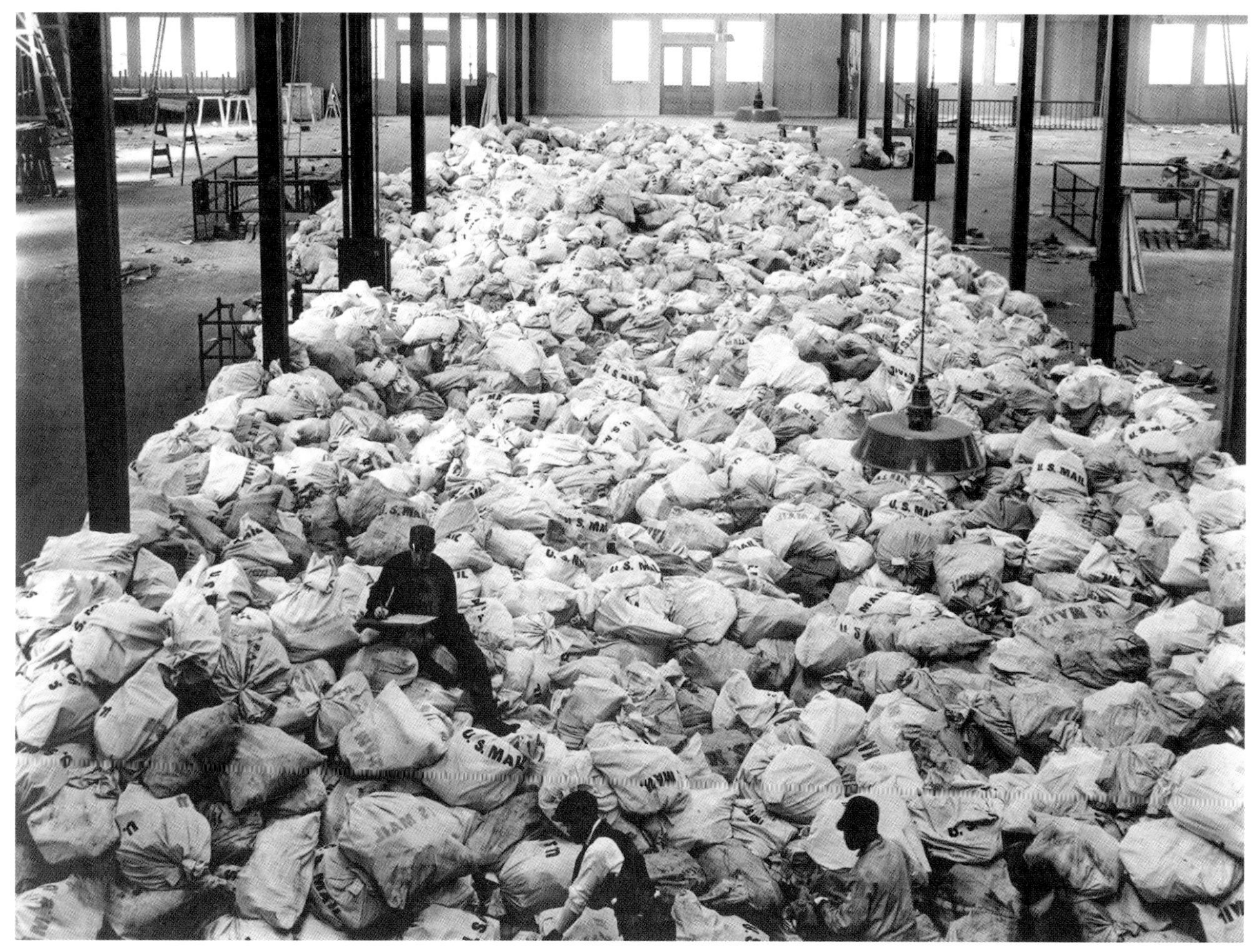

Christmas mail destined for American soldiers in WWI,
New York, New York, USA, 1918

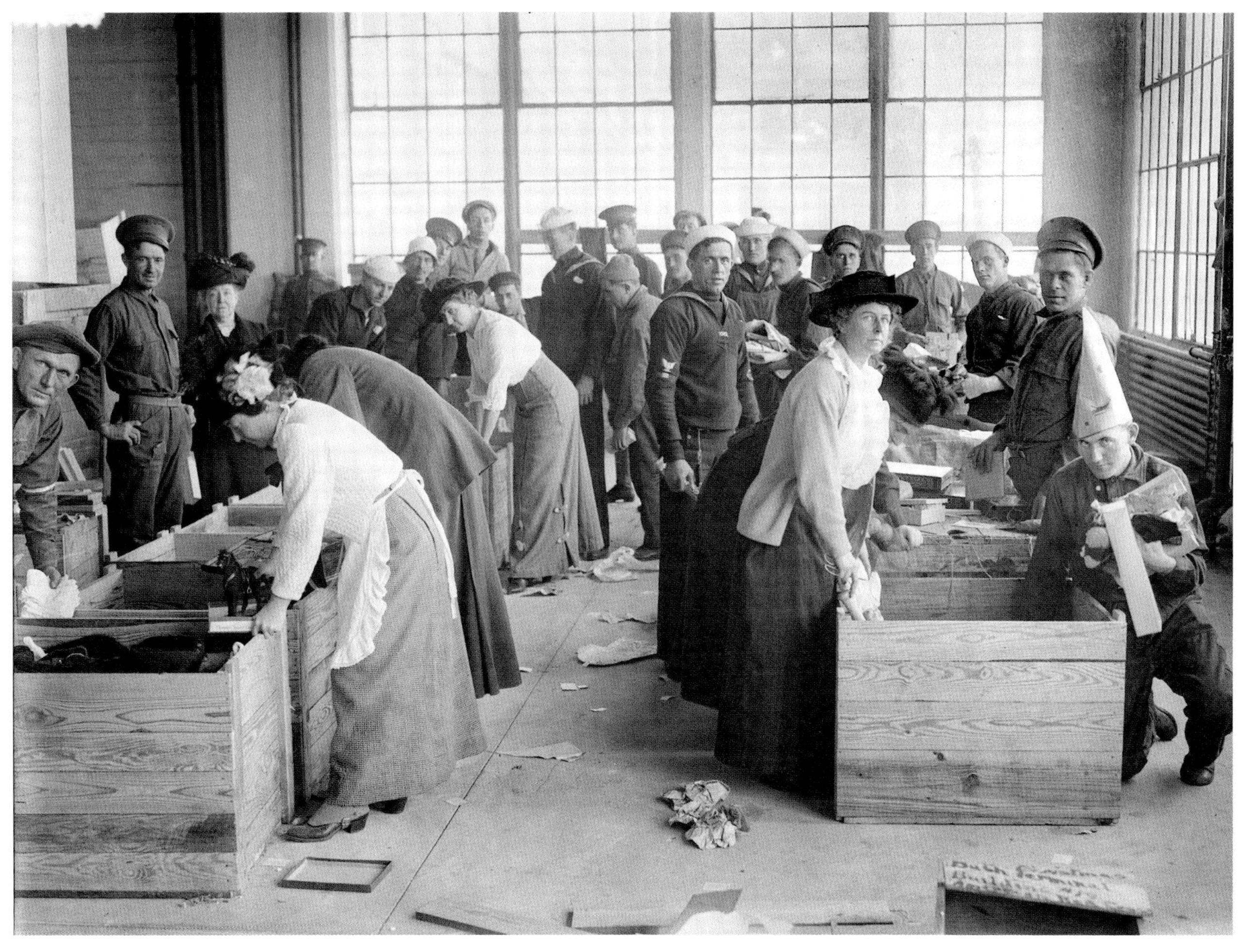

Packing six million gifts for European children affected by WWI,
New York, New York, USA, 1914

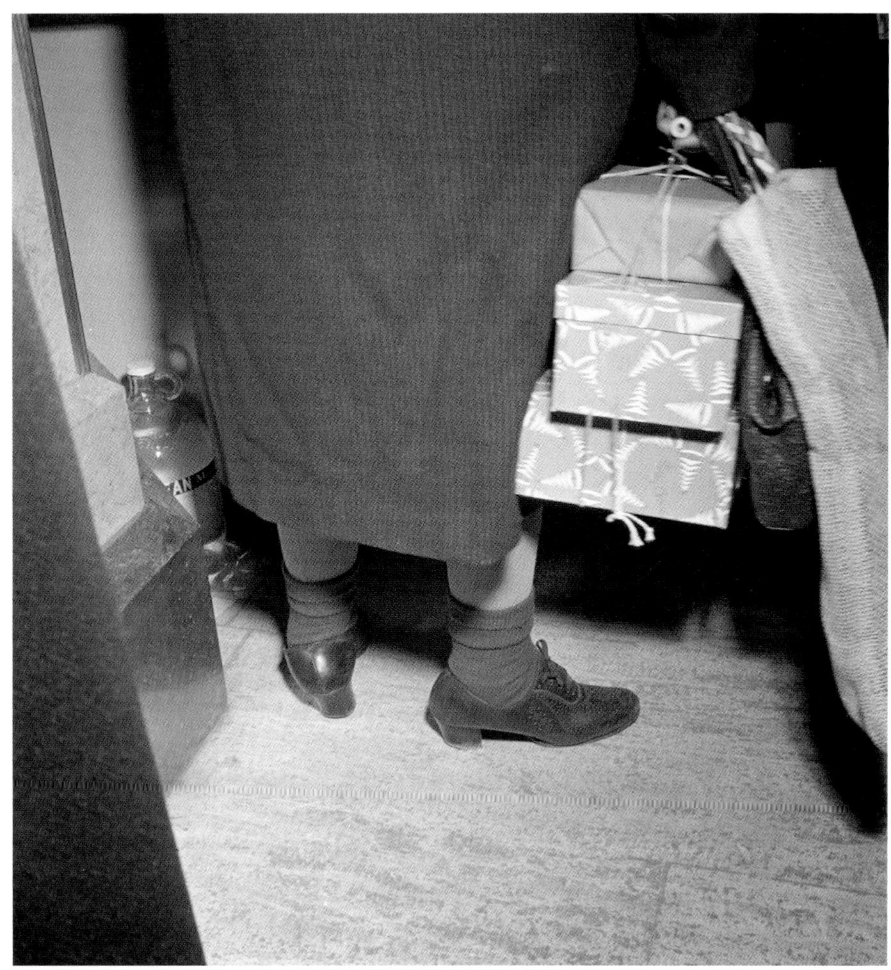

Macy's department store,
New York, New York, USA, 1942

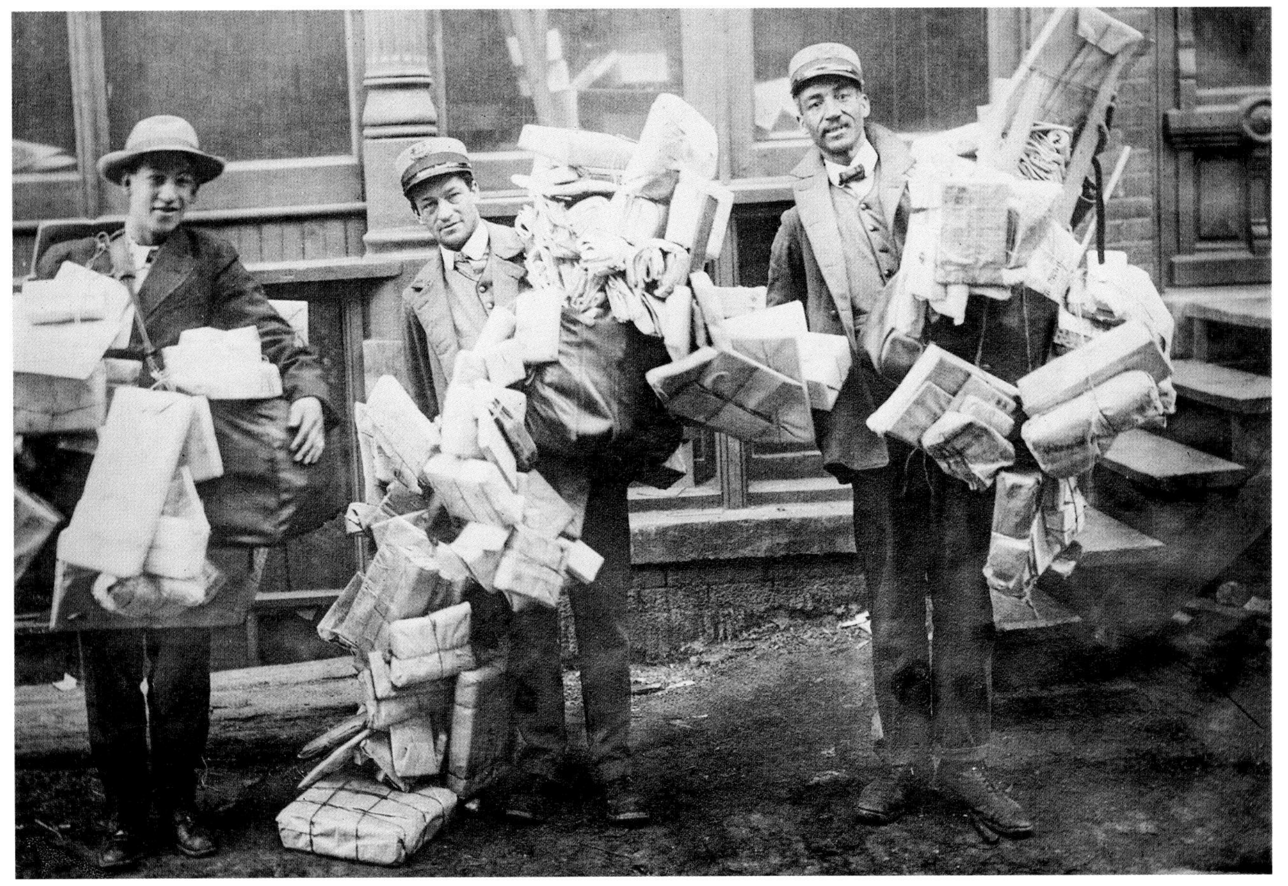

Mailmen loaded down with
Christmas parcels, USA, 1910s

Swapping a sleigh for a biplane,
USA, 1921

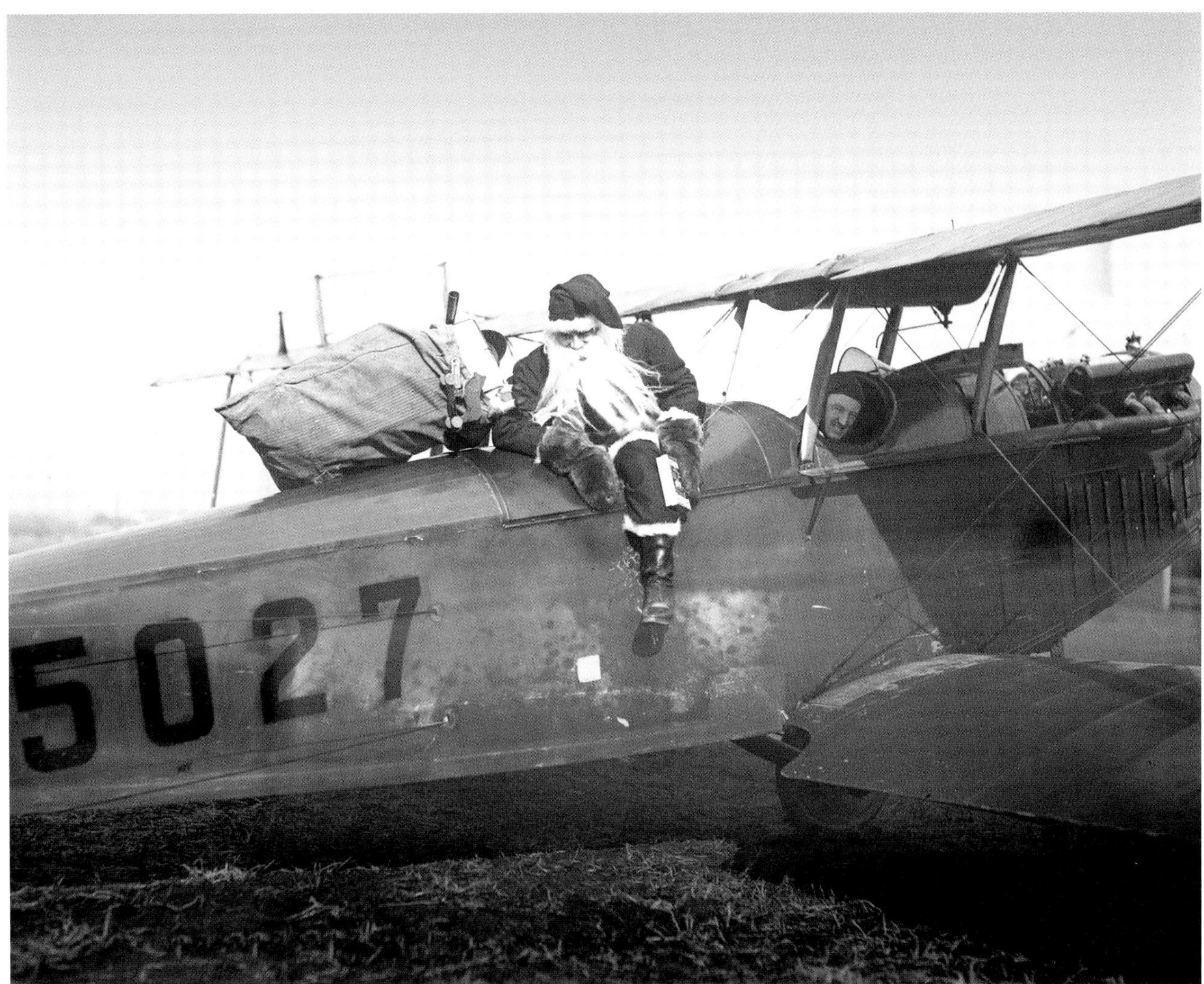

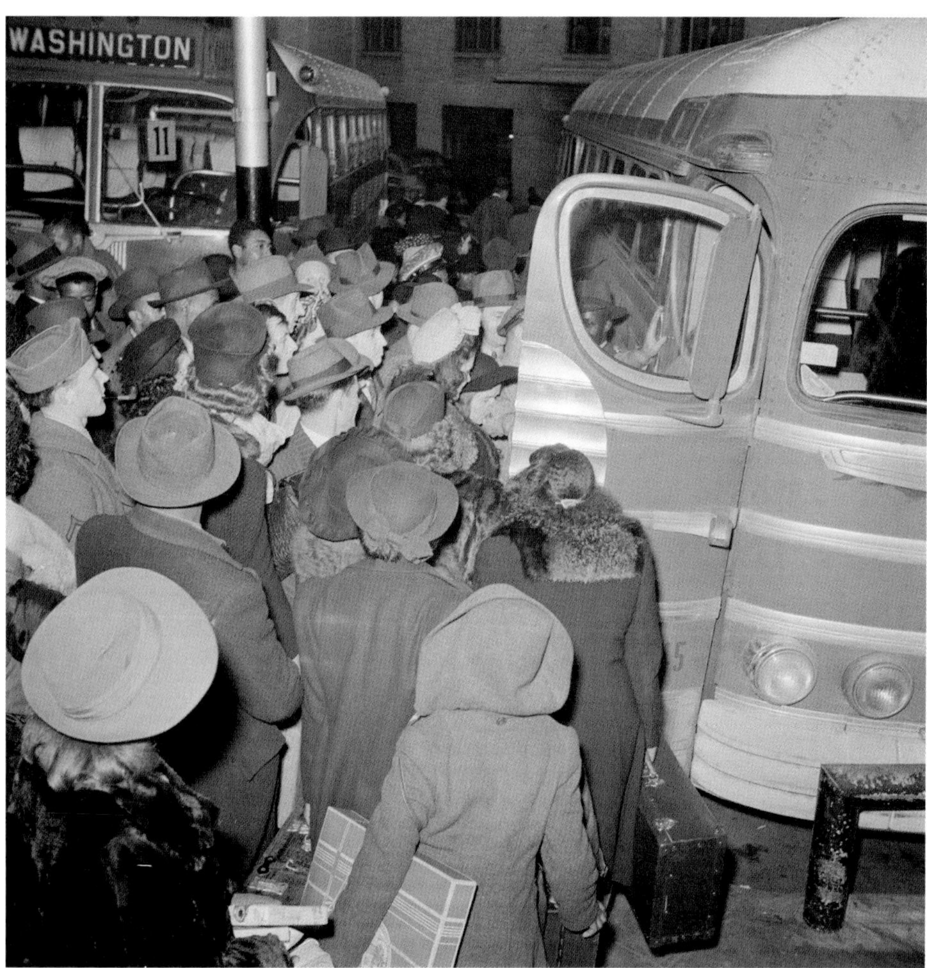

Christmas rush at the Greyhound bus terminal,
Washington, D.C., USA, 1941

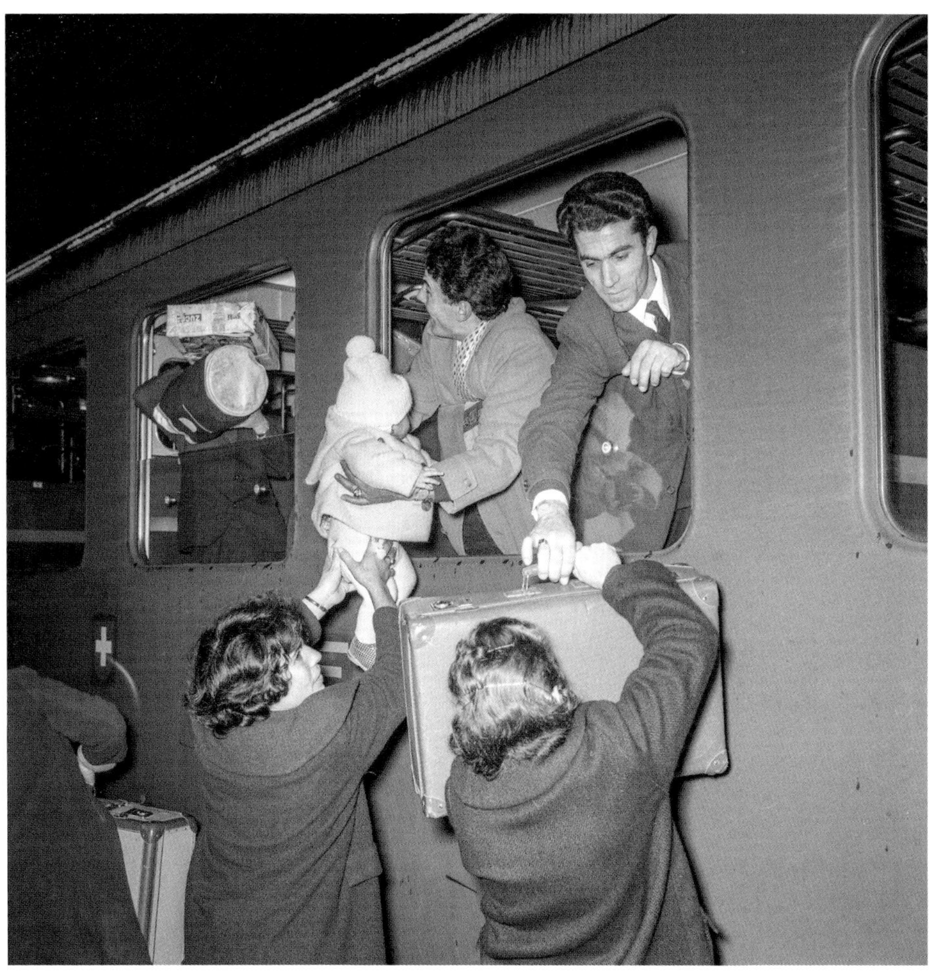

Italian guest workers headed home for Christmas,
Bern, Switzerland, 1962

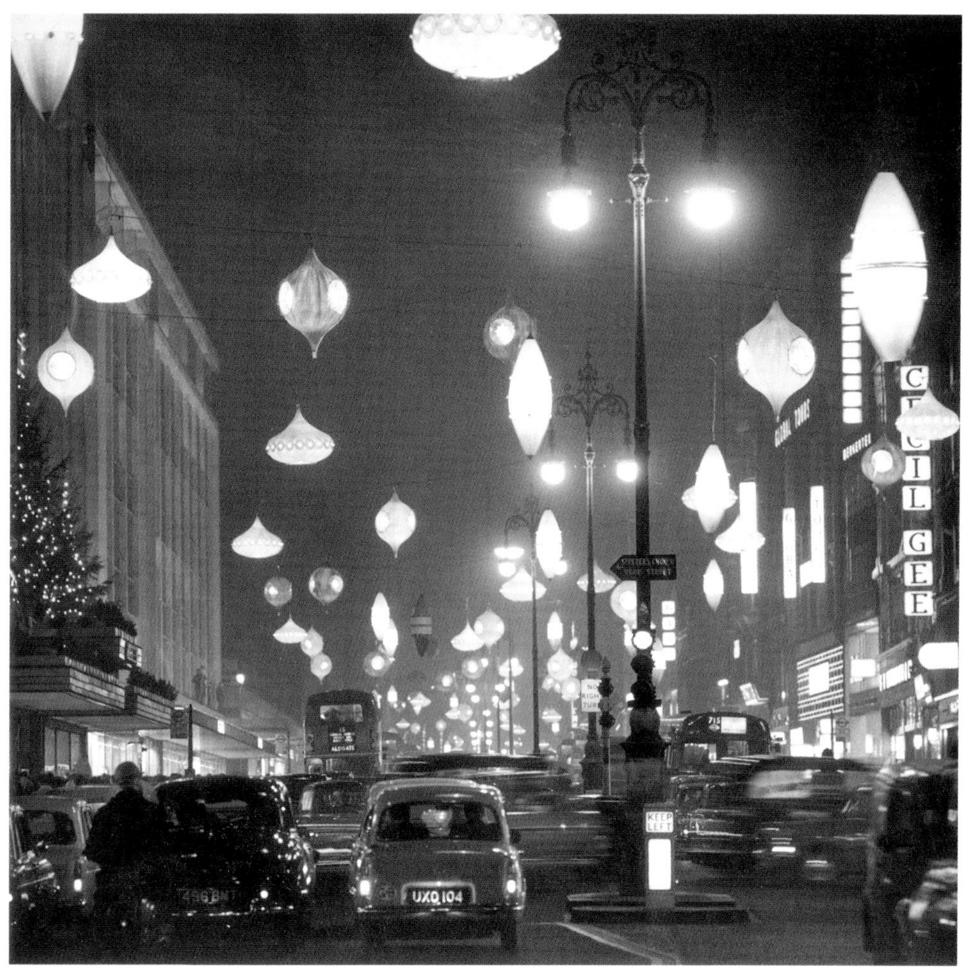

Christmas decorations on
Oxford Street, London, UK, 1961

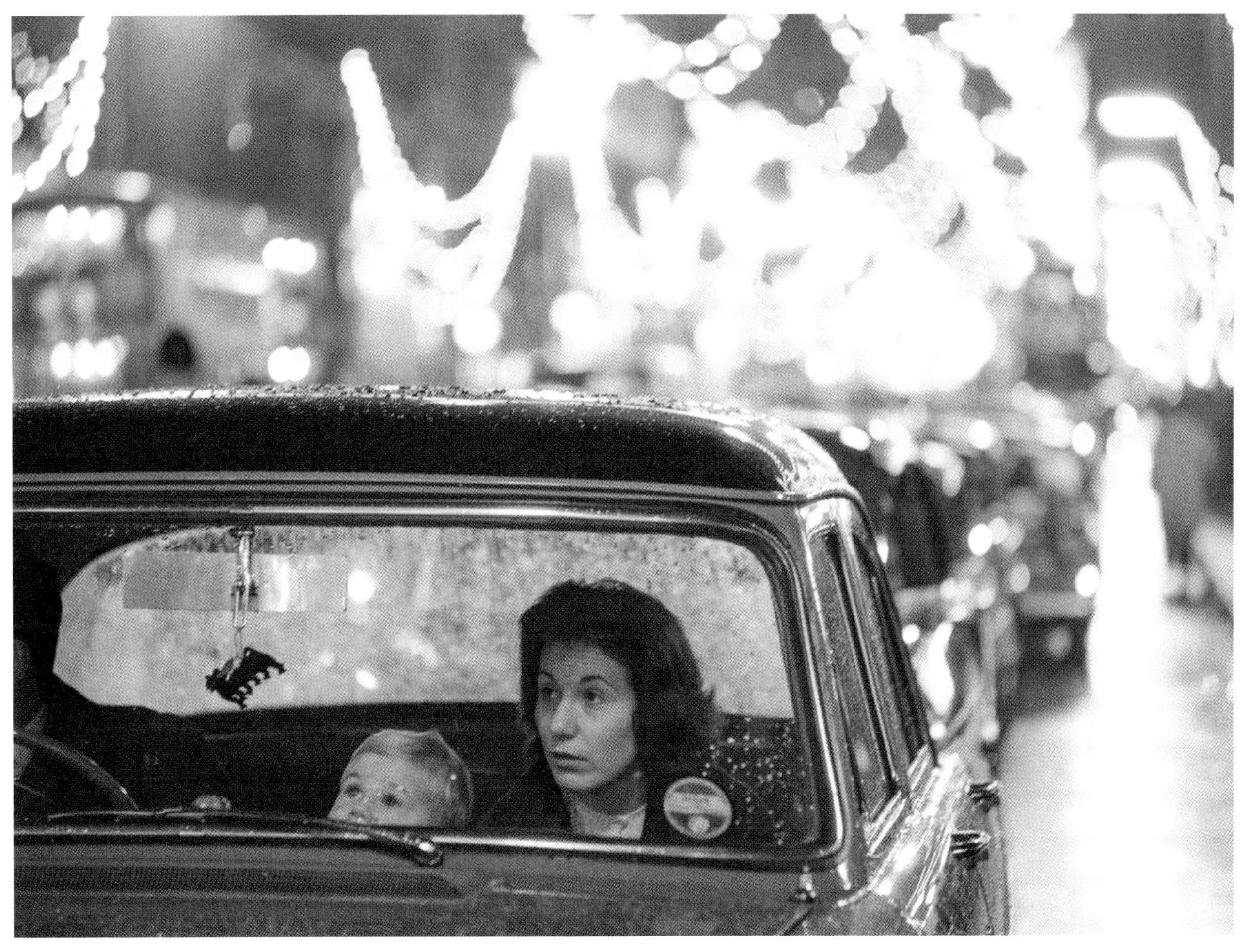

Admiring Regent Street's Christmas lights
from a traffic jam, London, UK, 1960

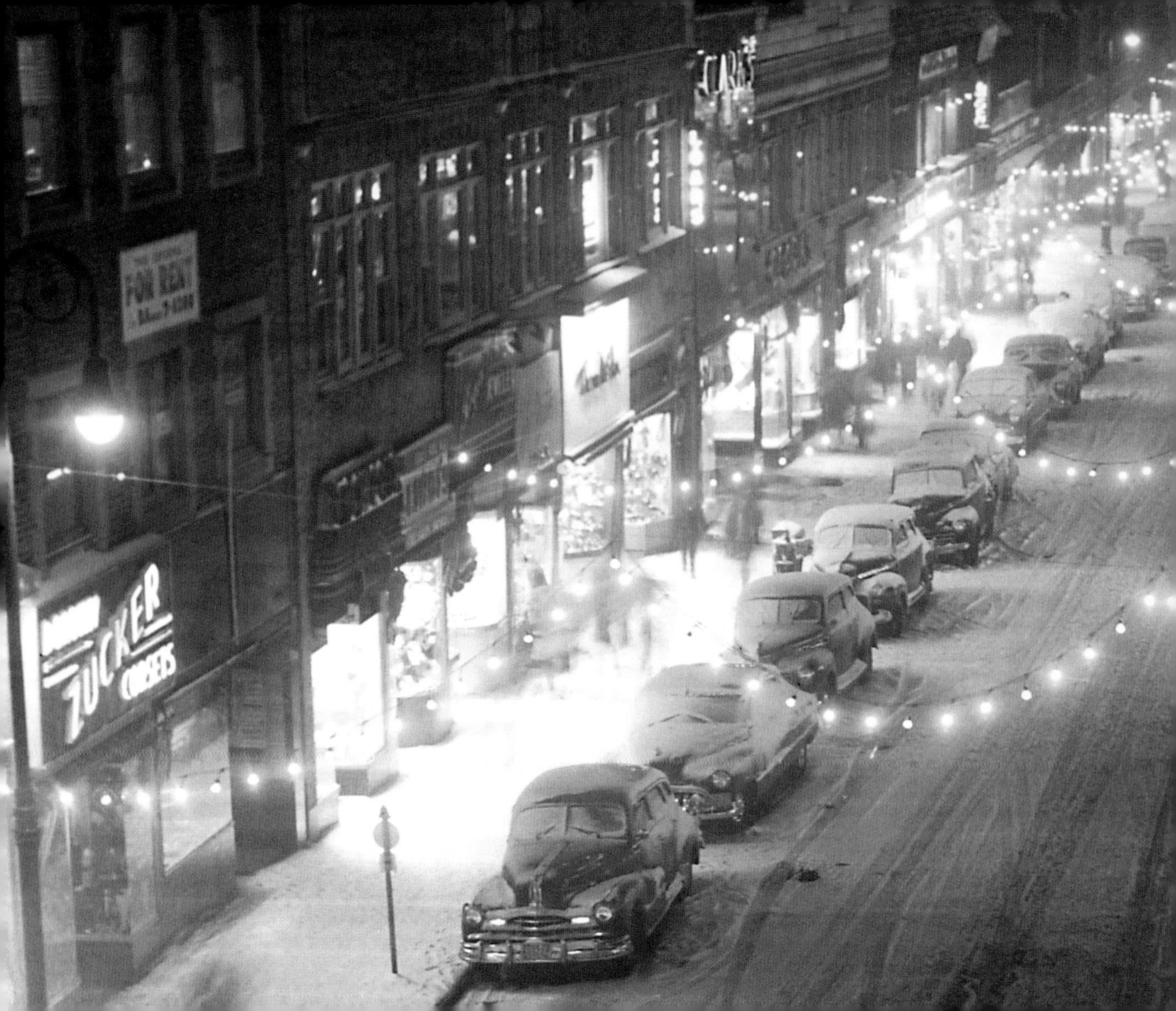

FOR RENT
TUCKER

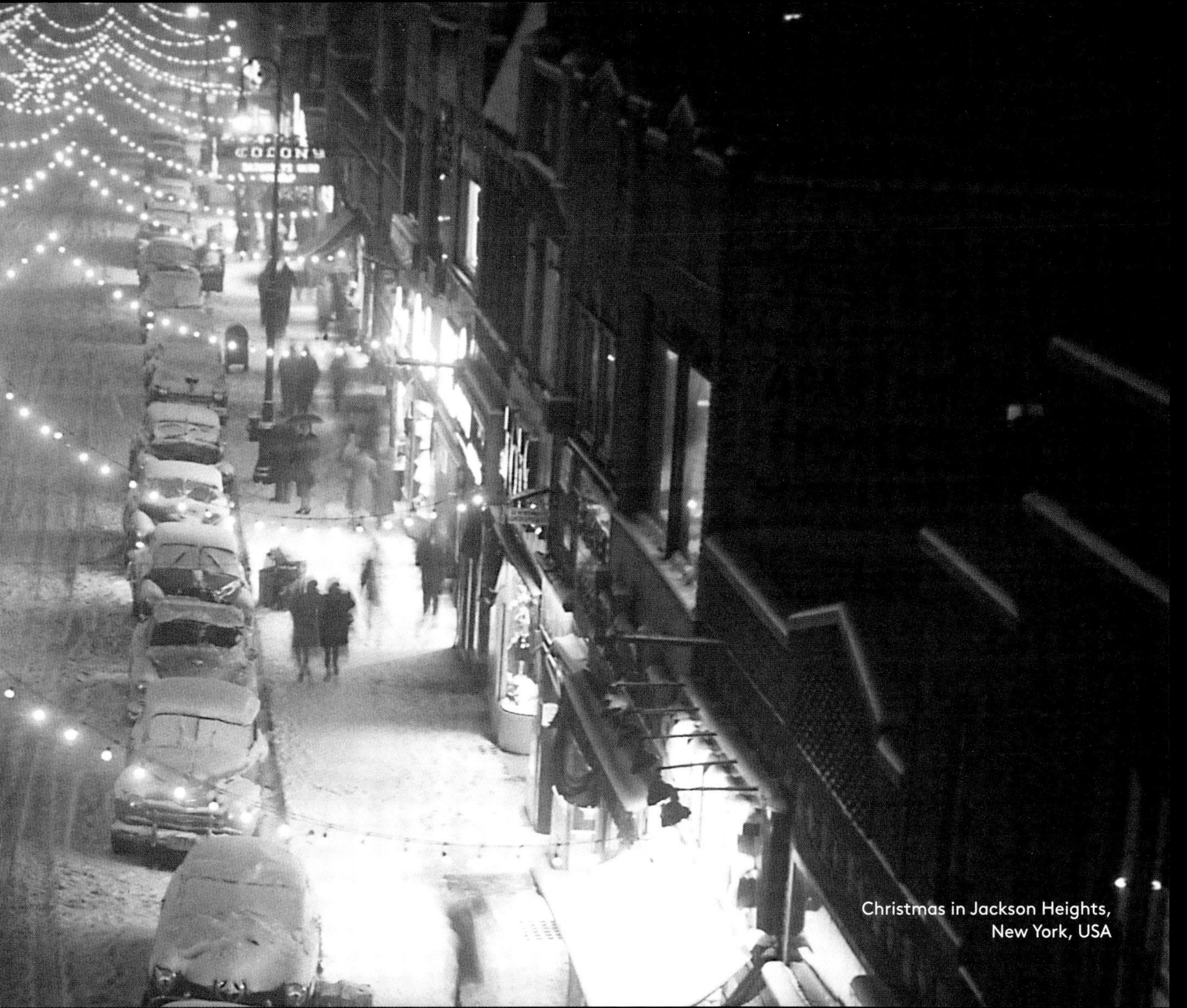

Christmas in Jackson Heights,
New York, USA

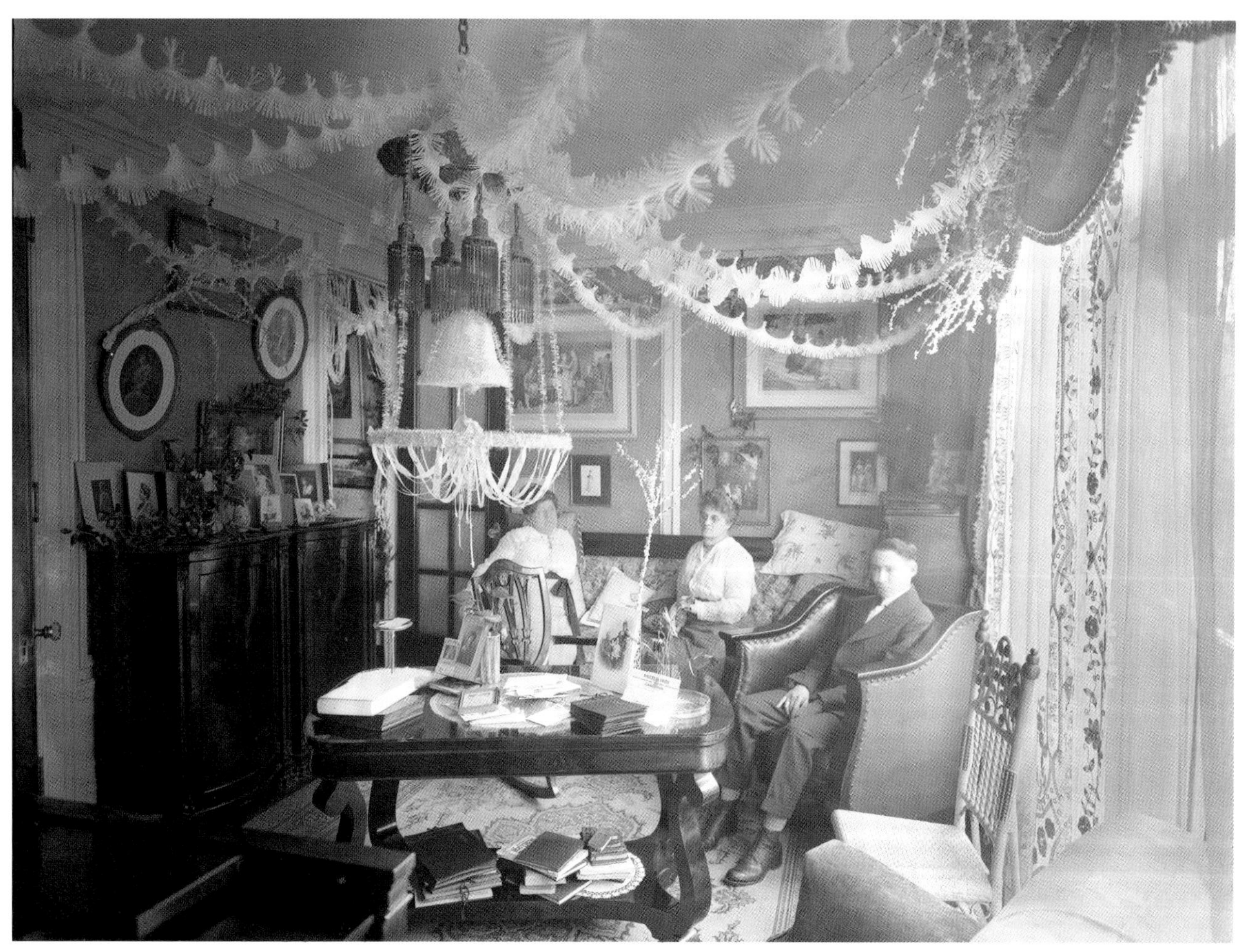

Private residence decorated for Christmas,
New York, New York, USA, 1917

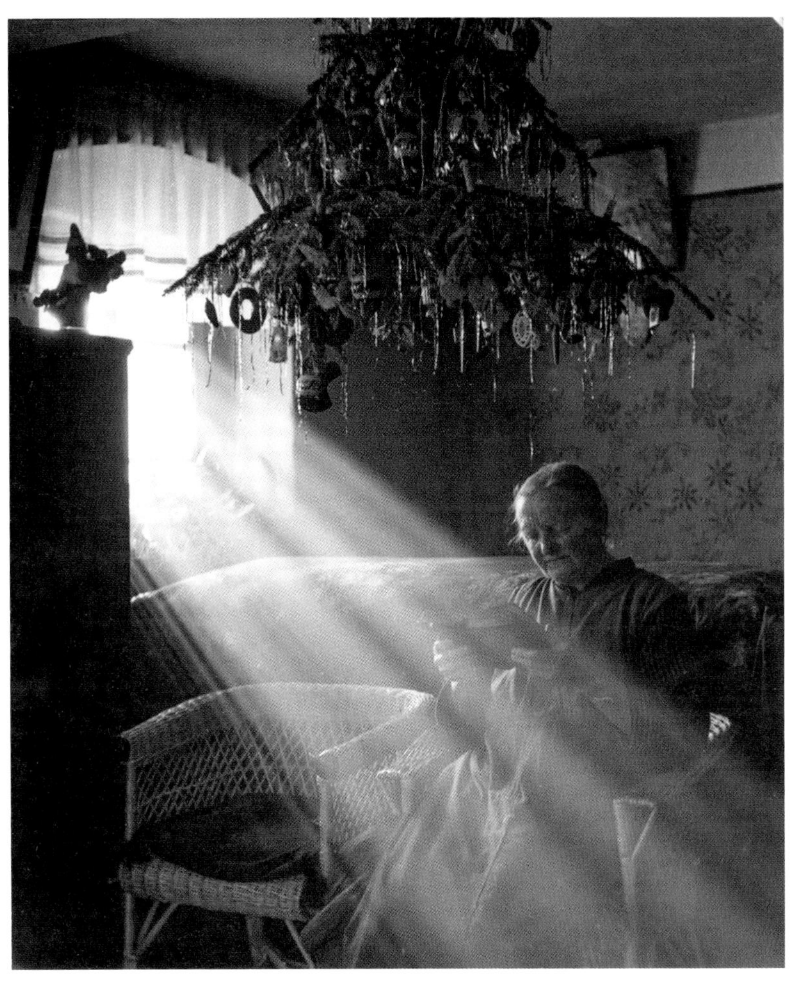

Elderly woman sits in a beam of light with a
Christmas tree overhead, Czech Republic, 1938

Children performing a nativity scene at
school in Lakkegata, Oslo, Norway, 1948

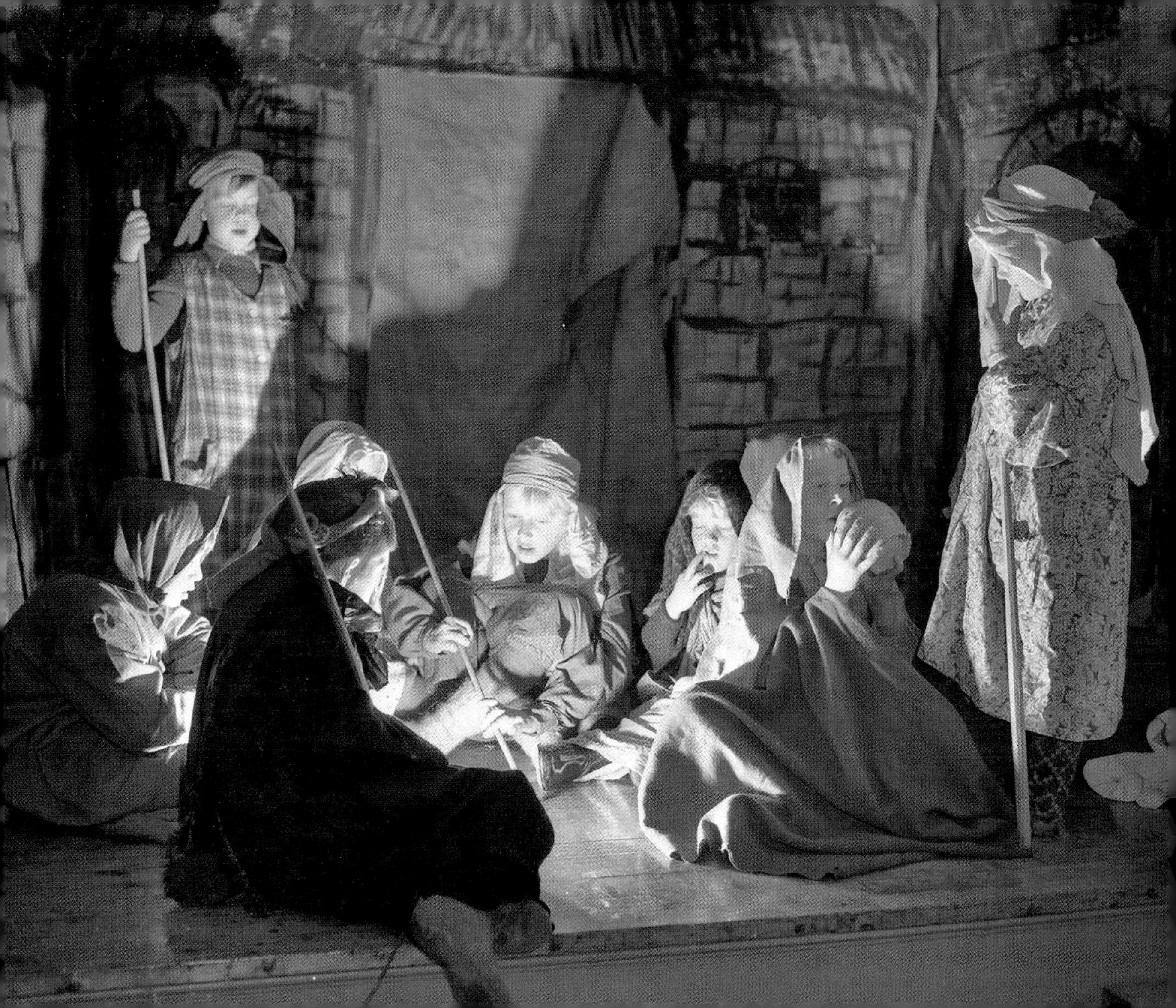

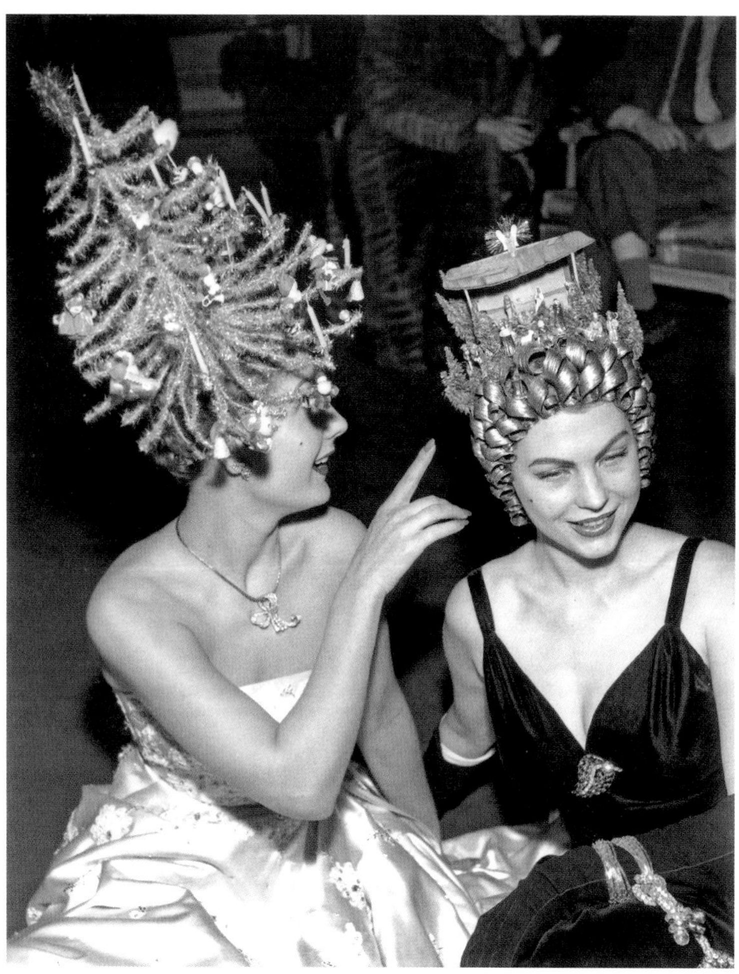

Christmas hairstyles,
France, 1952

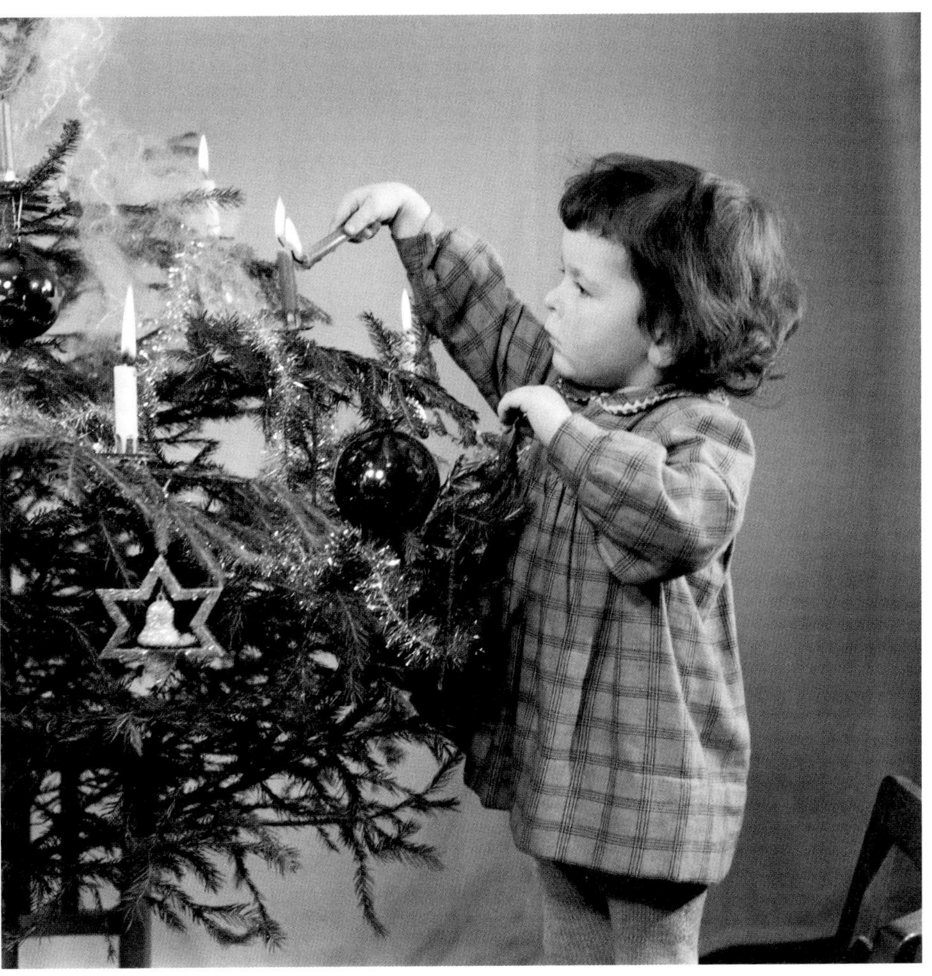

Lighting up the tree,
Switzerland, 1953

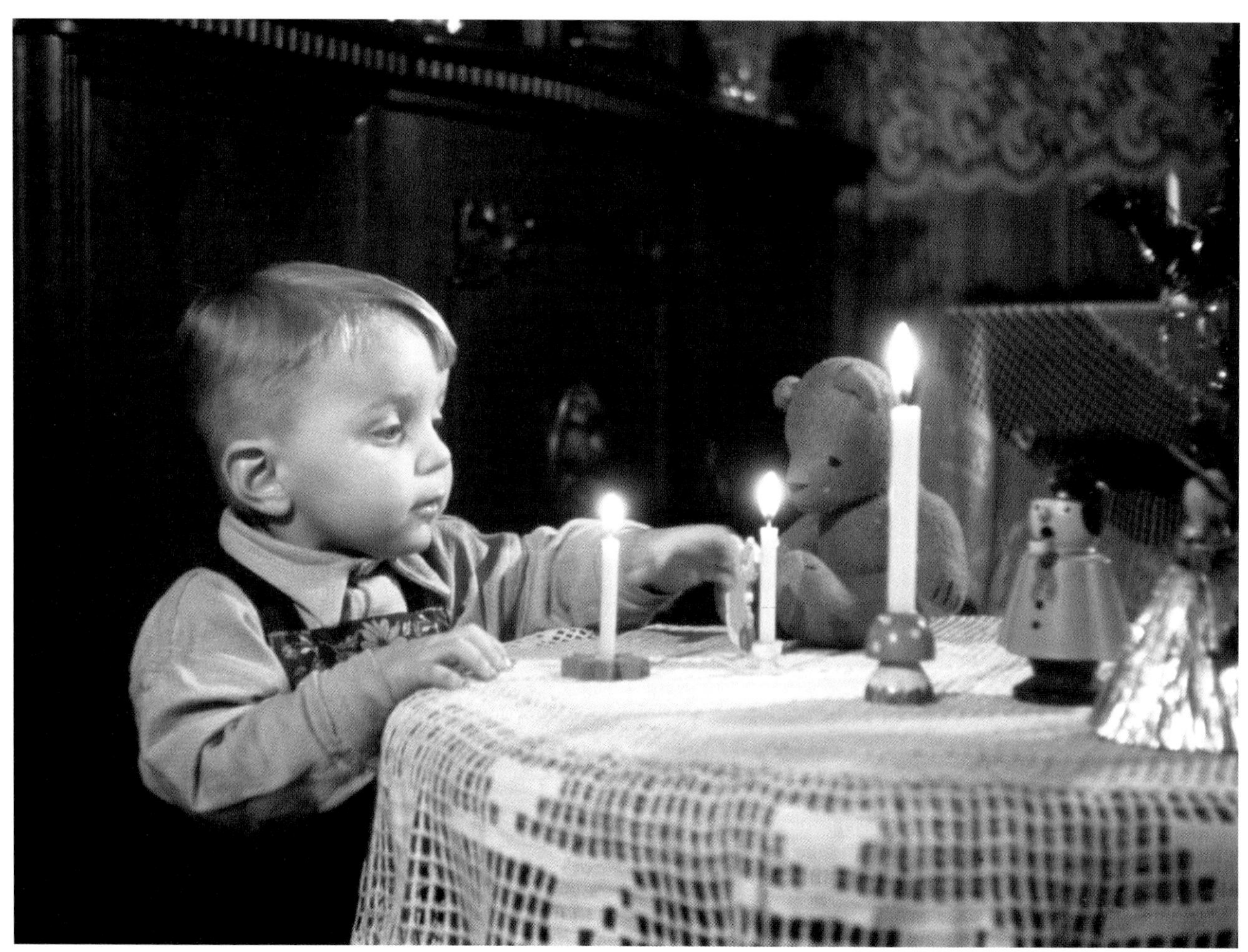

Young boy arranging Christmas toys
and candles, Germany, 1951

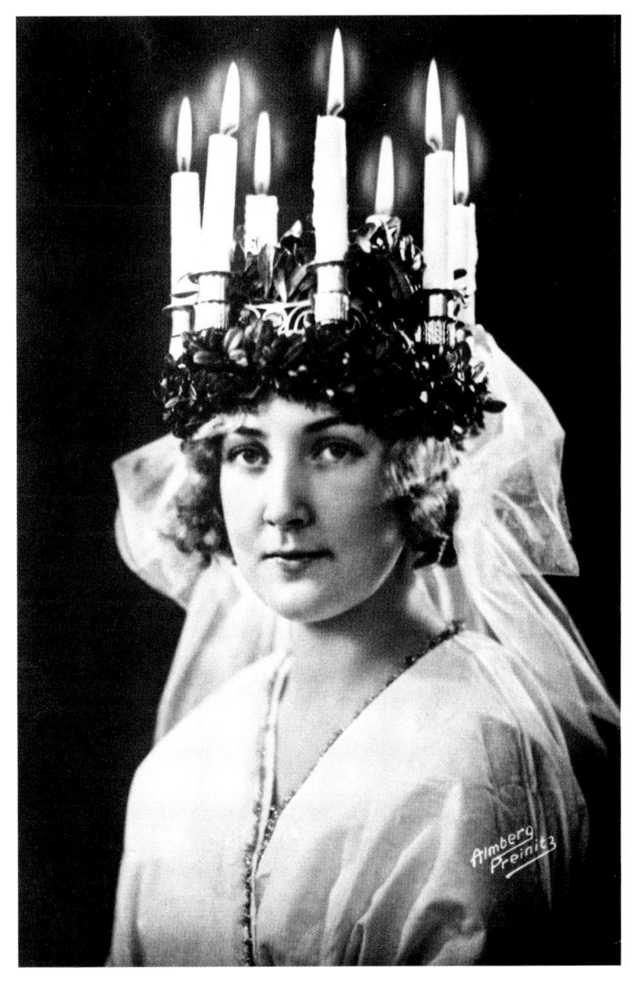

The Lucia Queen with candle crown, a Swedish
tradition since Roman times, Stockholm, Sweden, 1931

Children's choir sings at Dr Barnardo's Farm Hill
in Kelvedon, Essex, UK, 1963

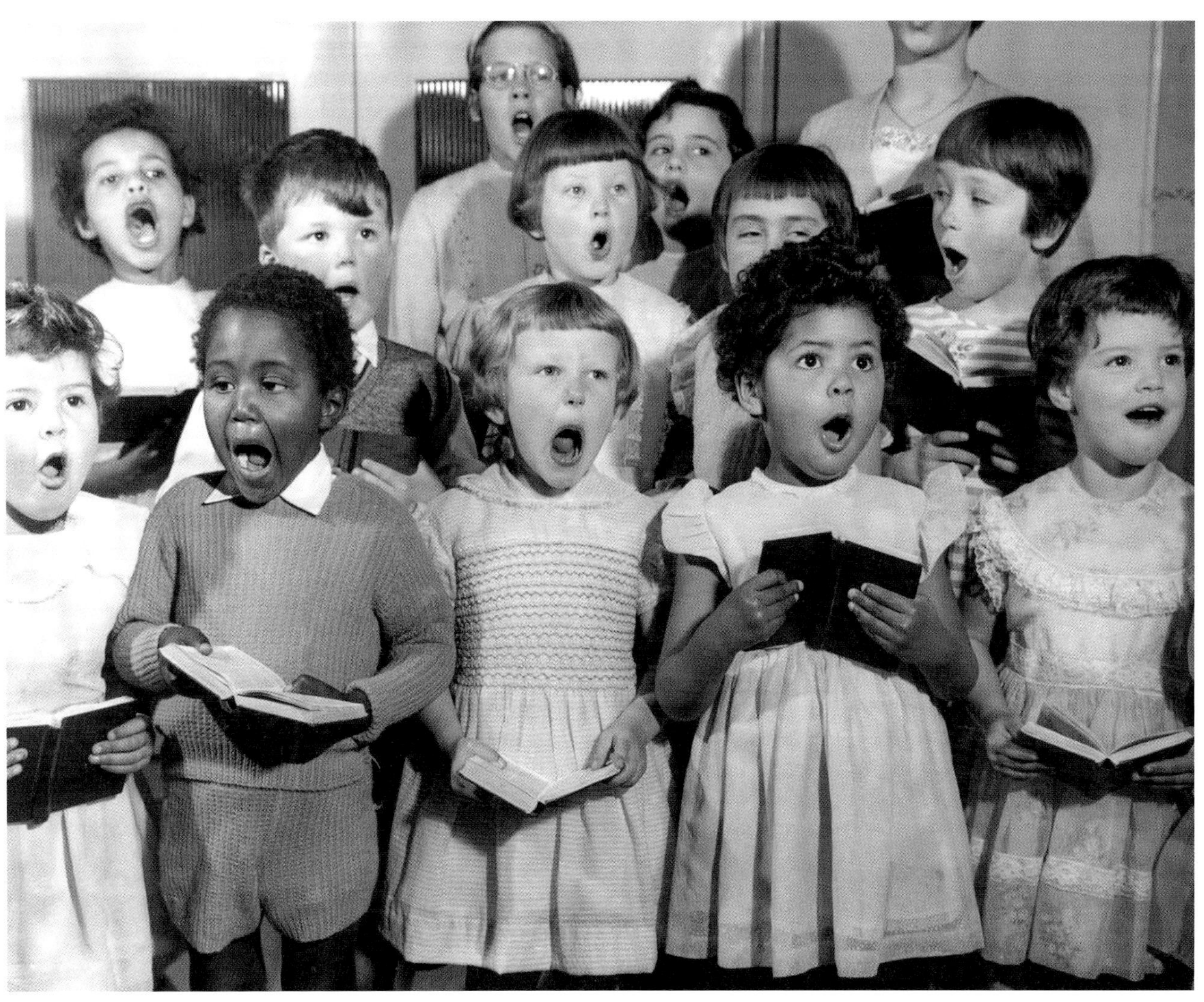

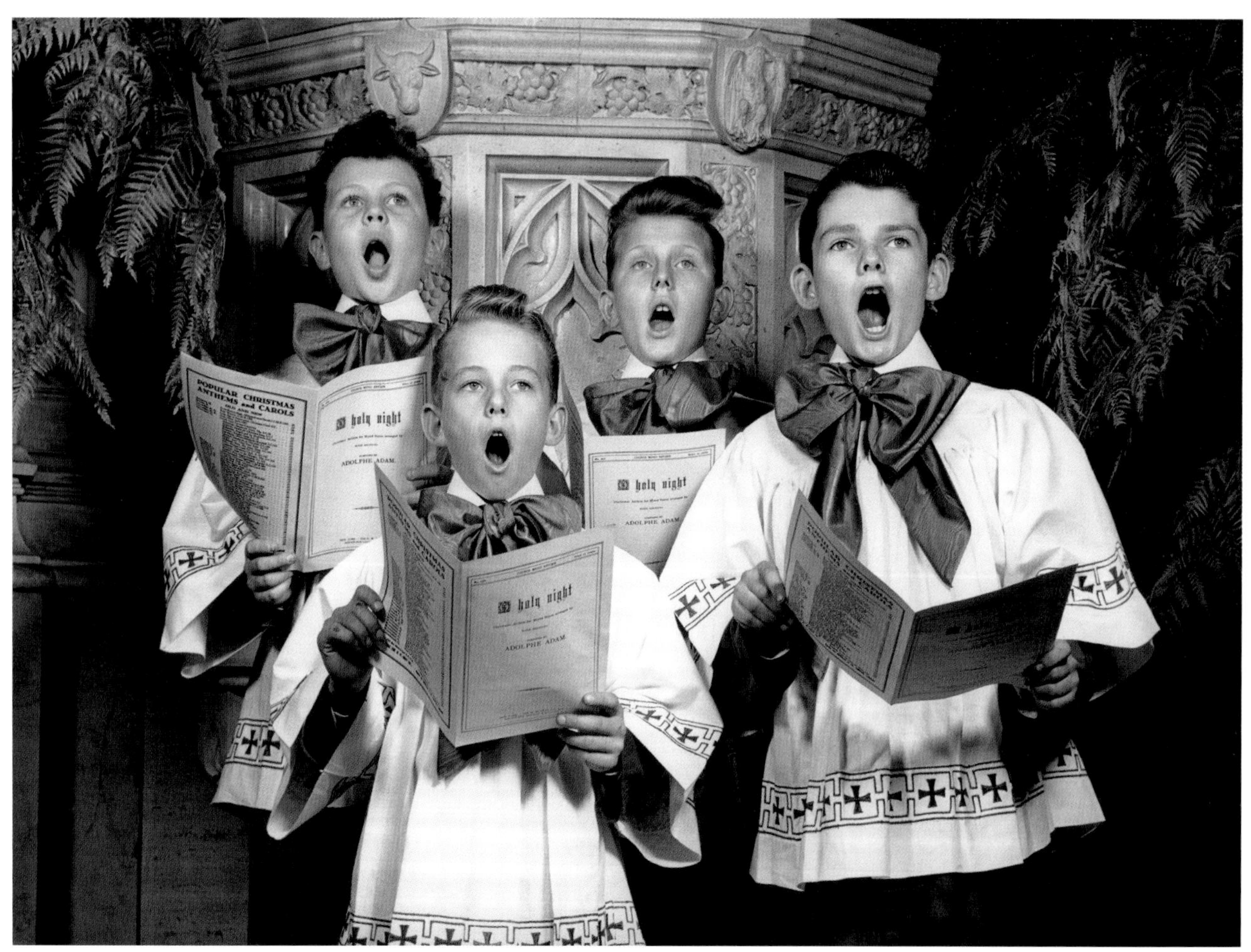

Choirboys singing 'O Holy Night',
1949

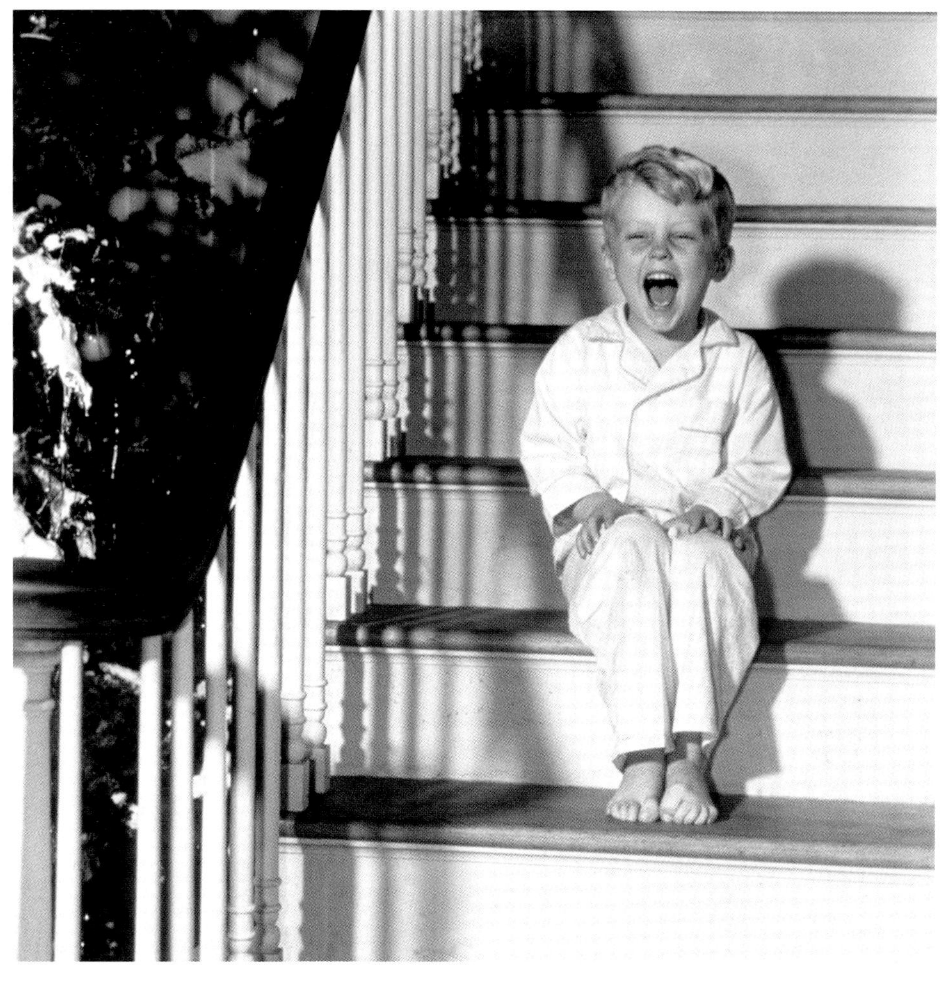

Christmas morning,
USA, 1950s

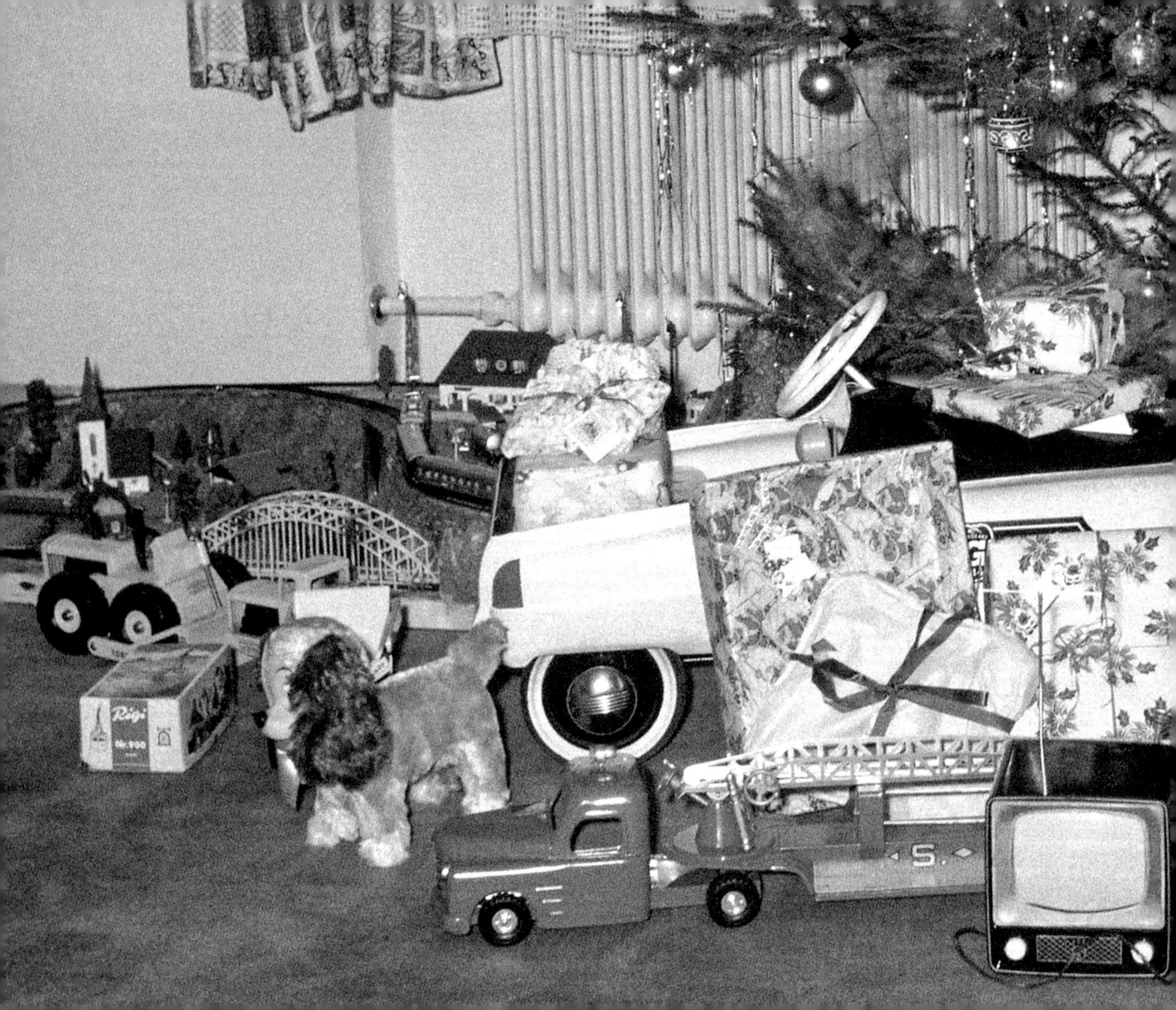

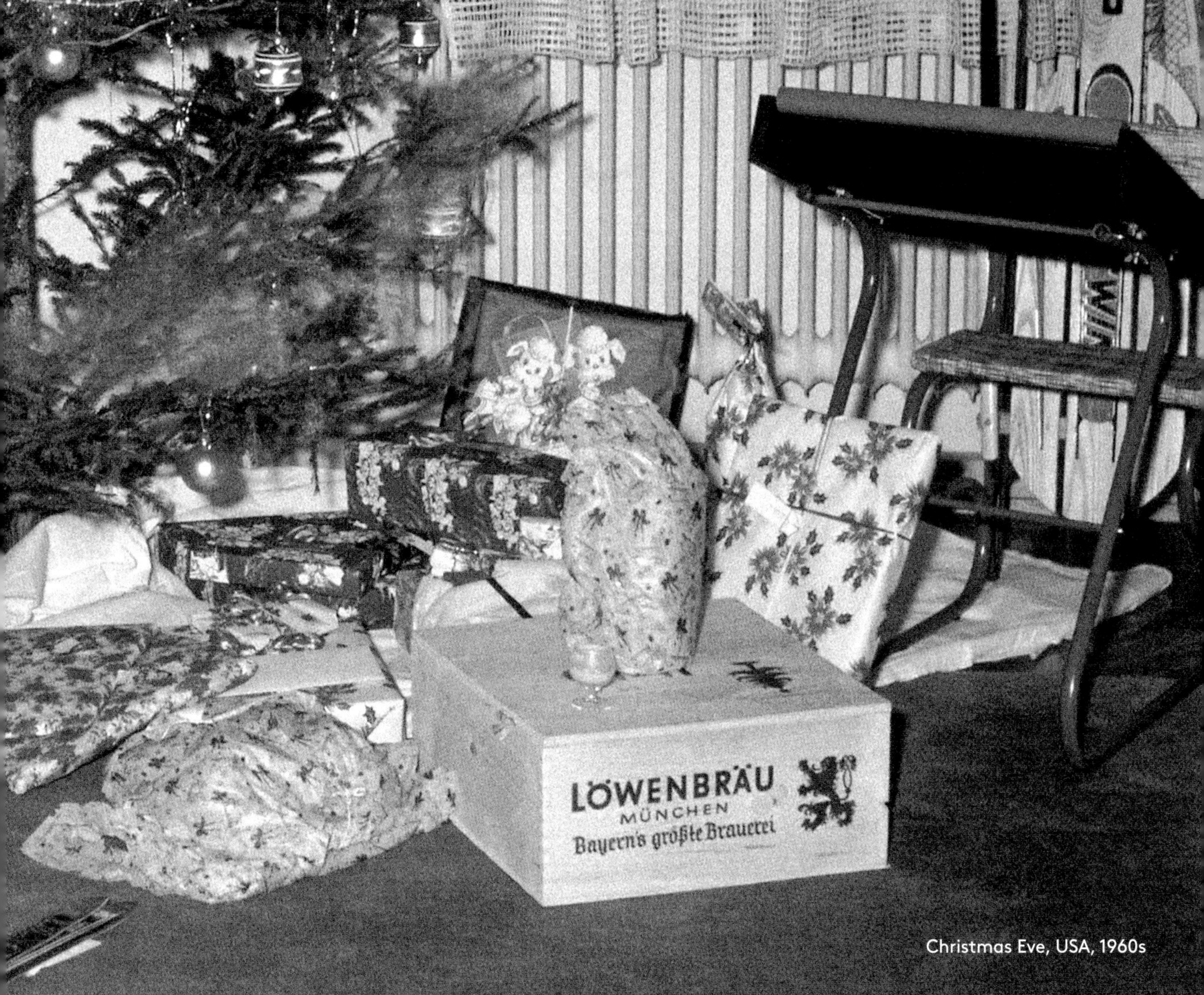

Christmas Eve, USA, 1960s

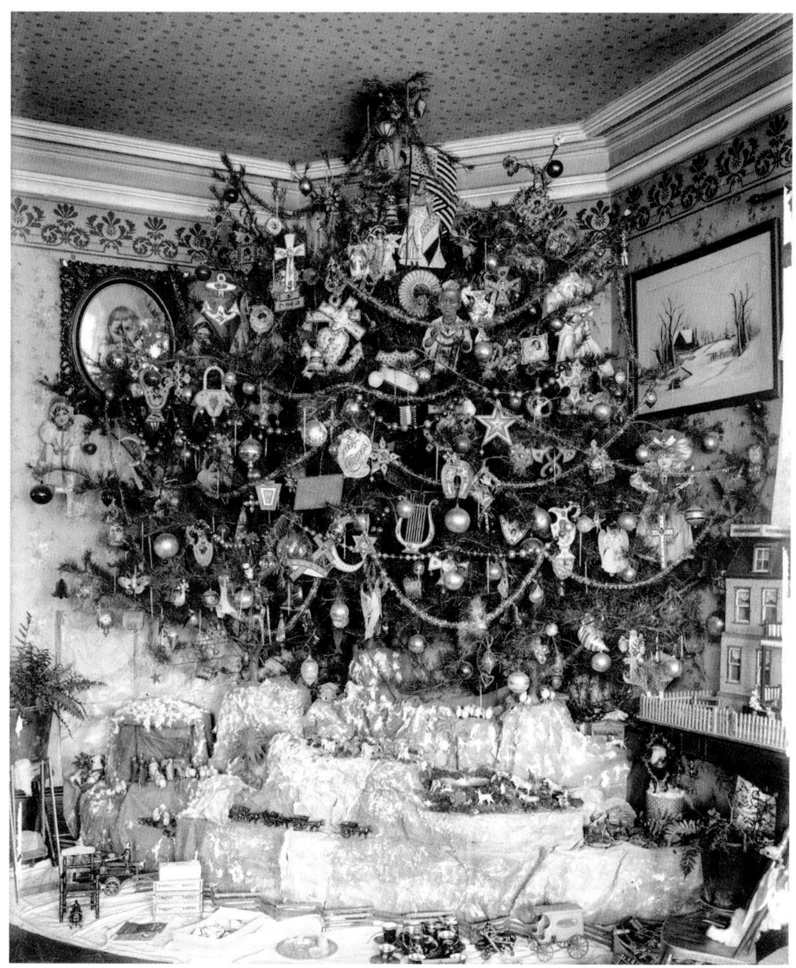

Family Christmas tree,
USA, 1910

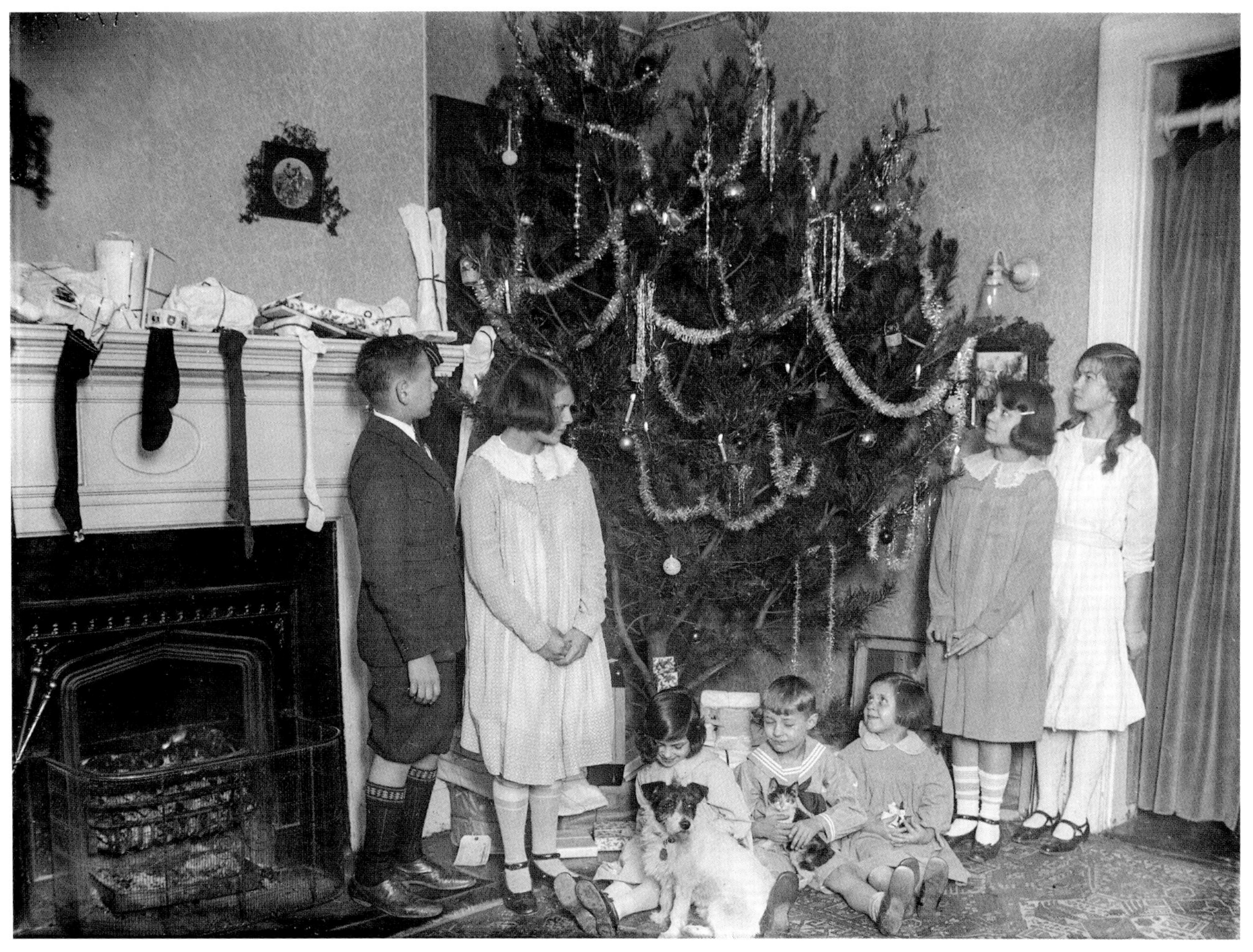

Lined up for a family photo with
the Christmas tree, USA, 1920s

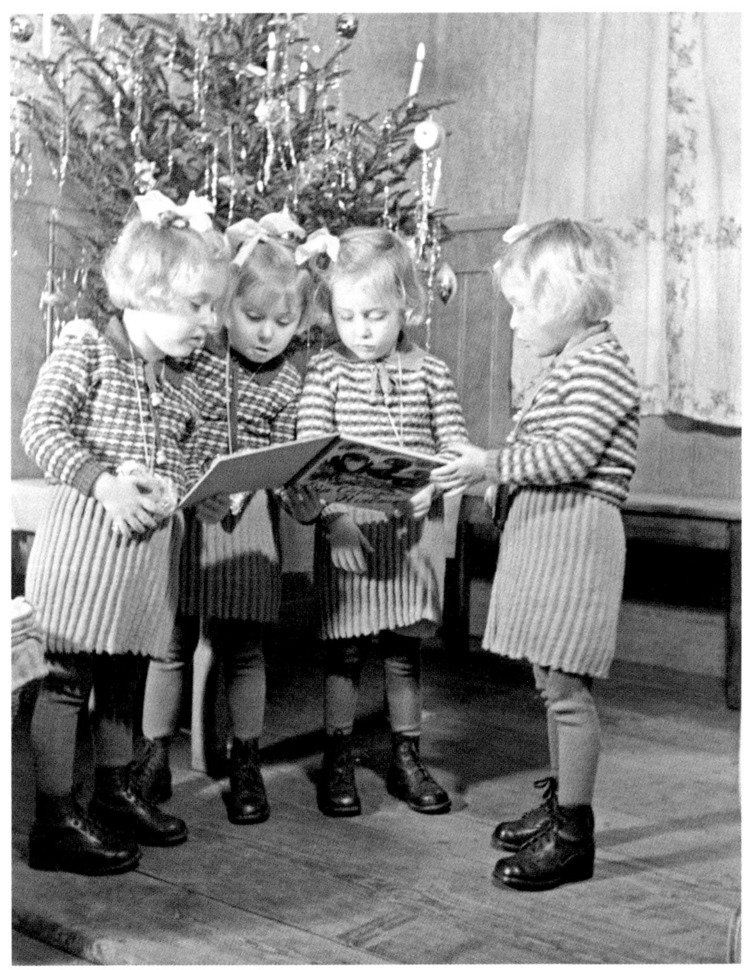

Christmas with quadruplets,
Germany, 1930s

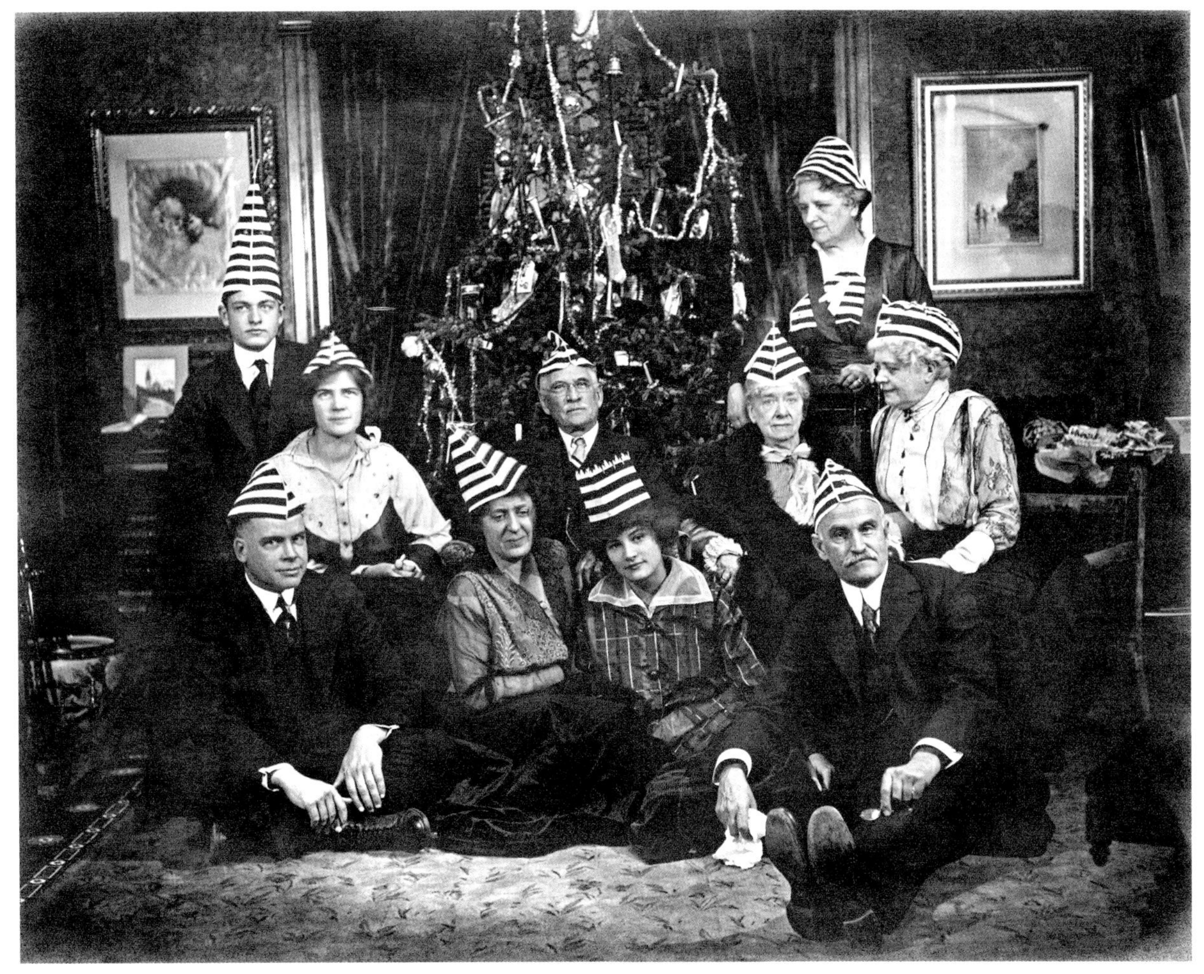

Christmas with fine hats,
USA, 1915

Anna Coleman Ladd (seated in foreground) of
the American Red Cross with her patients on
Christmas Day, France, 1918

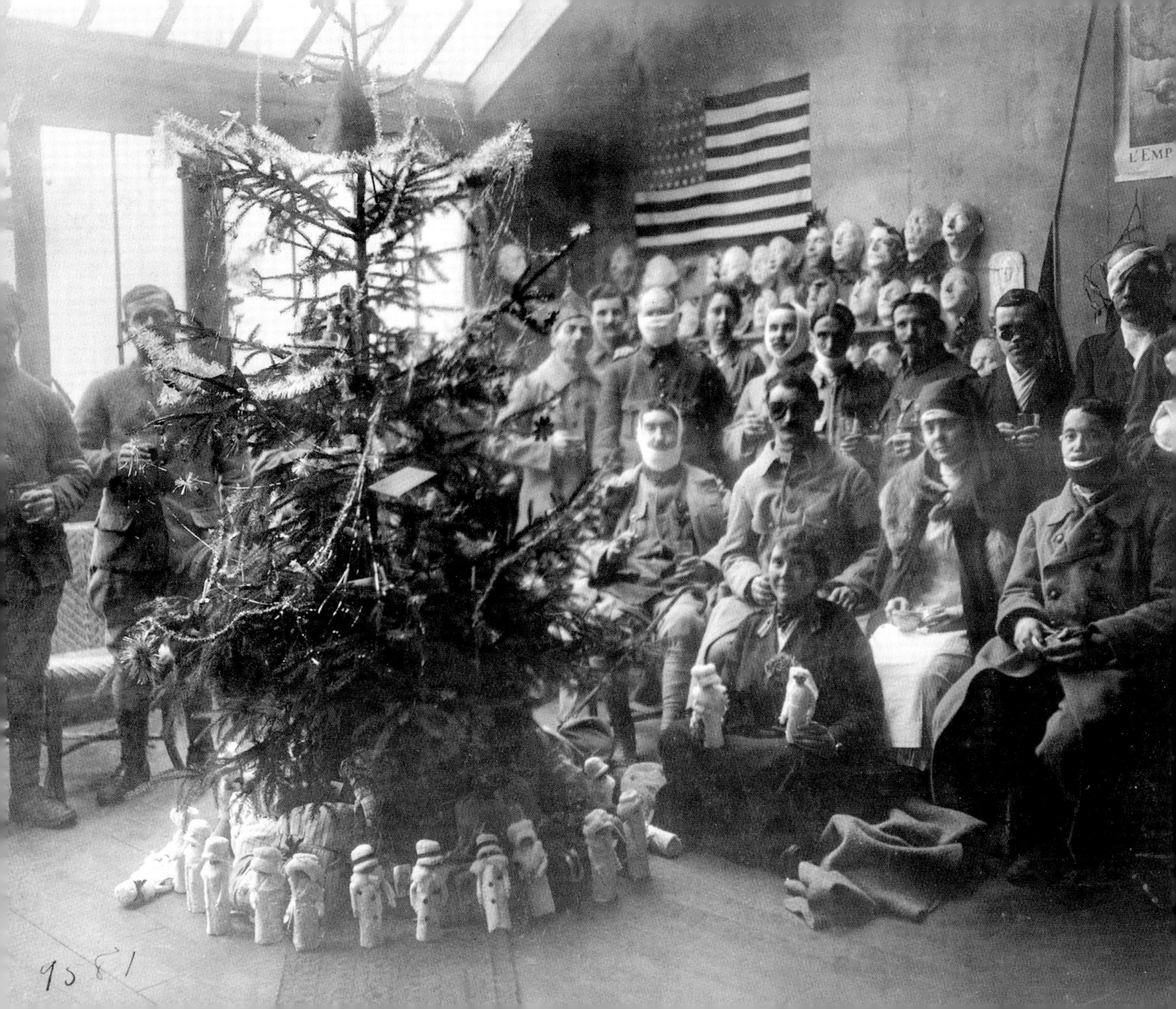

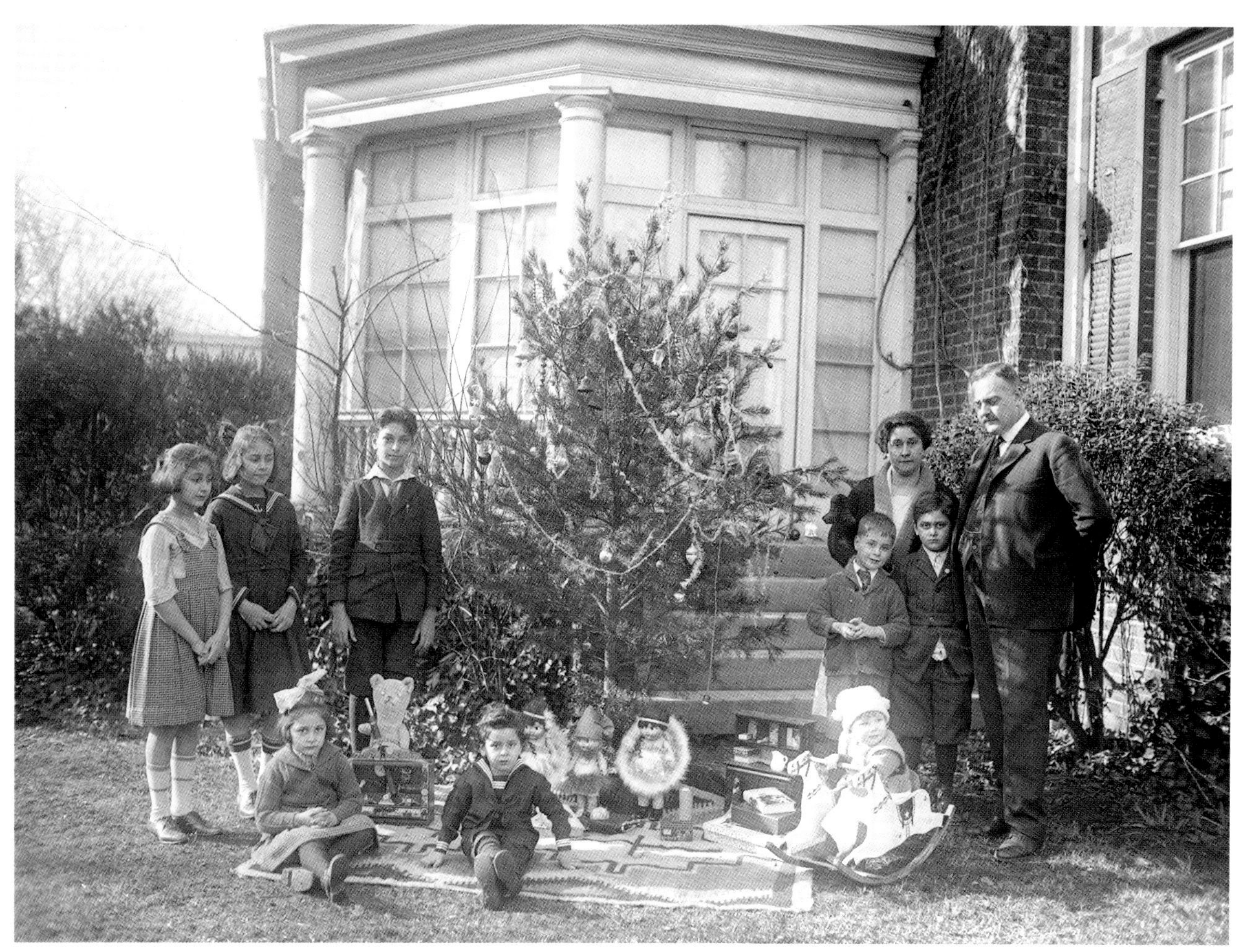

Guatemalan minister Dr Julio Bianchi with wife and children at
the ambassador's embassy residence, Washington, D.C., USA, 1921

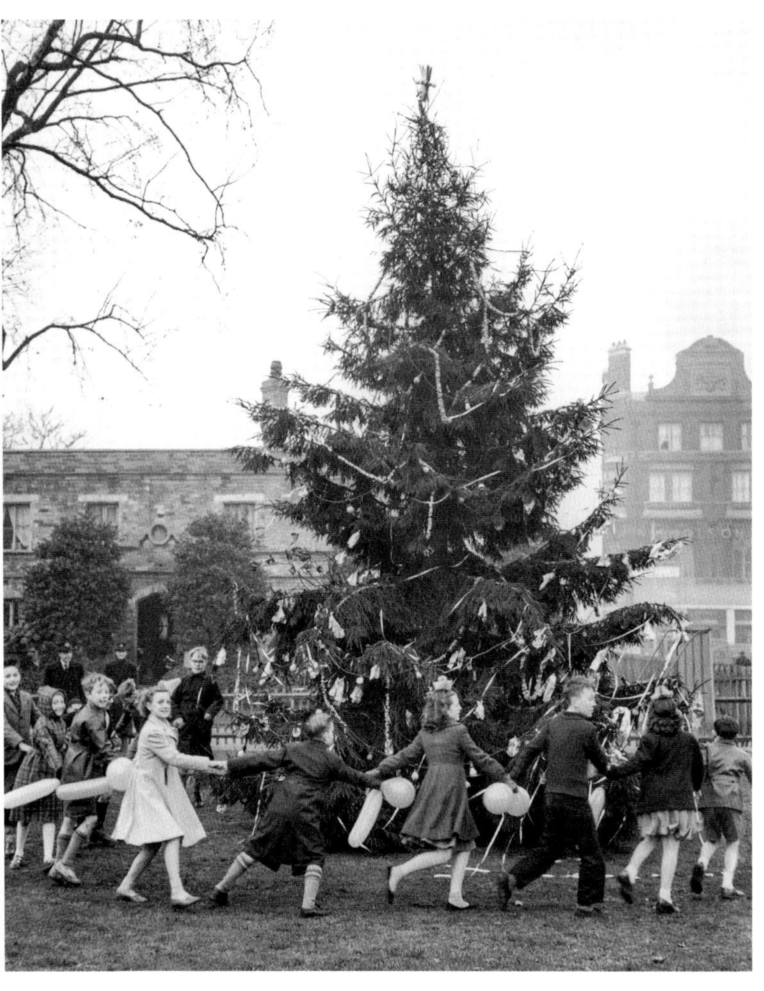

Children dancing around a Christmas tree
in Kennington Park, London, UK, 1955

Jailhouse Christmas tree,
Washington, D.C., USA, 1919

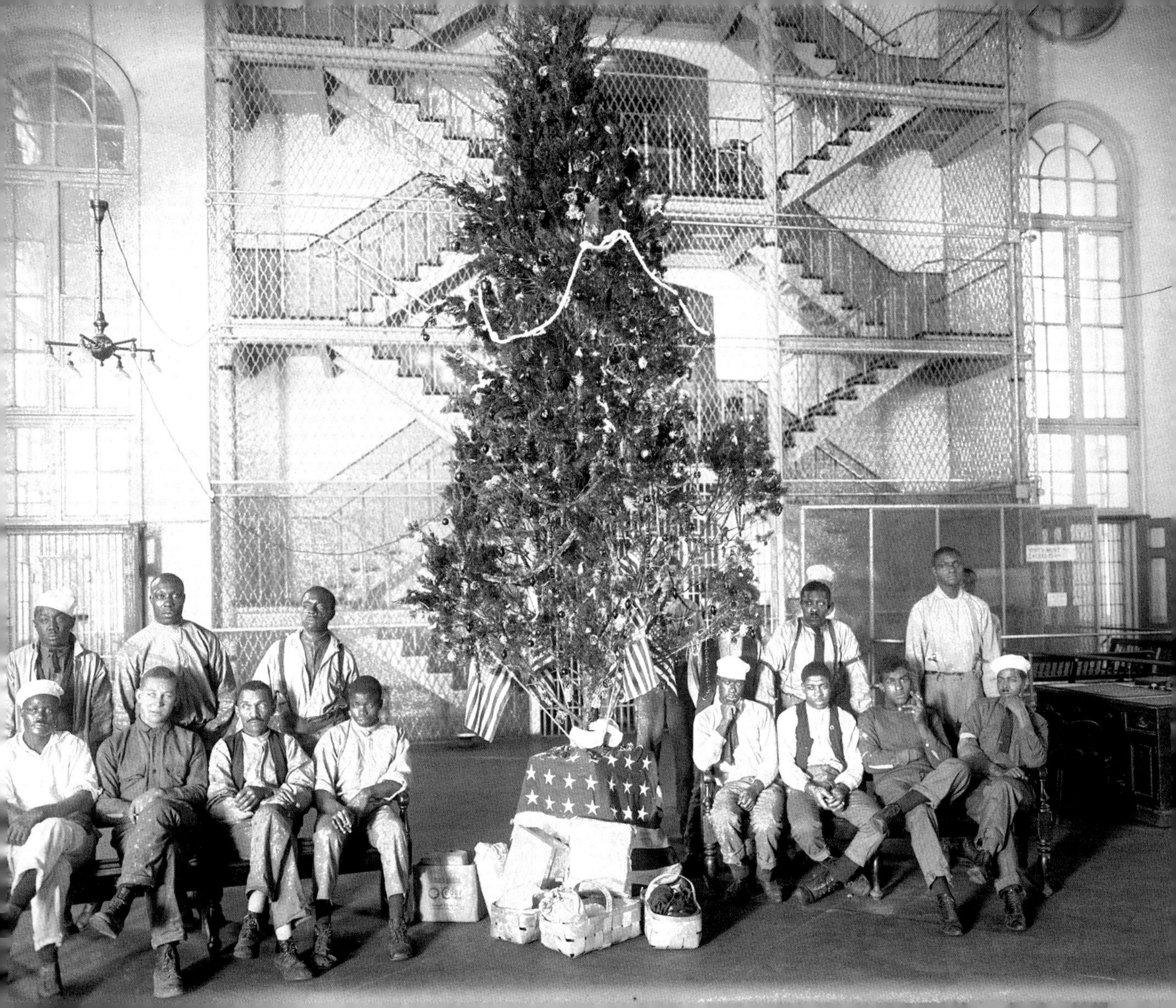

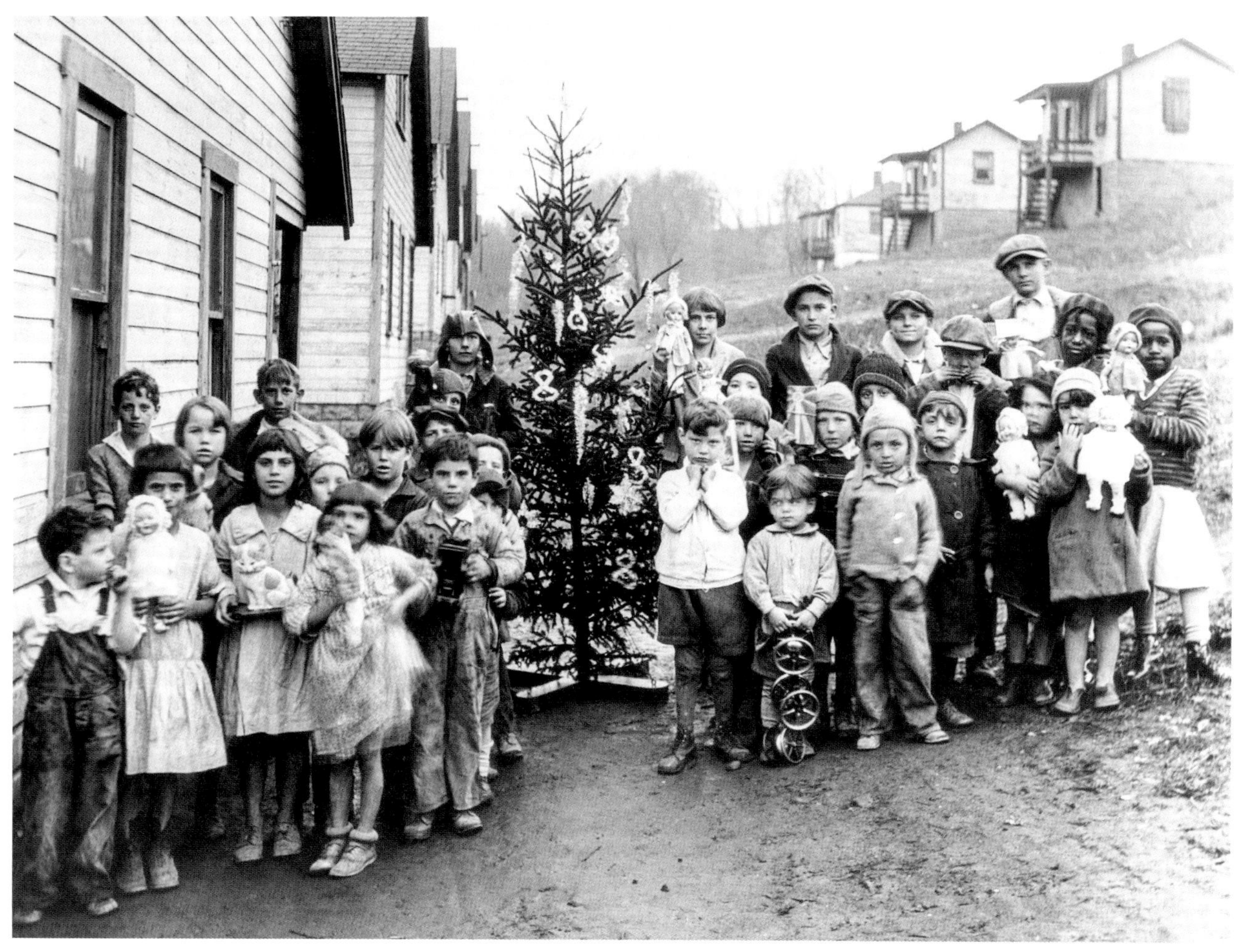

Miner's children holding gifts received from
First Lady Lou Hoover, West Virginia, USA, 1931

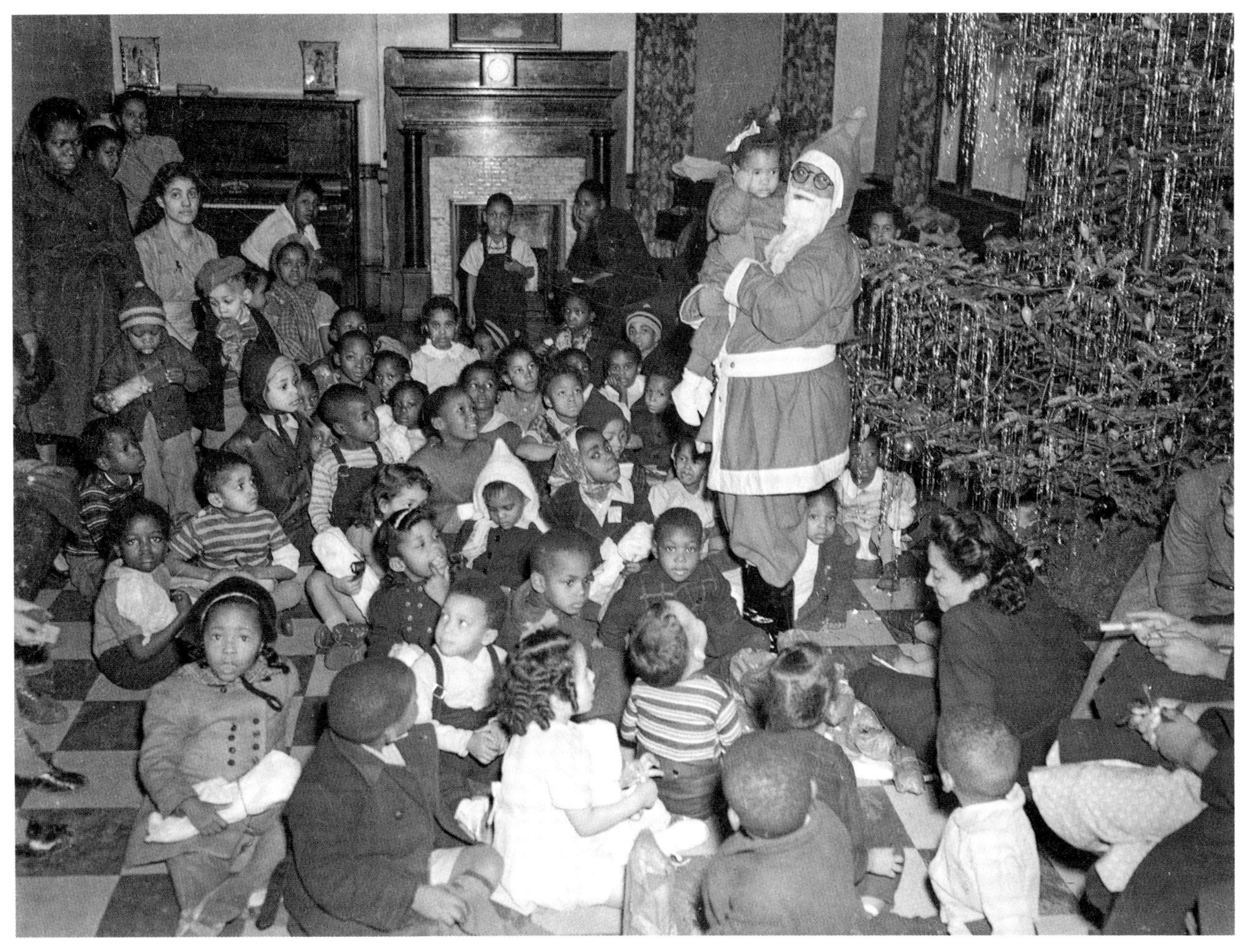

Santa at the YWCA crisis shelter, shot by
Charles 'Teenie' Harris, Pittsburgh, Pennsylvania, 1941

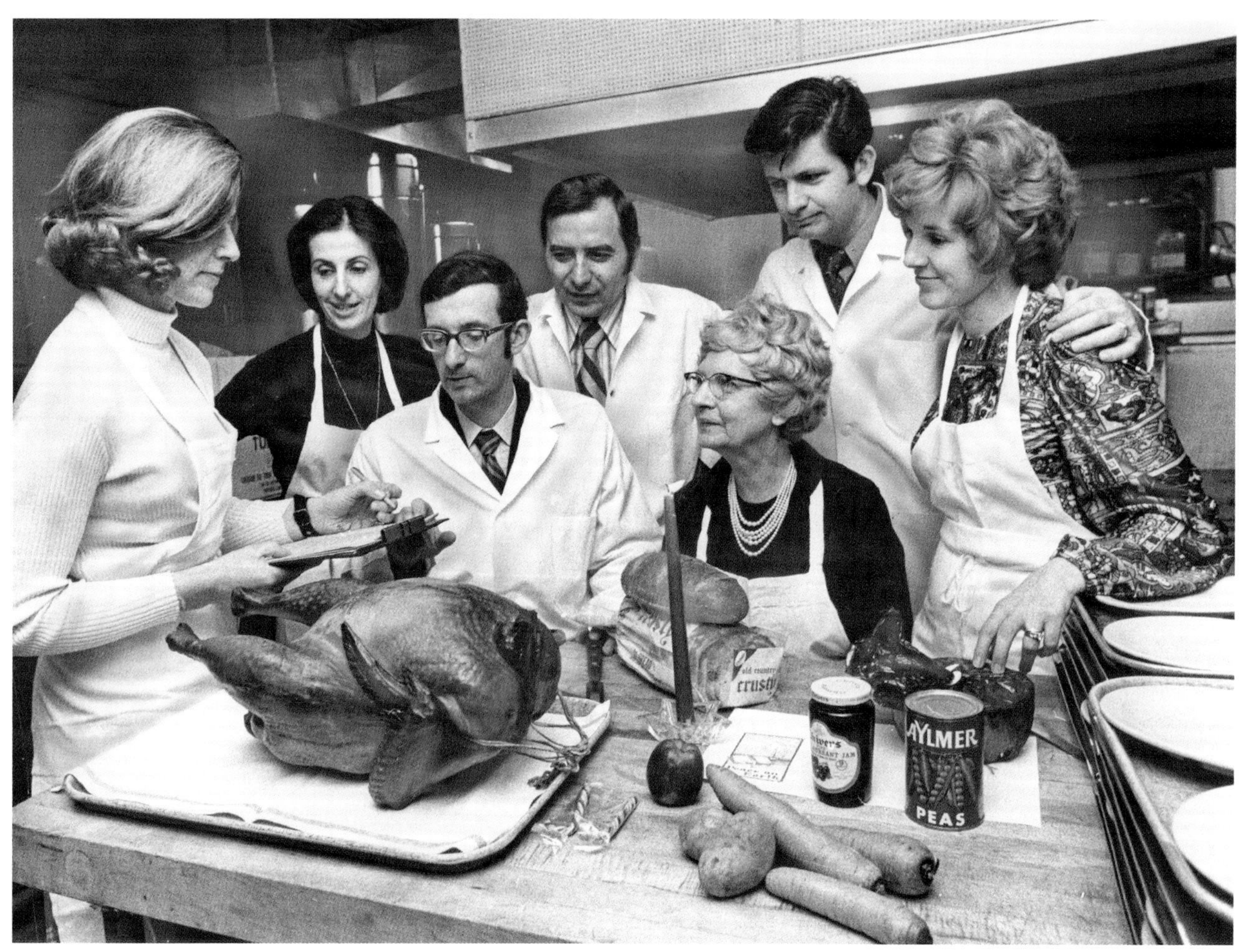

Preparing Christmas dinner at Scott Mission, a charity
fighting homelessness and hunger, Toronto, Canada, 1971

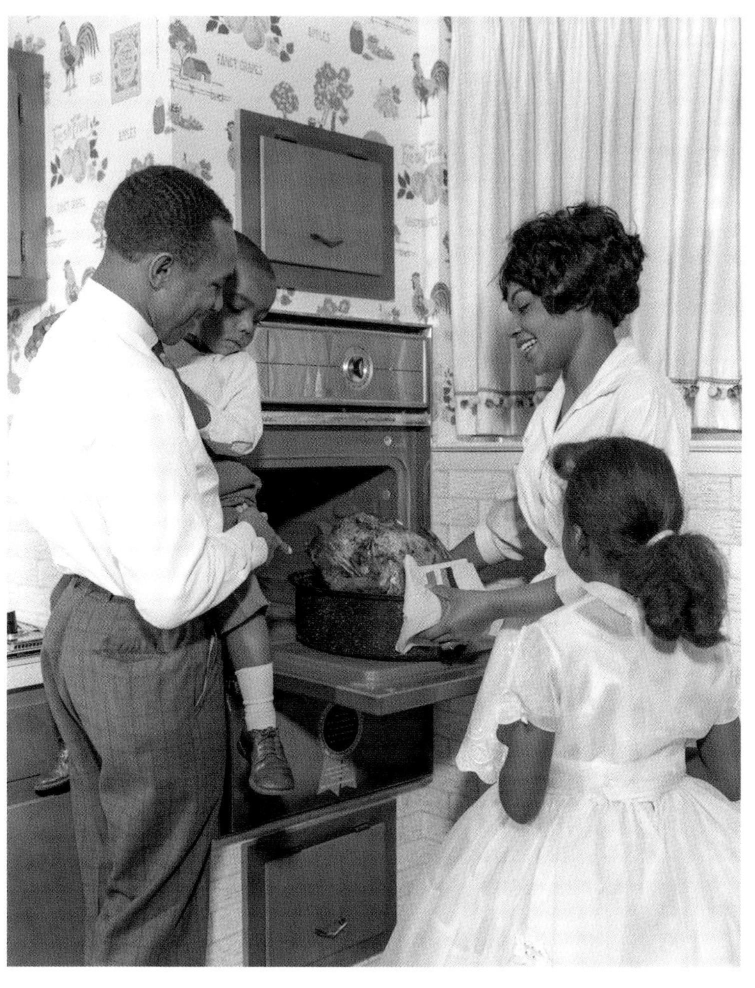

The turkey is ready,
USA, 1960s

USA, 1955

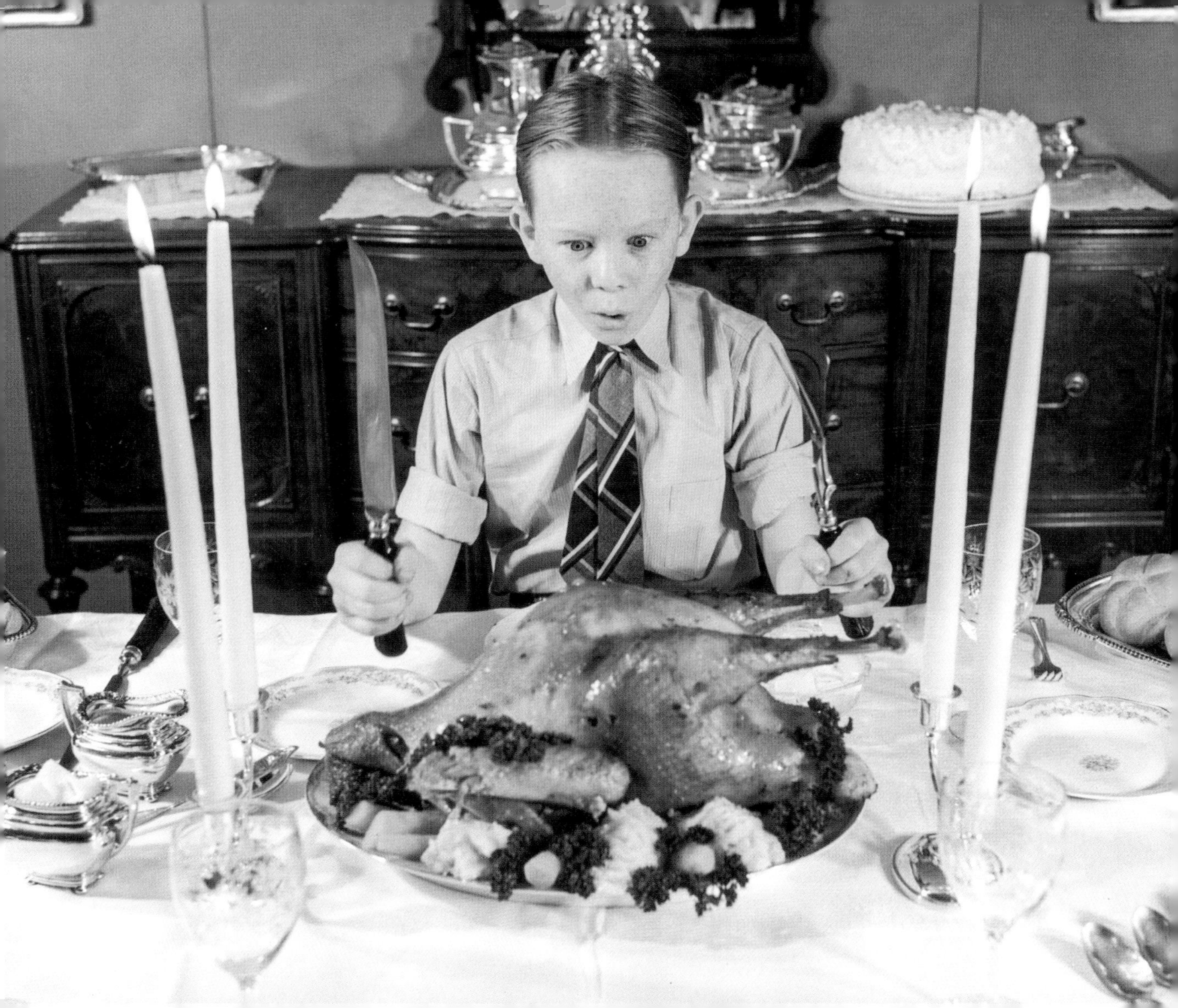

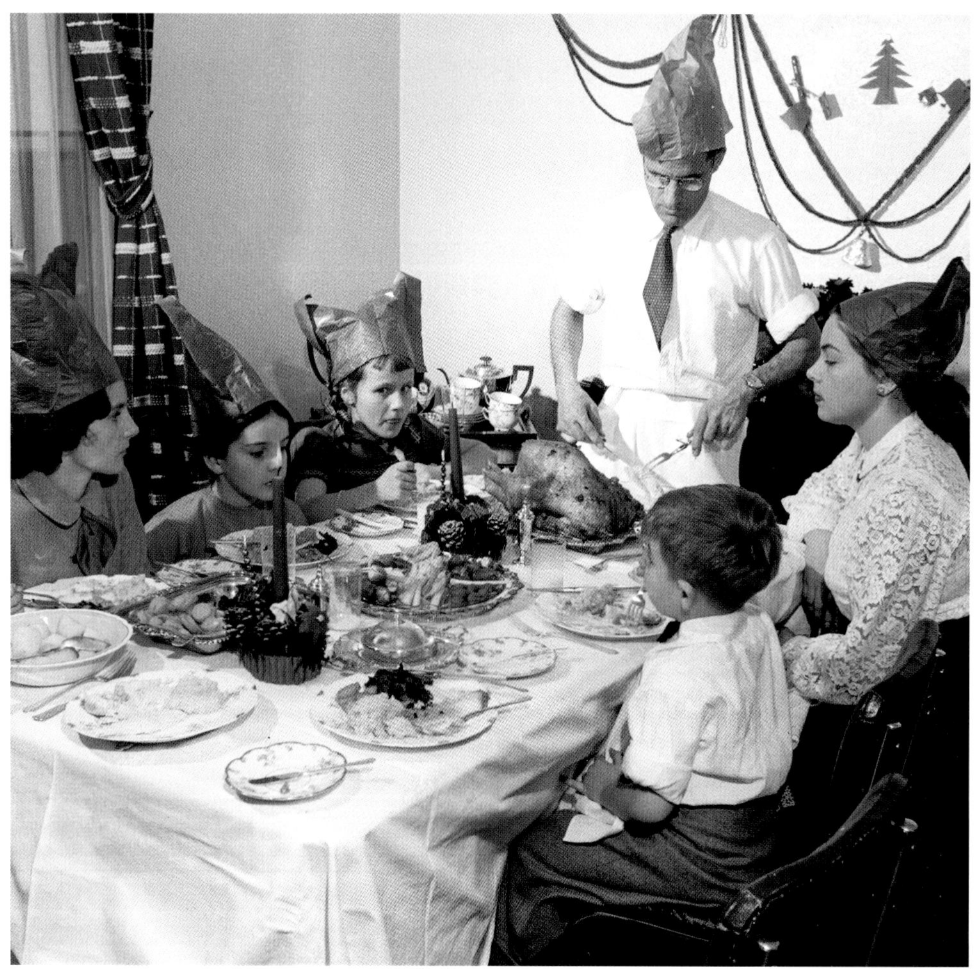

The turkey is carved, 1955

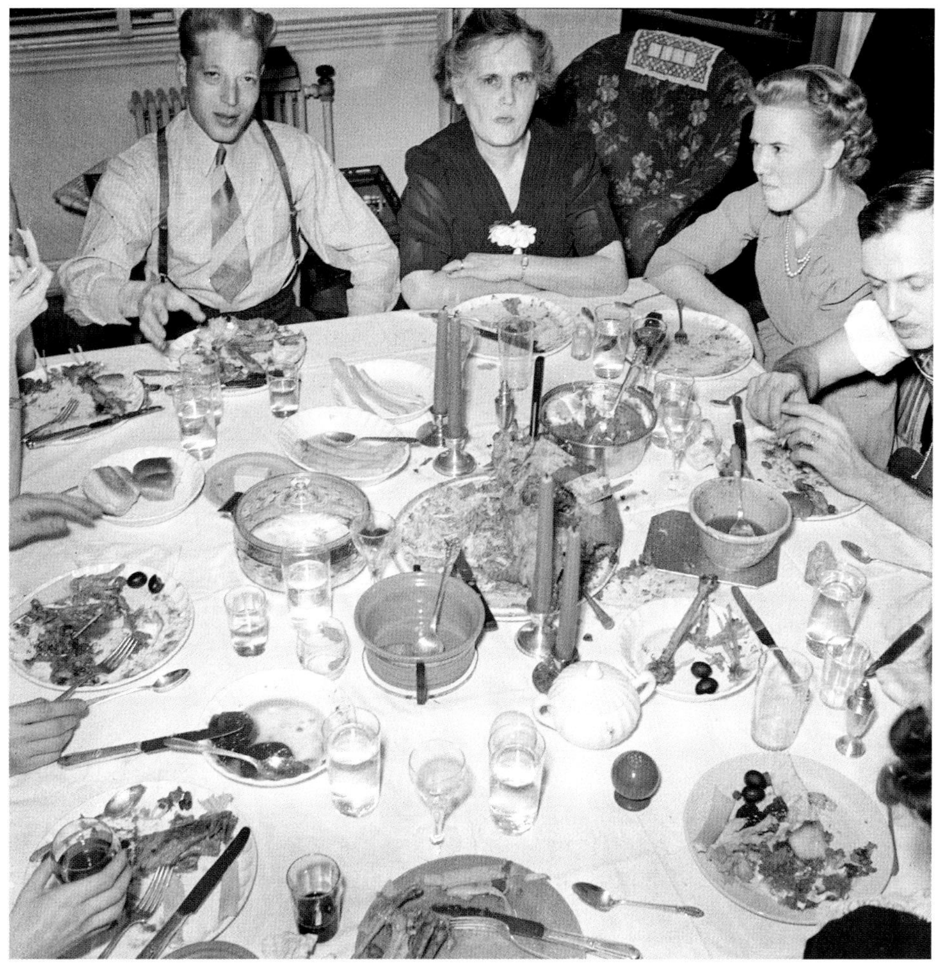

Washington, D.C., USA, 1941

Elderly lady and a young boy pulling
a Christmas cracker, 1944

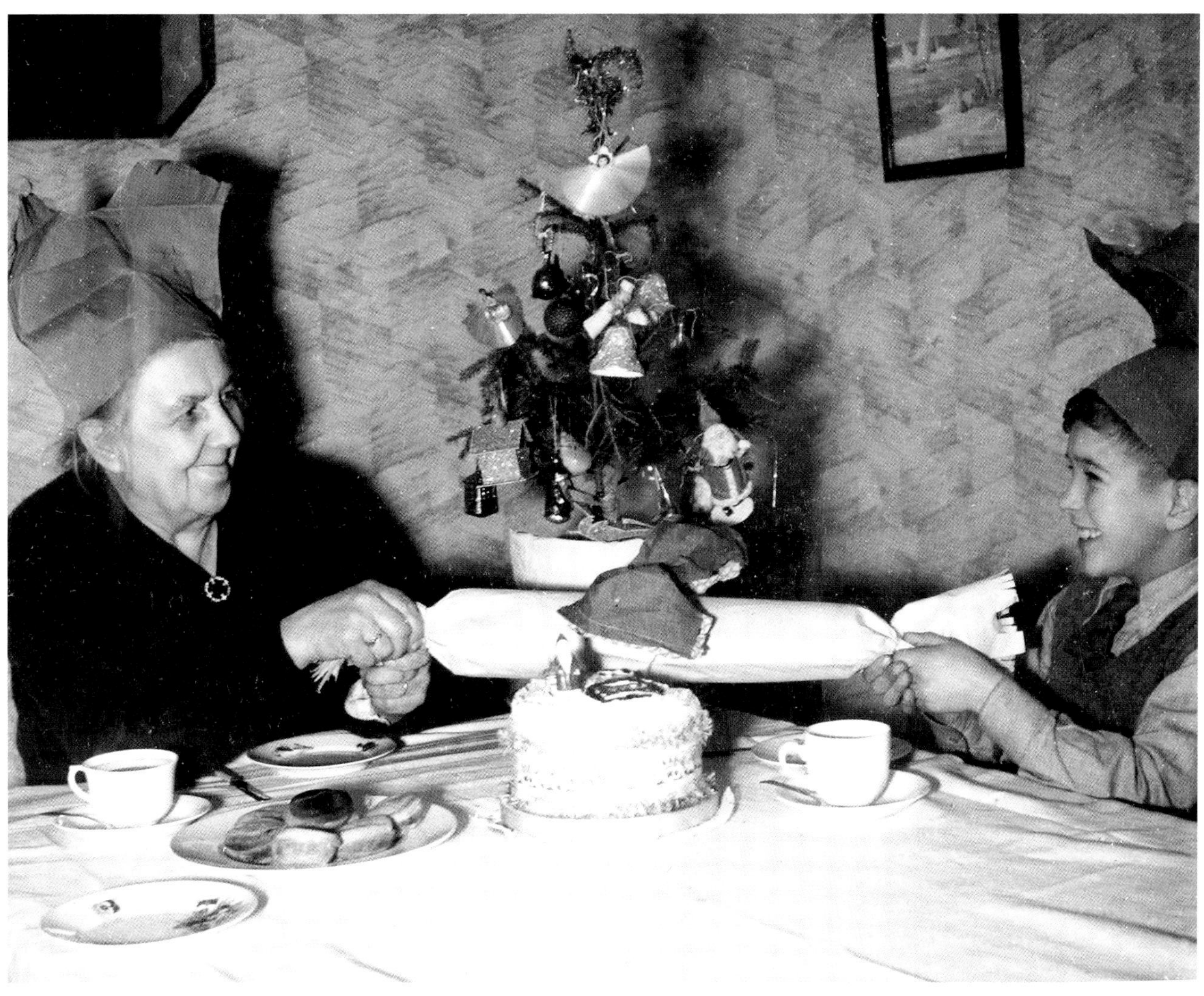

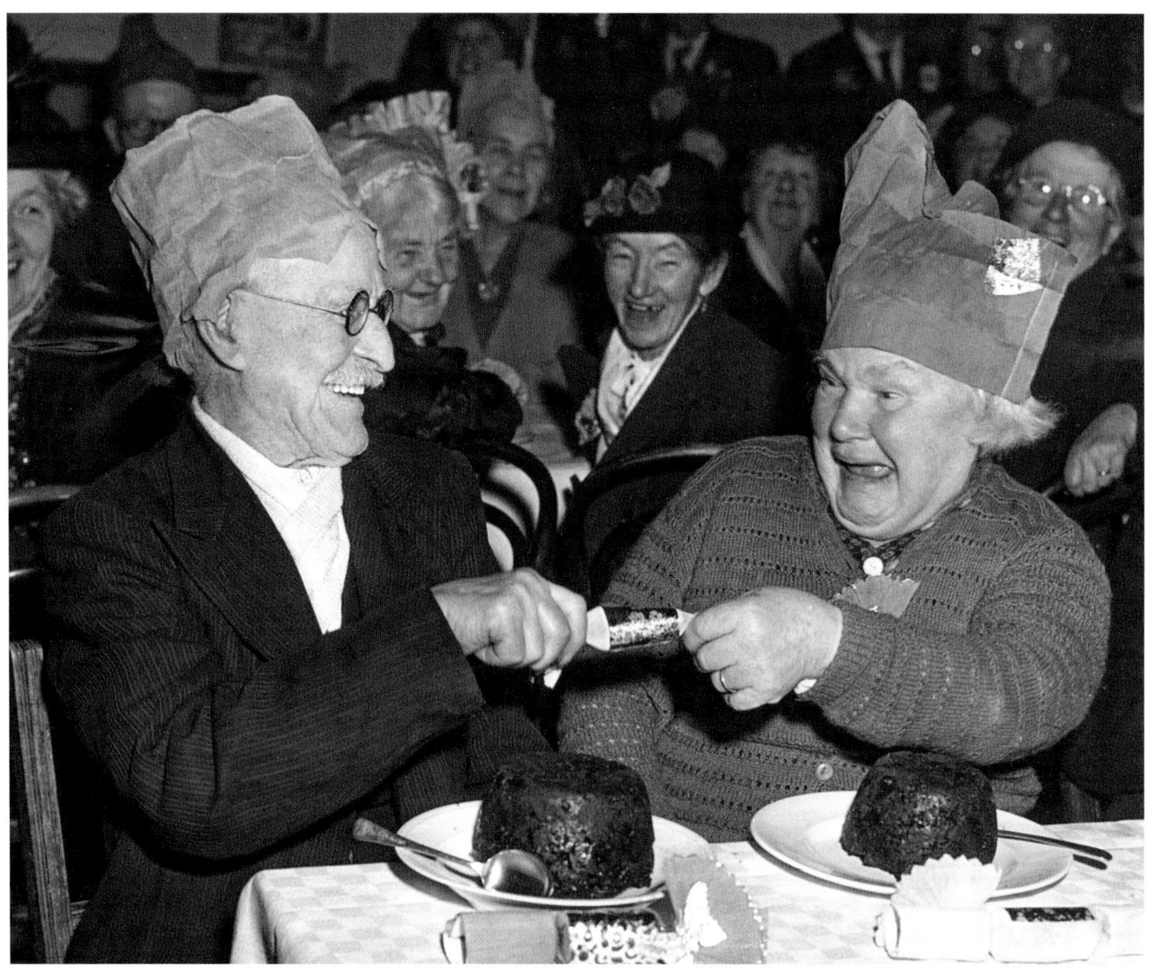

A married couple share a Christmas cracker,
Essex, UK, 1951

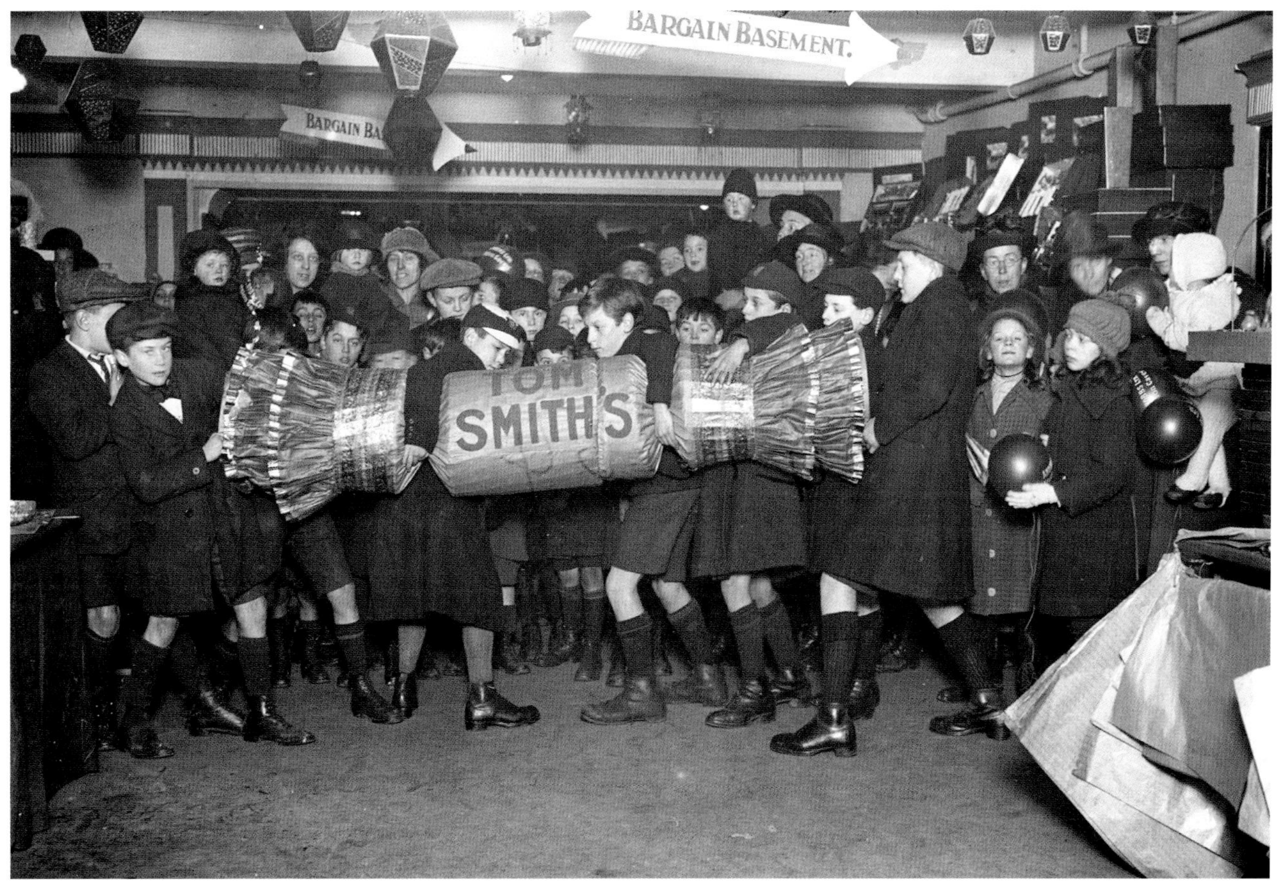

Schoolchildren try to pull apart a giant cracker at an Arding & Hobbs
department store Christmas event, London, UK, 1922

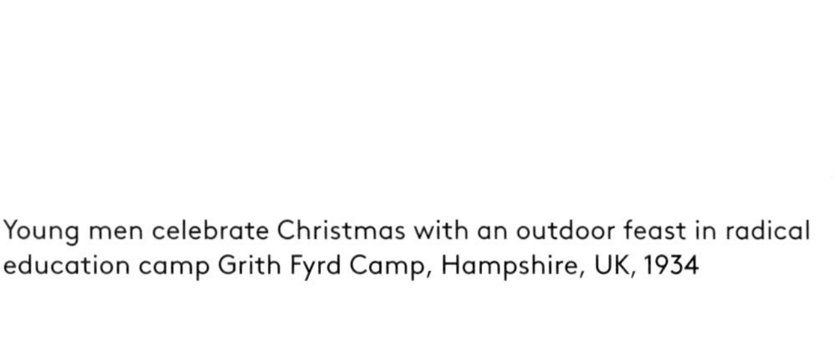

Young men celebrate Christmas with an outdoor feast in radical
education camp Grith Fyrd Camp, Hampshire, UK, 1934

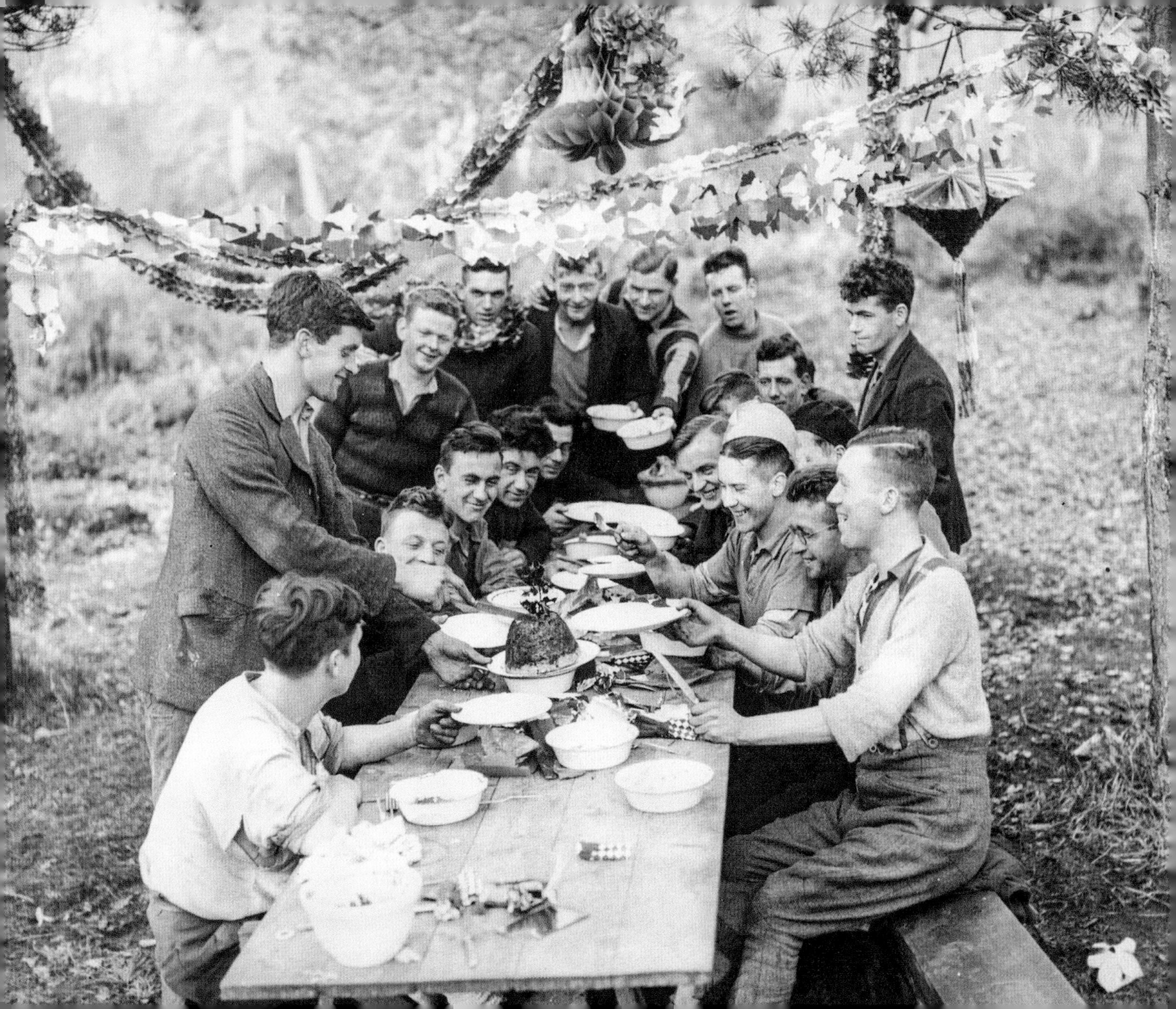

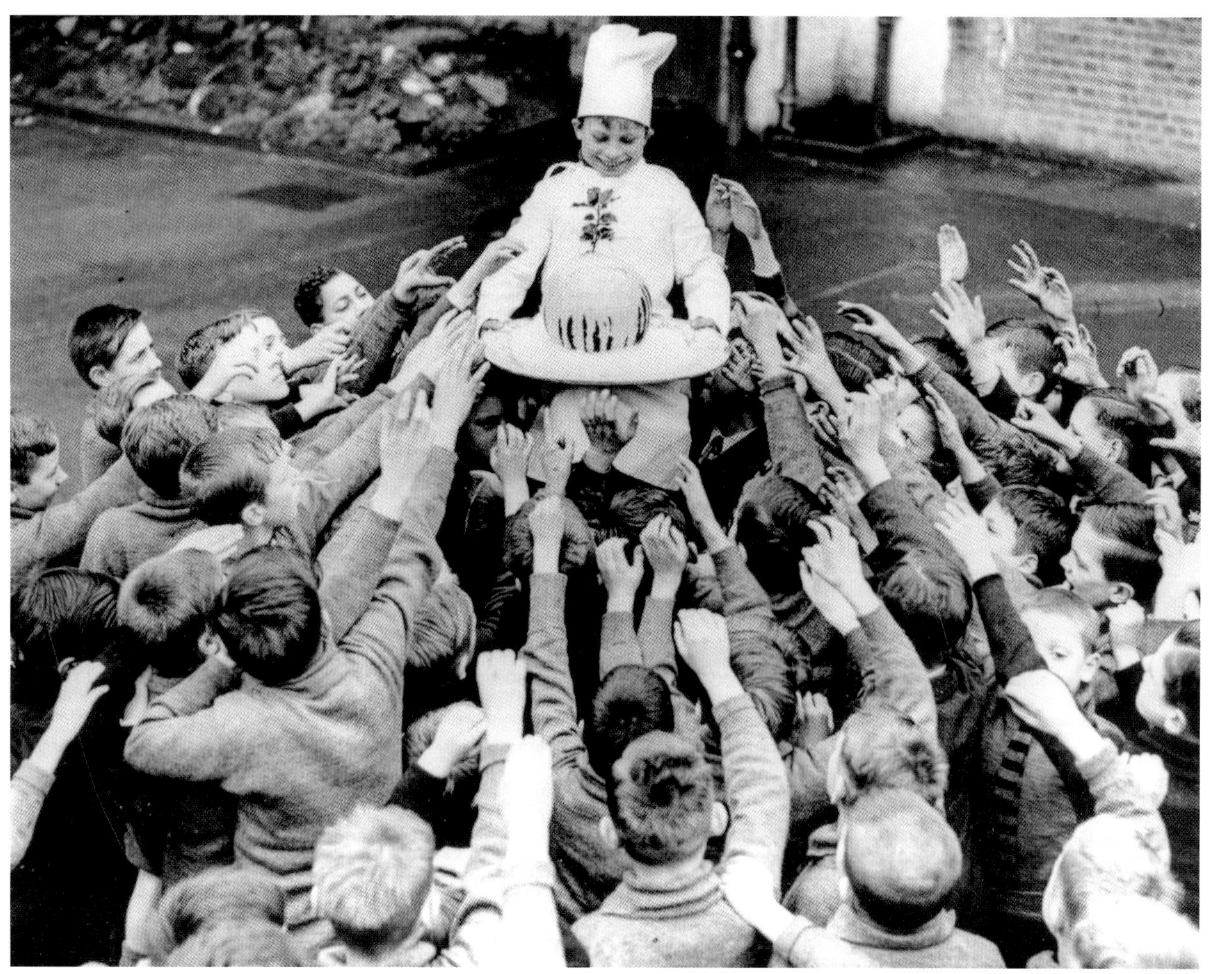

Boys at a Dr Barnardo's home eagerly reaching for
the traditionally piped Christmas pudding, UK, 1935

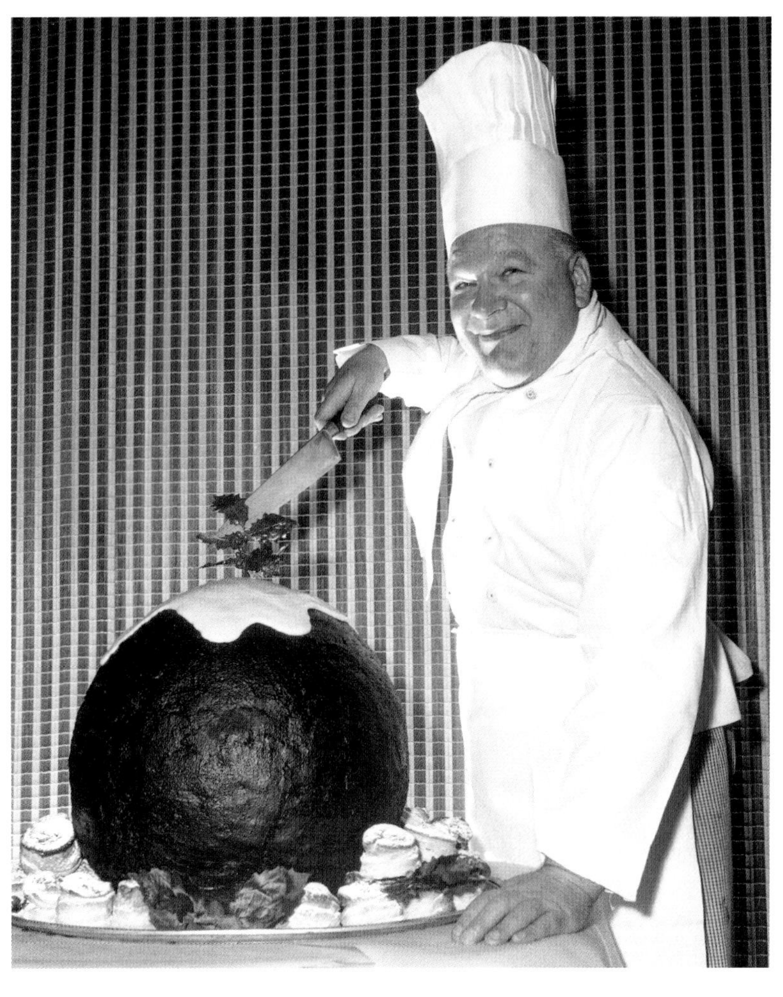

Chef A.W. Valsler ready to cut a gigantic
Christmas pudding surrounded by mince pies, UK, 1958

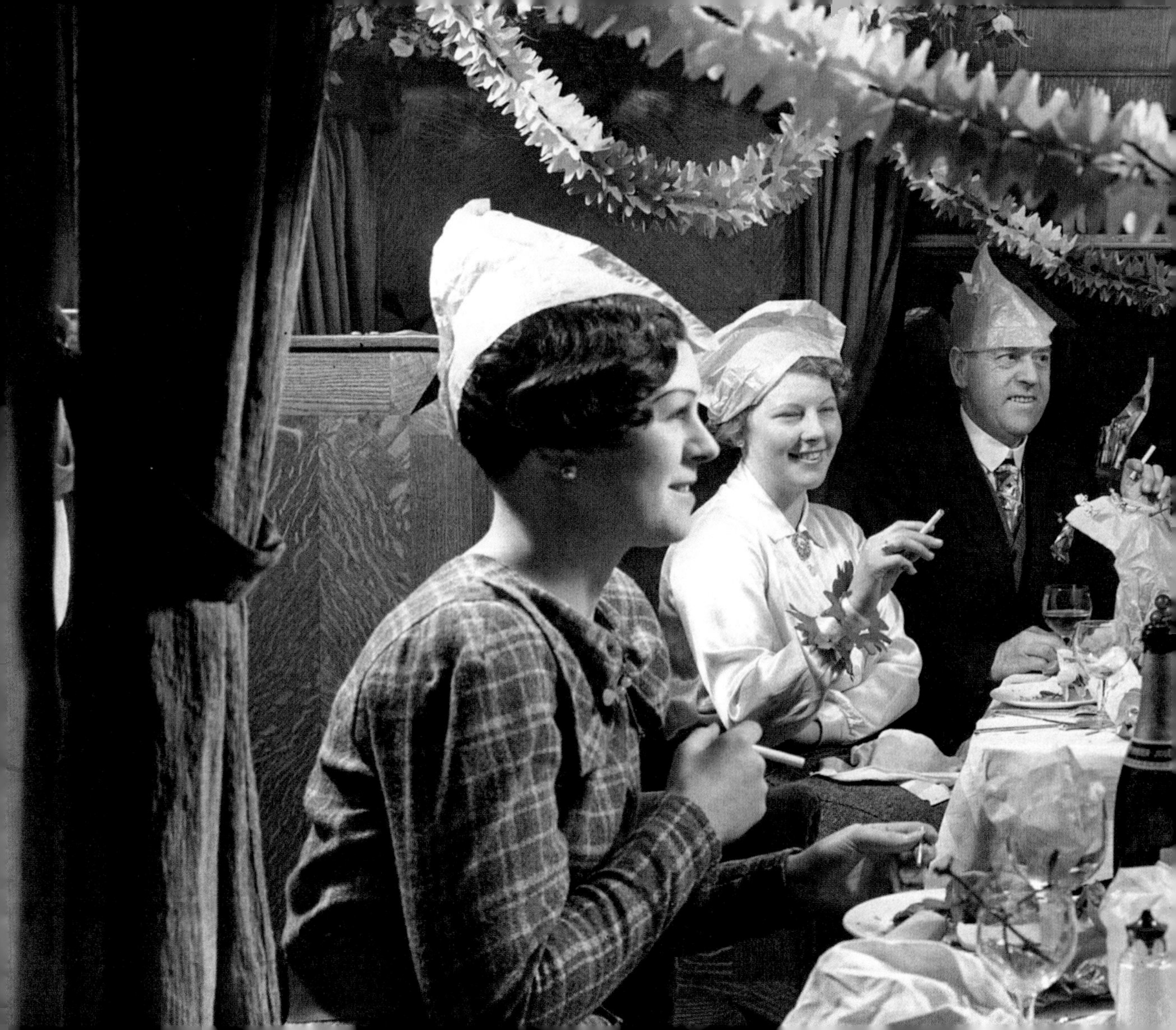

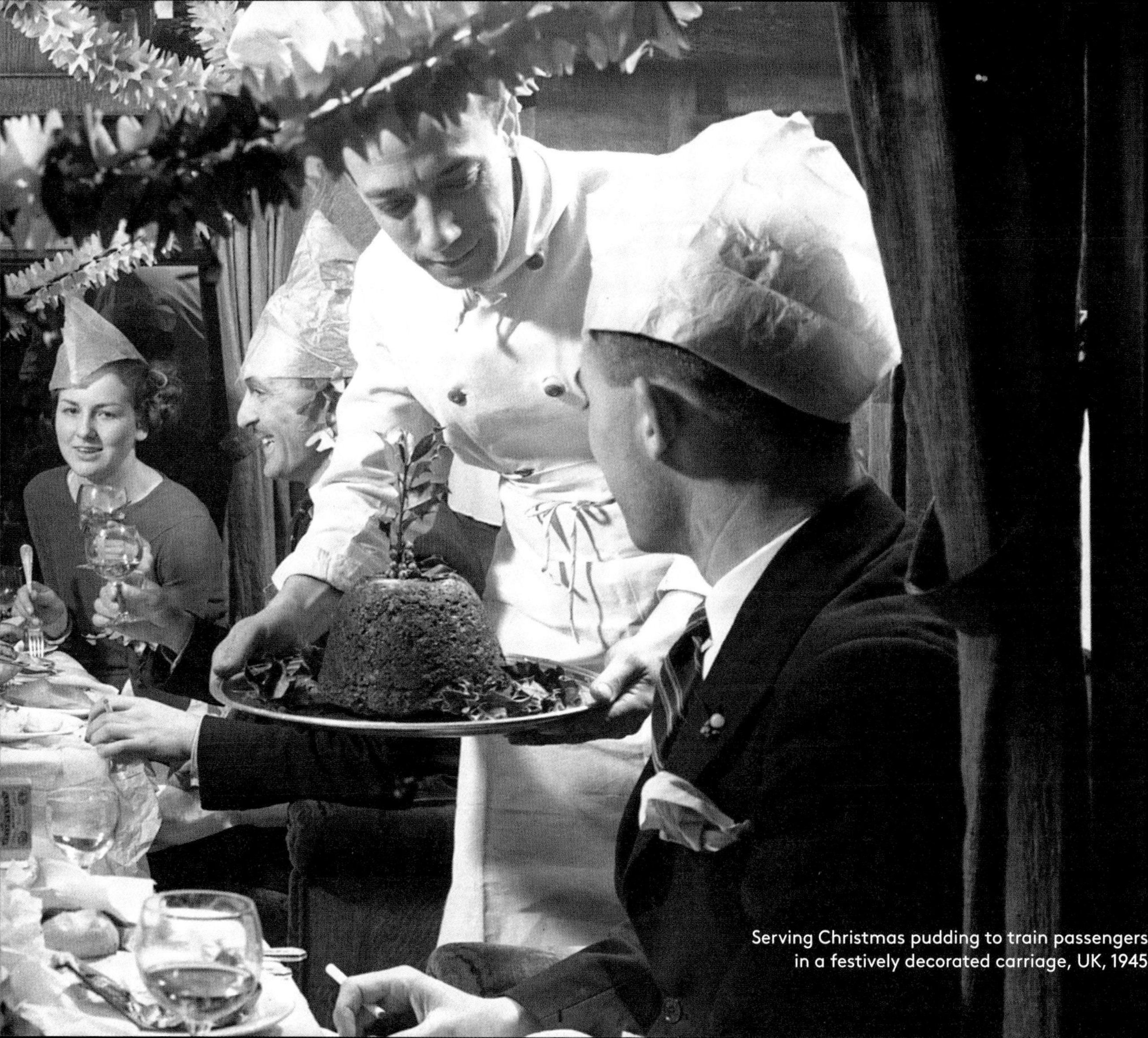

Serving Christmas pudding to train passengers in a festively decorated carriage, UK, 1945

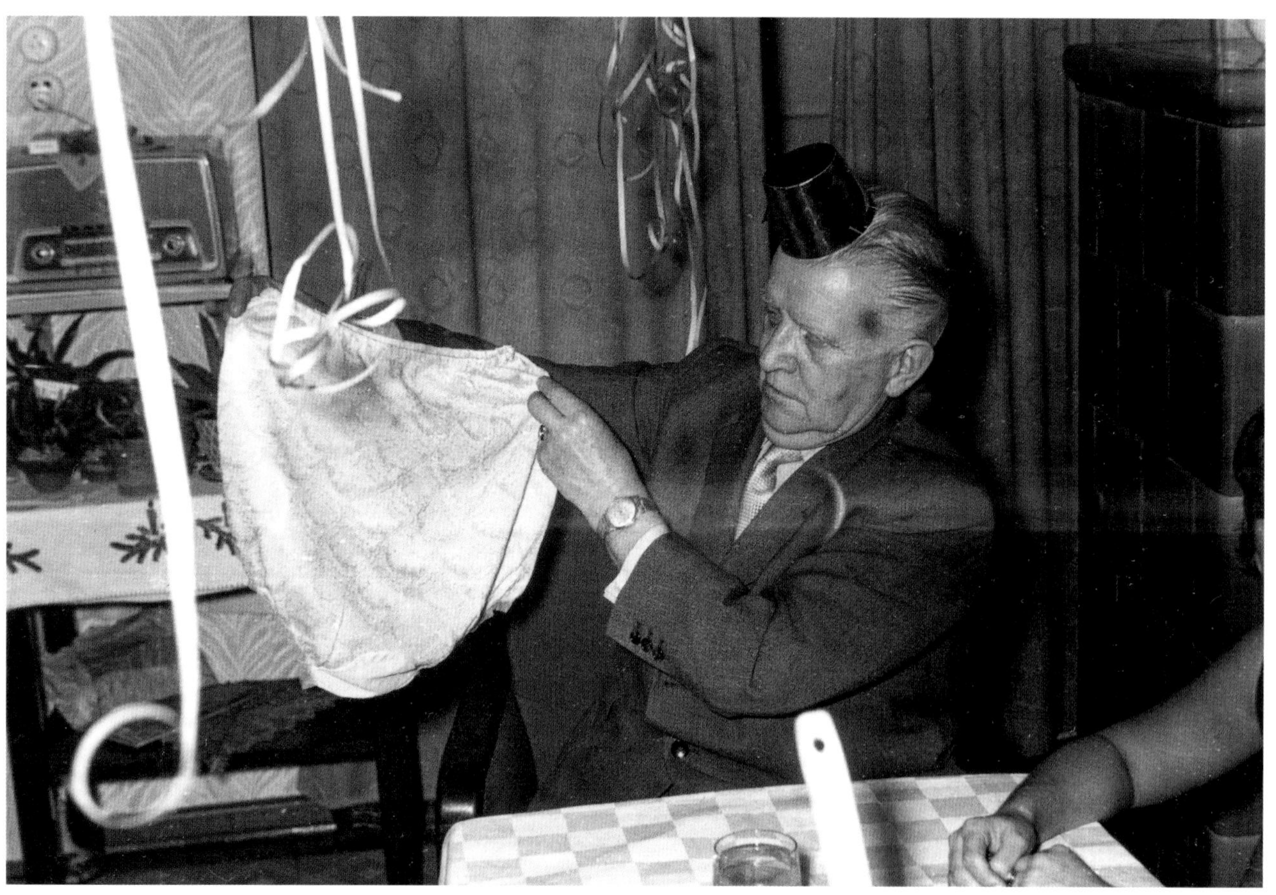

Unwrapping perplexing presents
at Christmas, Germany, 1960s

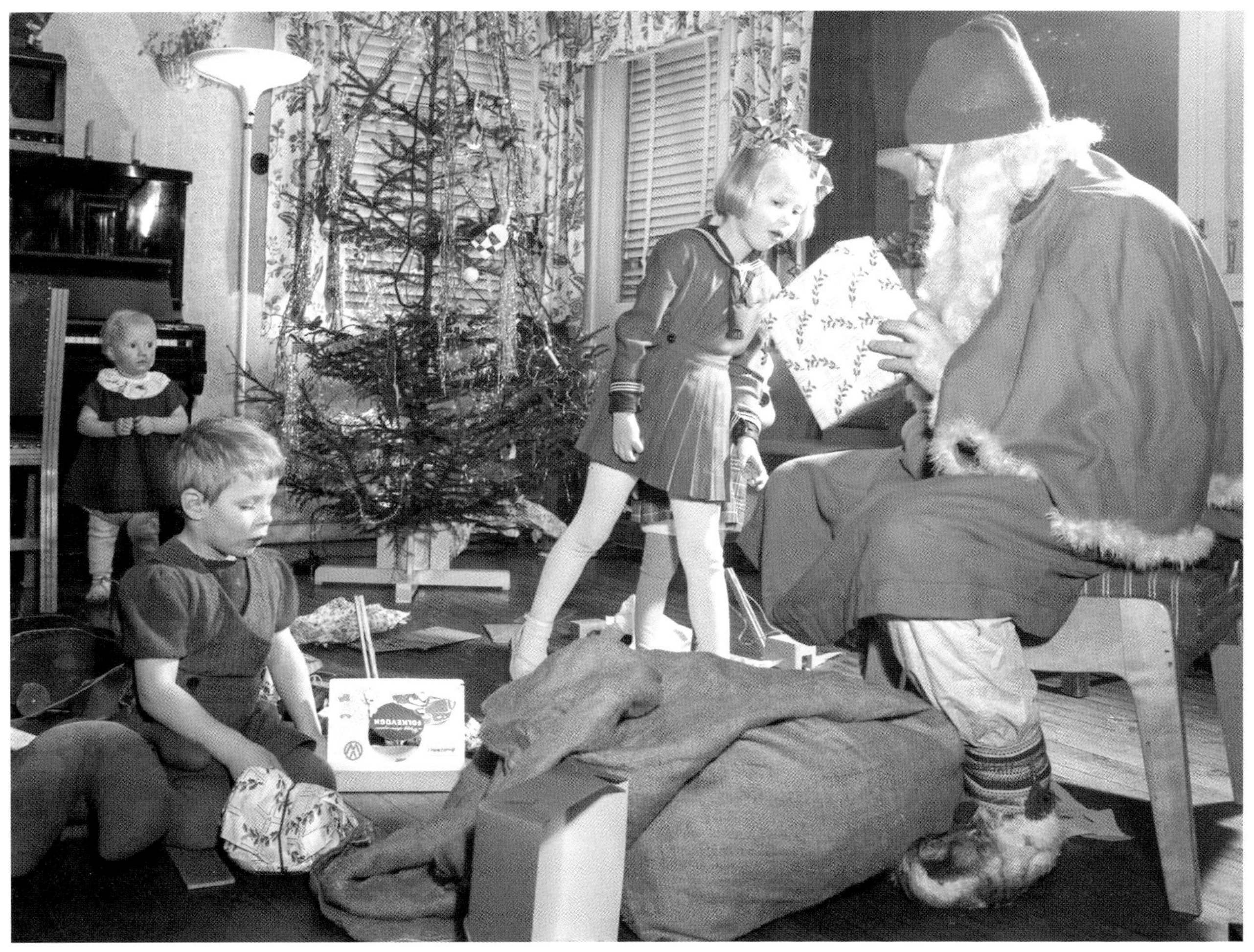

Christmas Eve gifts arrive,
Oslo, Norway, 1953

Children kitted out as cowboys enjoying the
holiday season, Pennsylvania, USA, 1960

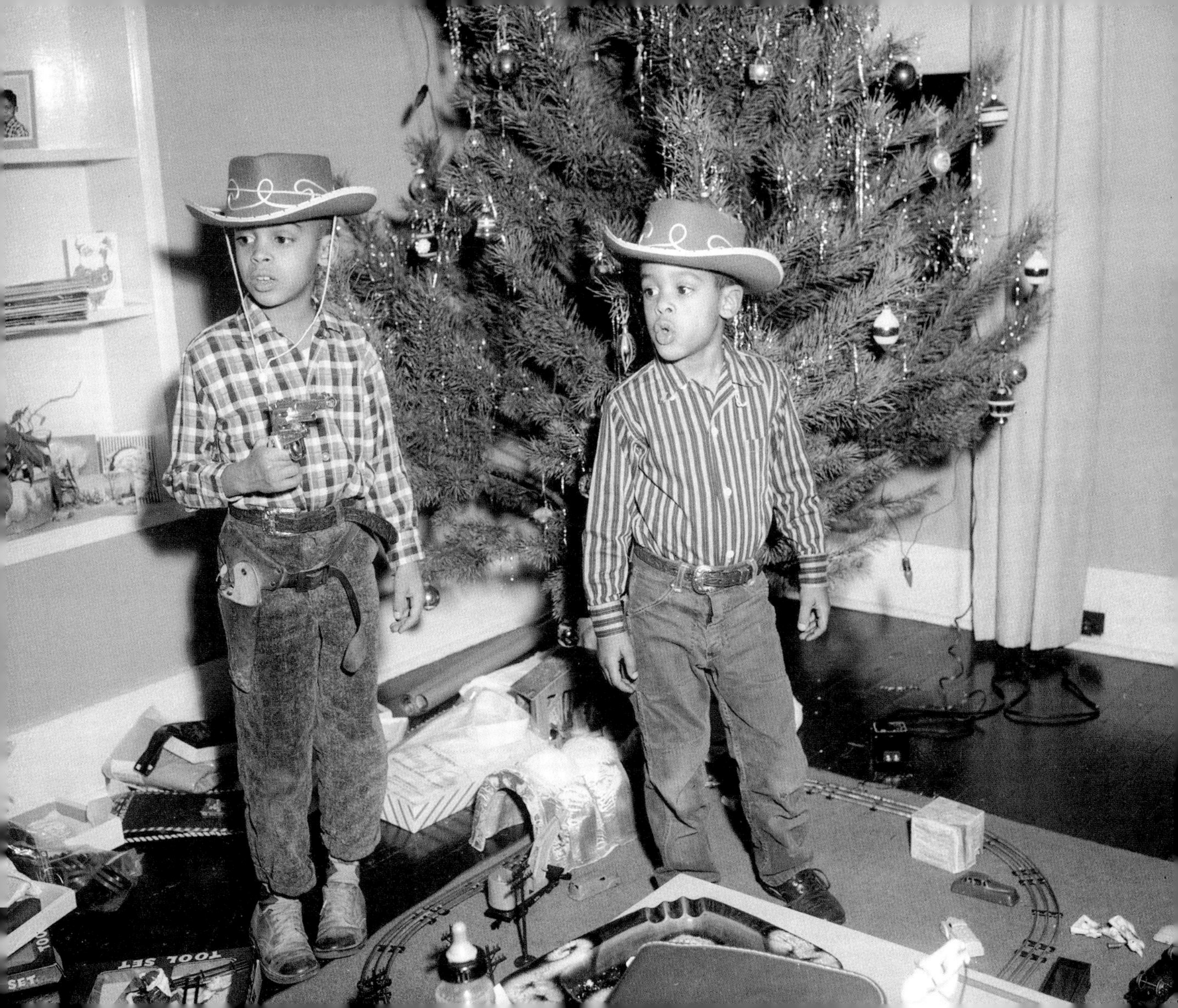
TOOL SET
SET

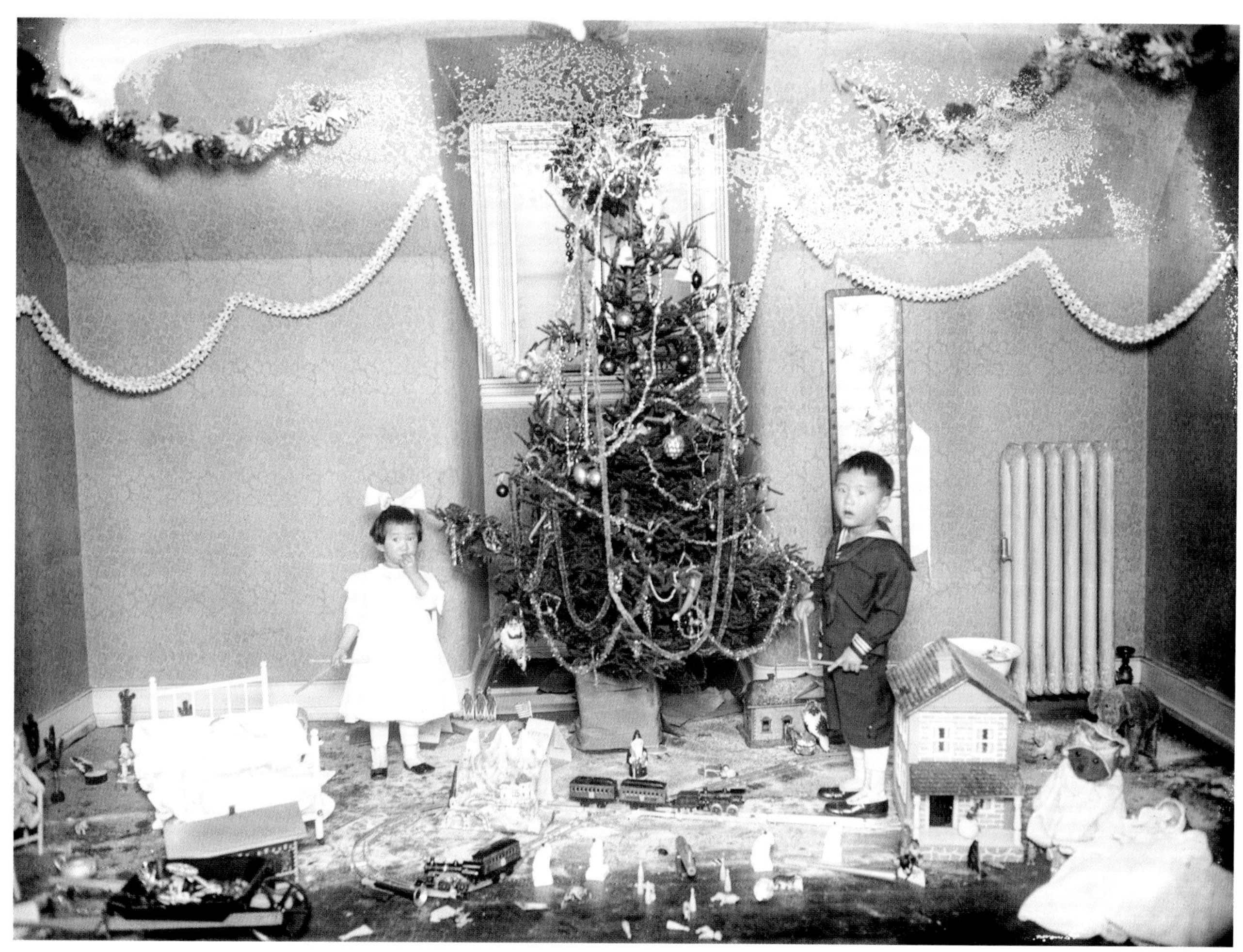

The children of Dr. Wellington Koo, Chinese Minister in
Washington, D.C., either side of the Christmas tree, USA, 1919

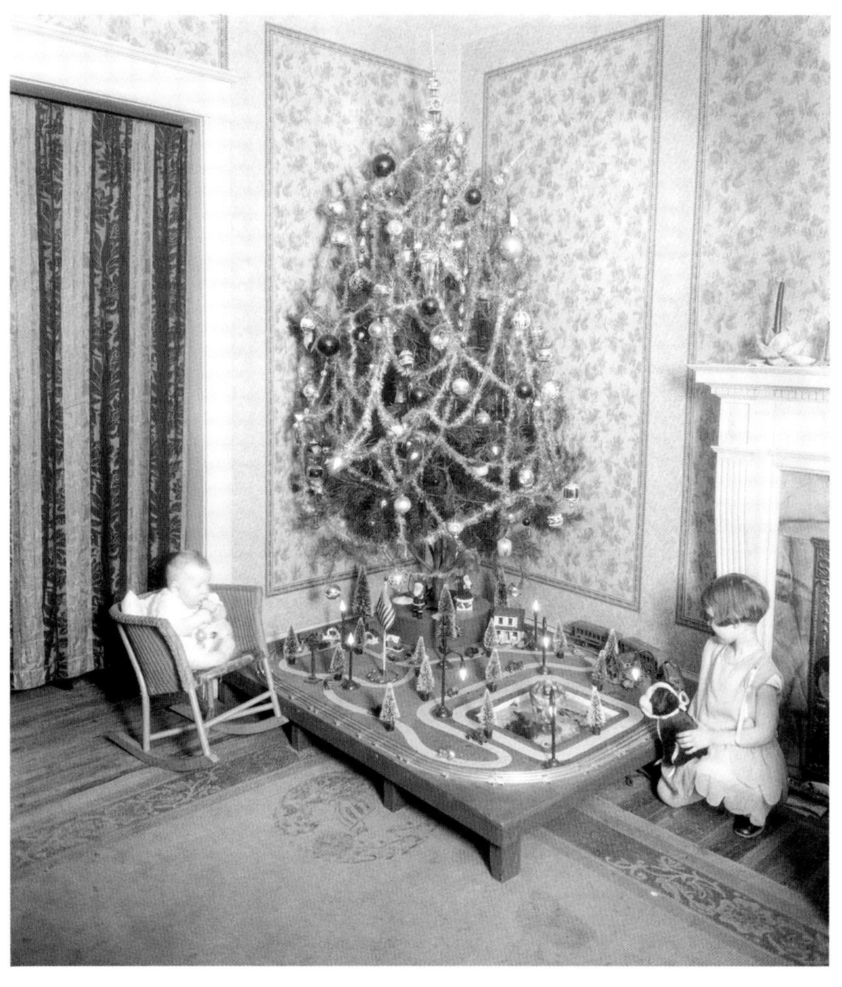

Playing with a model village beneath
the Christmas tree, USA, 1910s

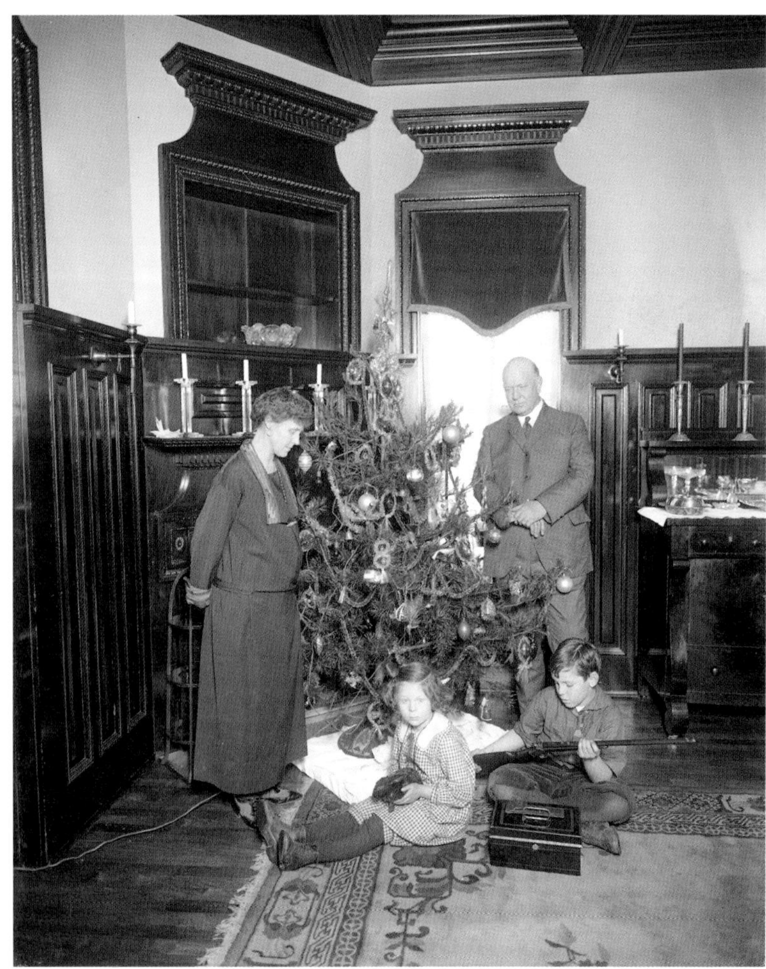

Around the Christmas tree,
USA, early 1900s

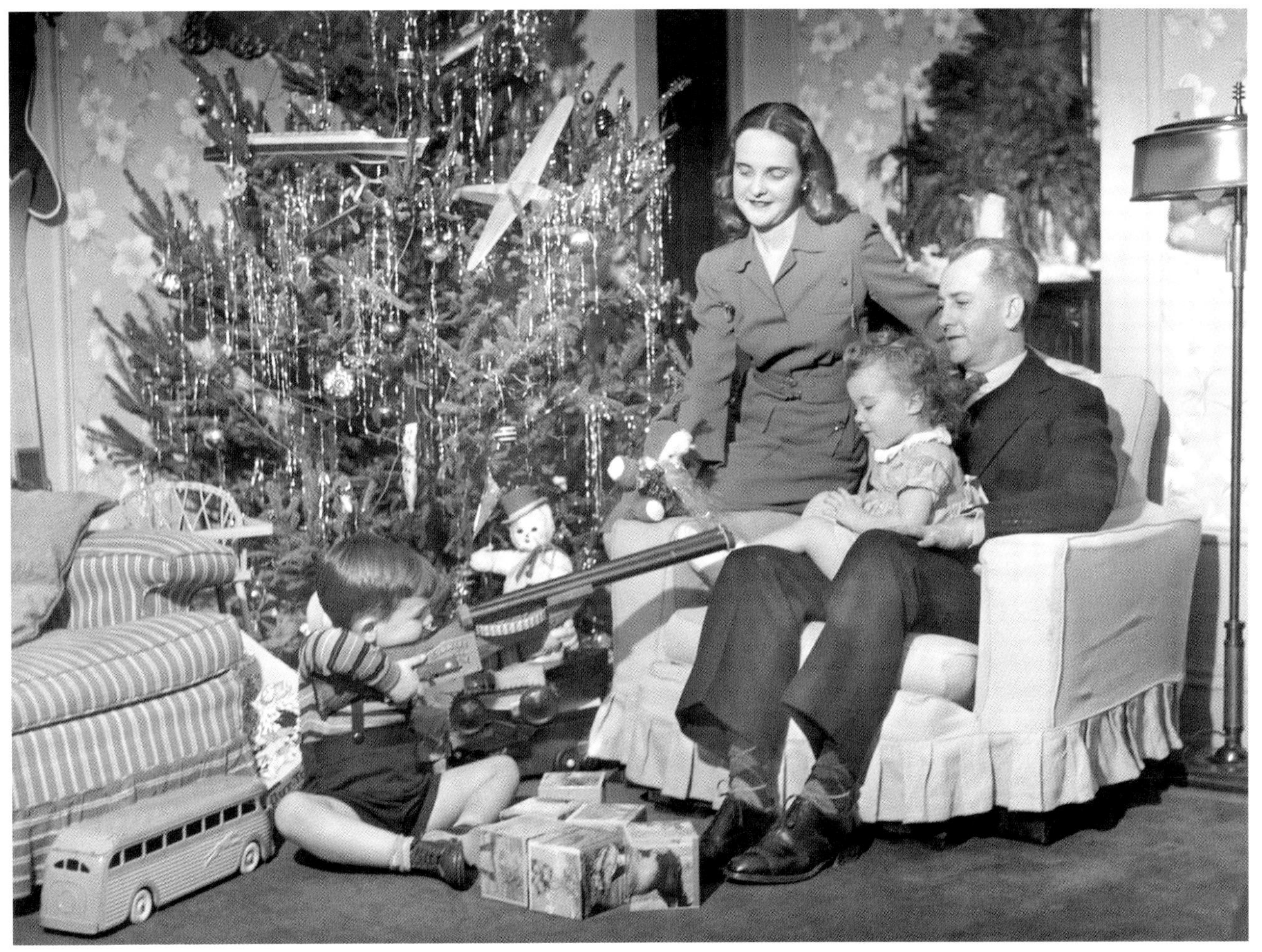

Taking aim with new Christmas toys,
USA, 1950s

Celebrating Christmas at home,
Pittsburgh, Pennsylvania, 1945

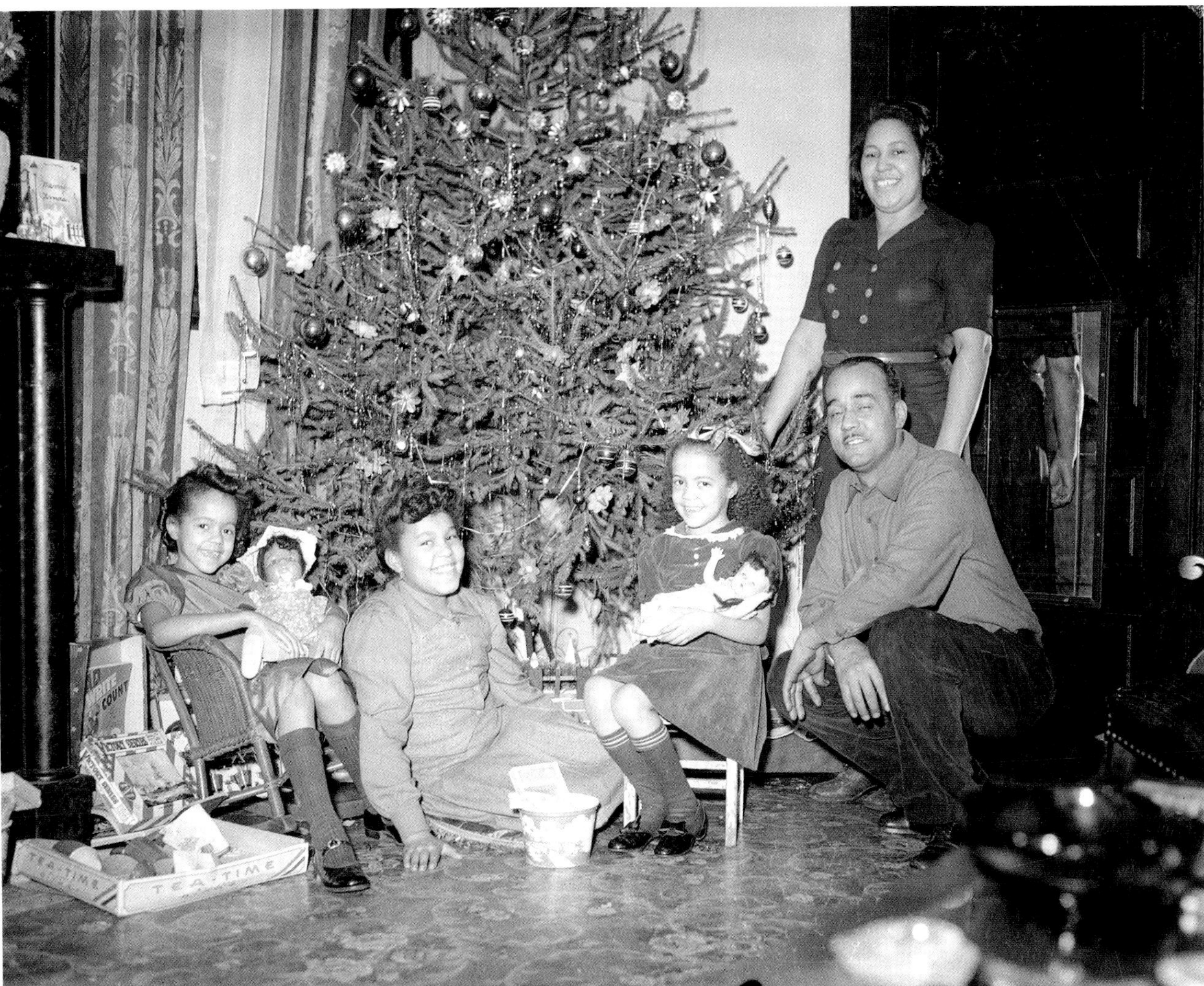

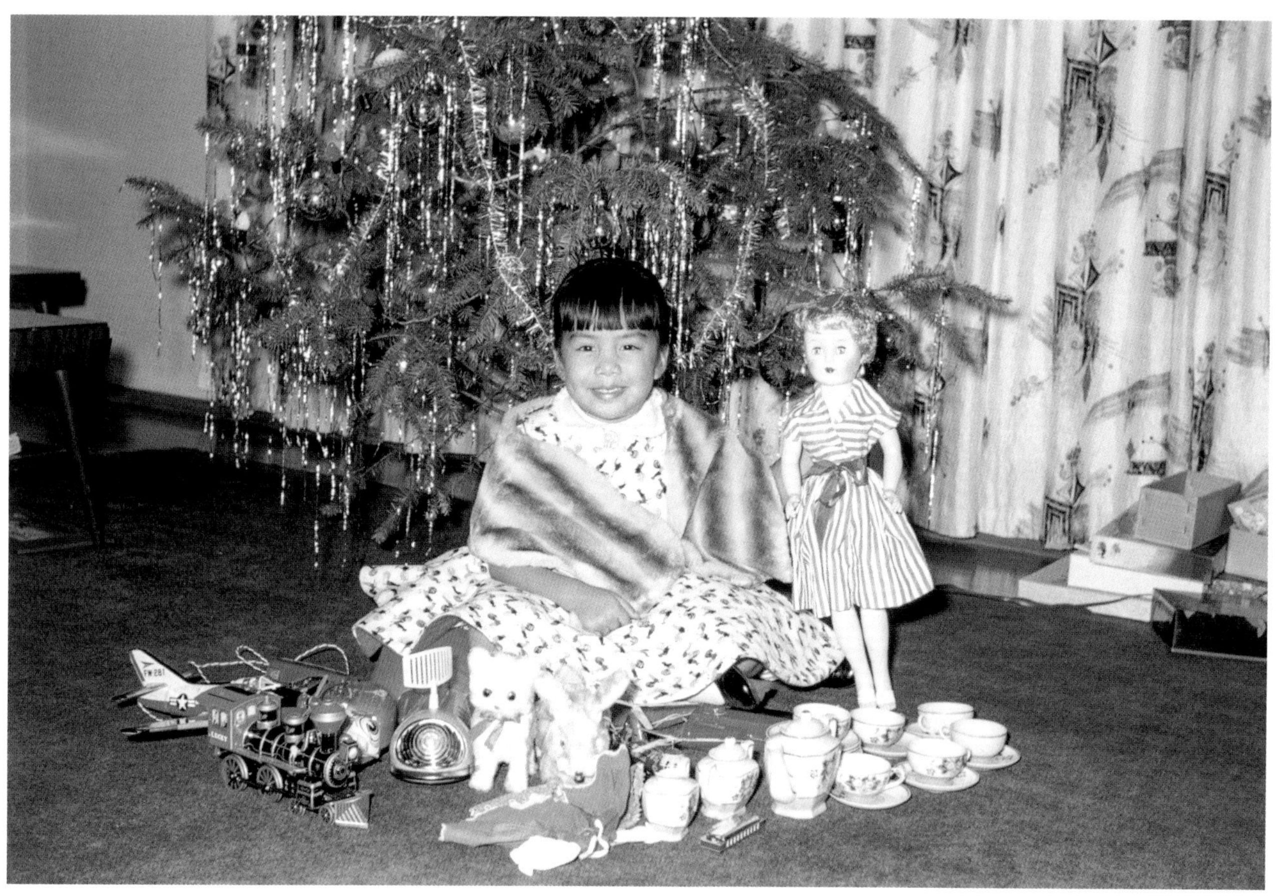

Gifts beneath the Christmas tree

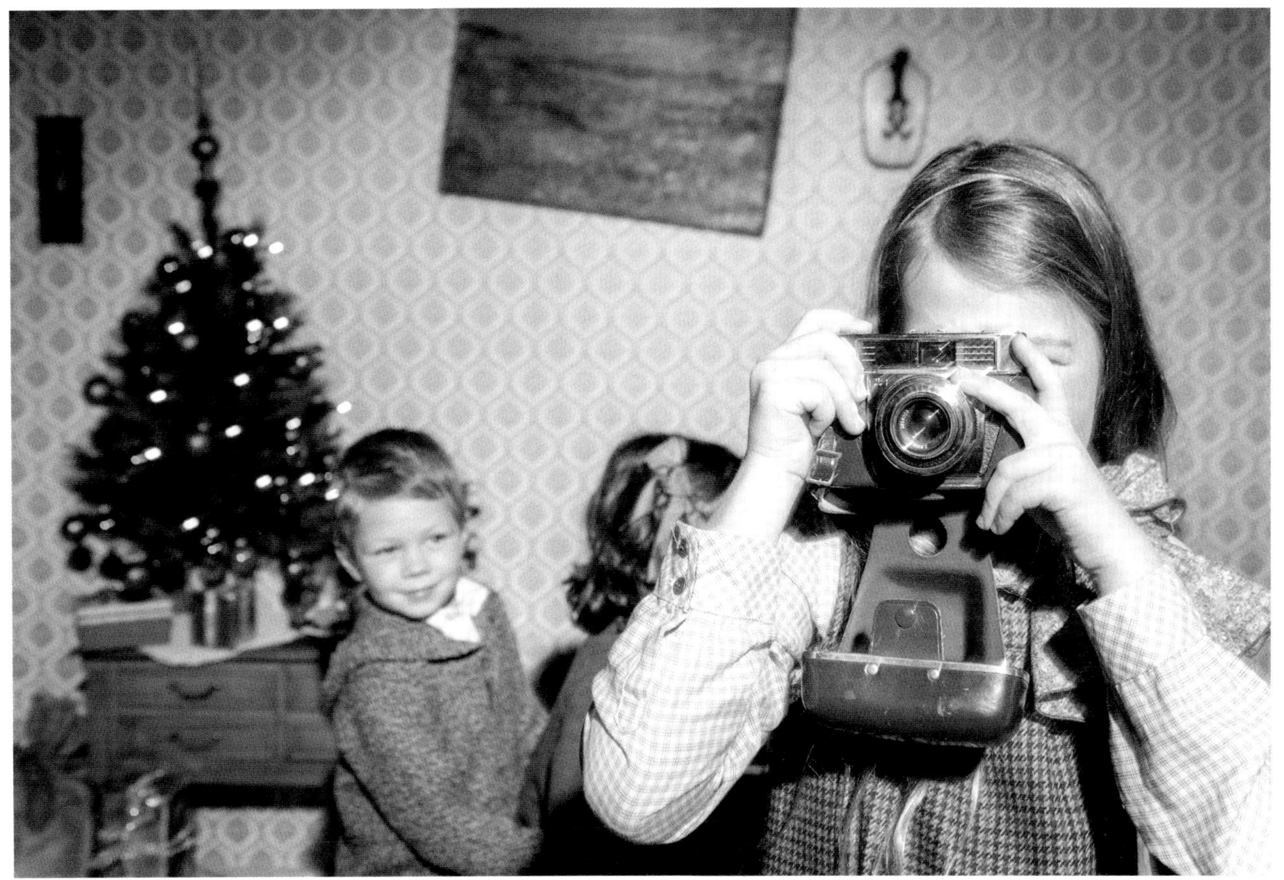

Capturing Christmas memories

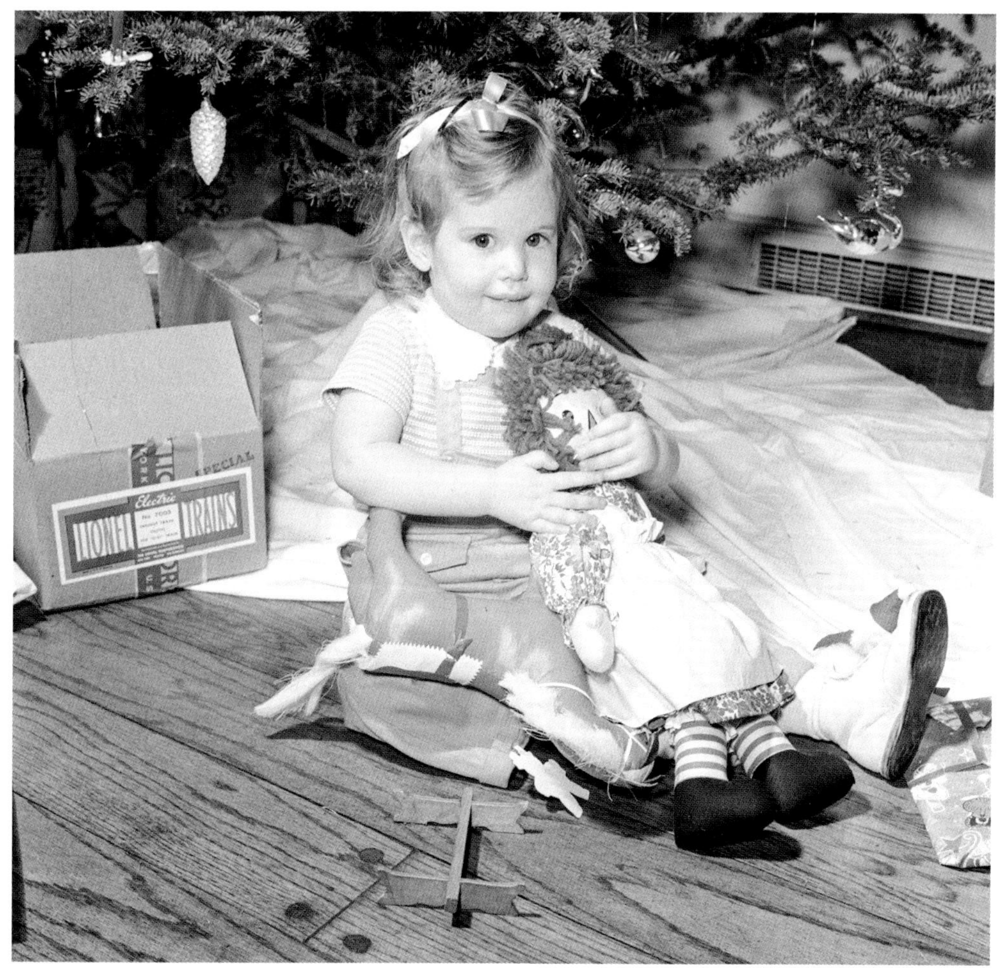

Young girl with a new Raggedy Ann doll,
Virginia, USA, 1941

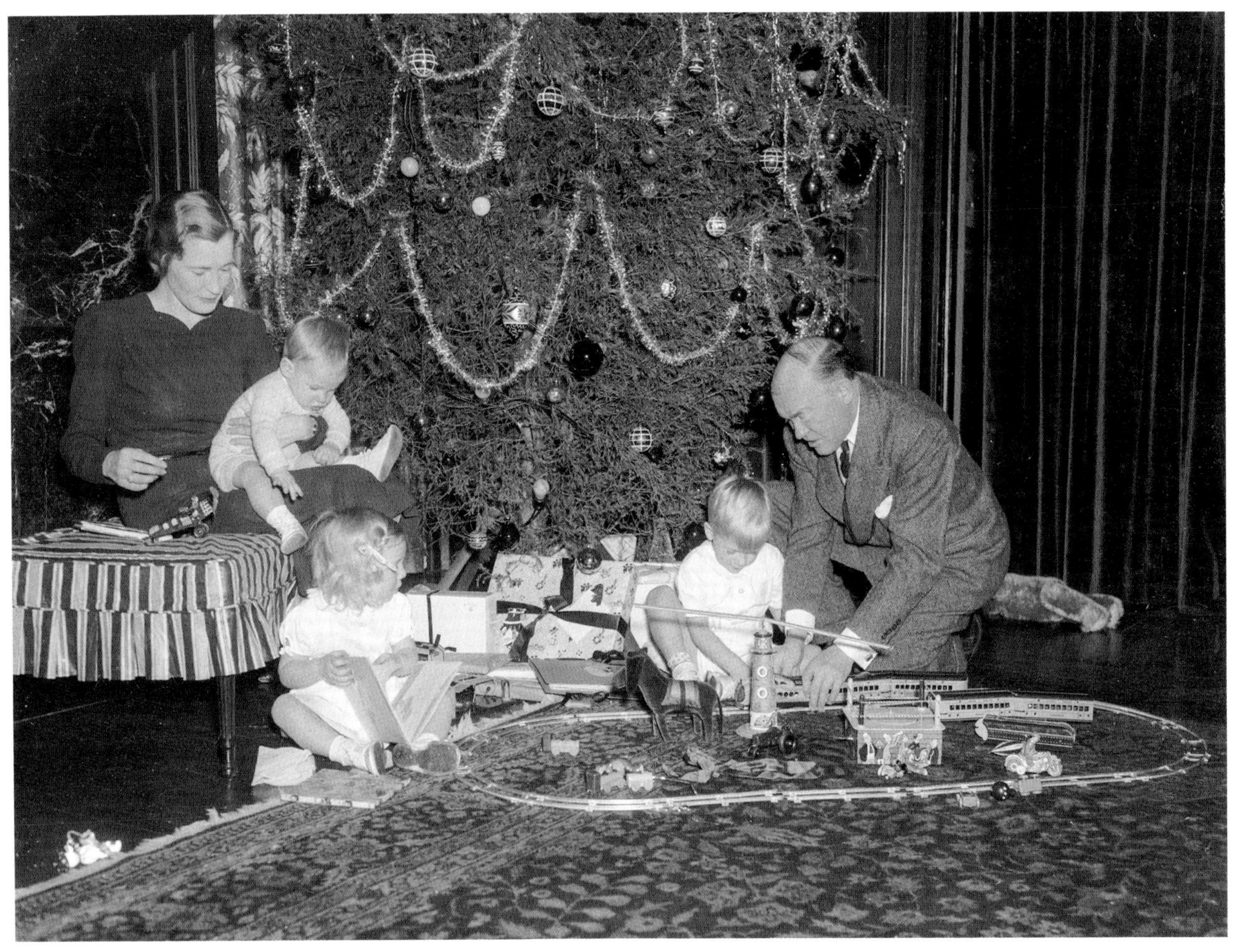

Children of government officials celebrating
Christmas, Washington, D.C., USA, 1937

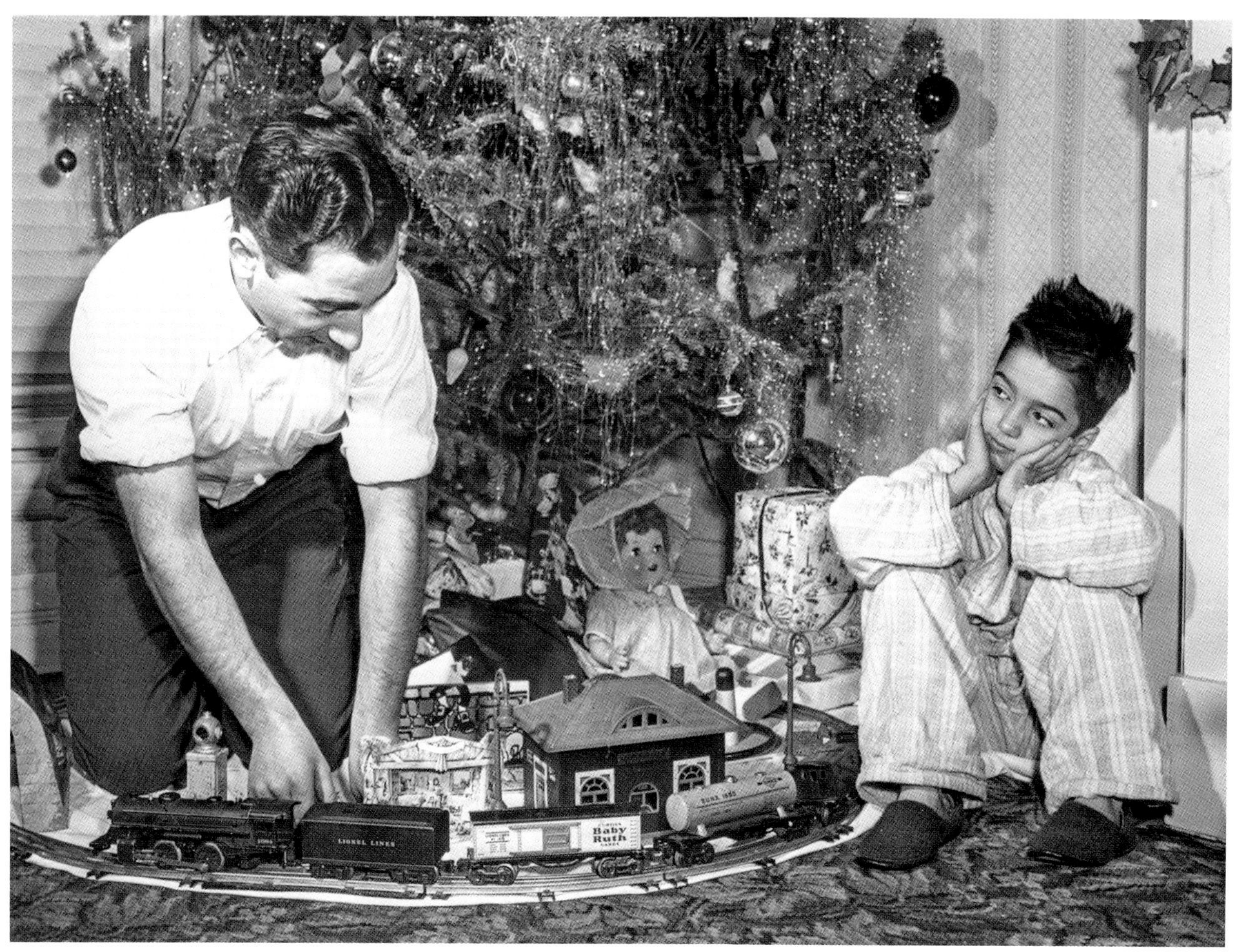

Parent hogging the electric train set,
Chicago, Illinois, USA, 1946

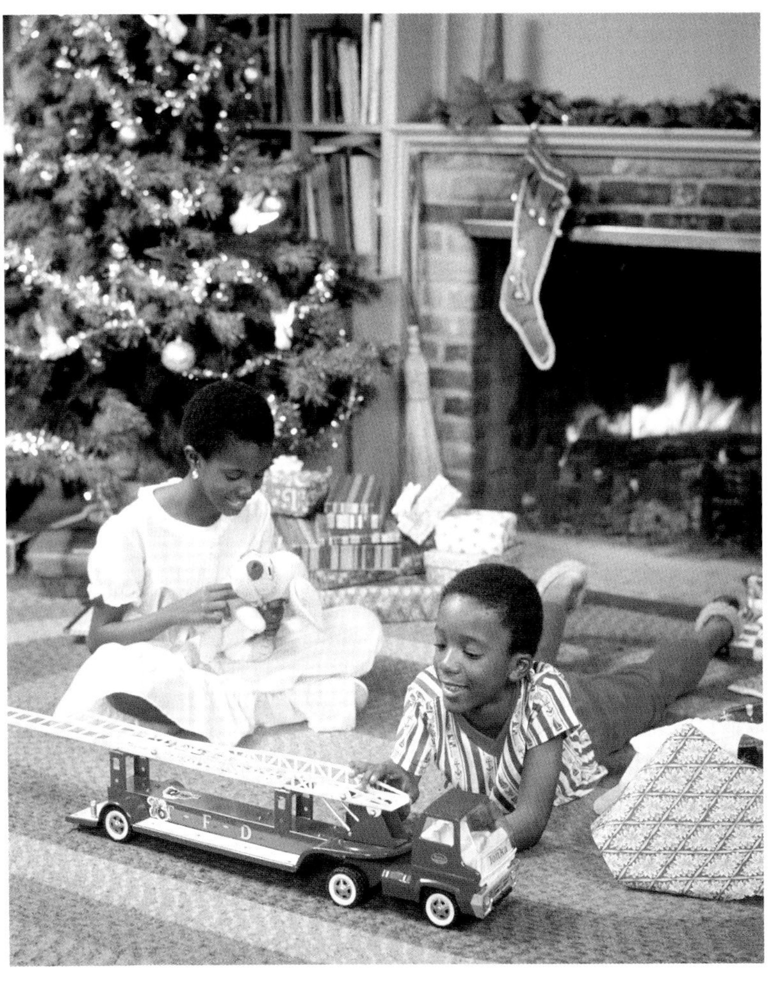

Christmas morning,
USA, 1972

Assembling a jumbo-sized electric
train set on Christmas morning, 1957

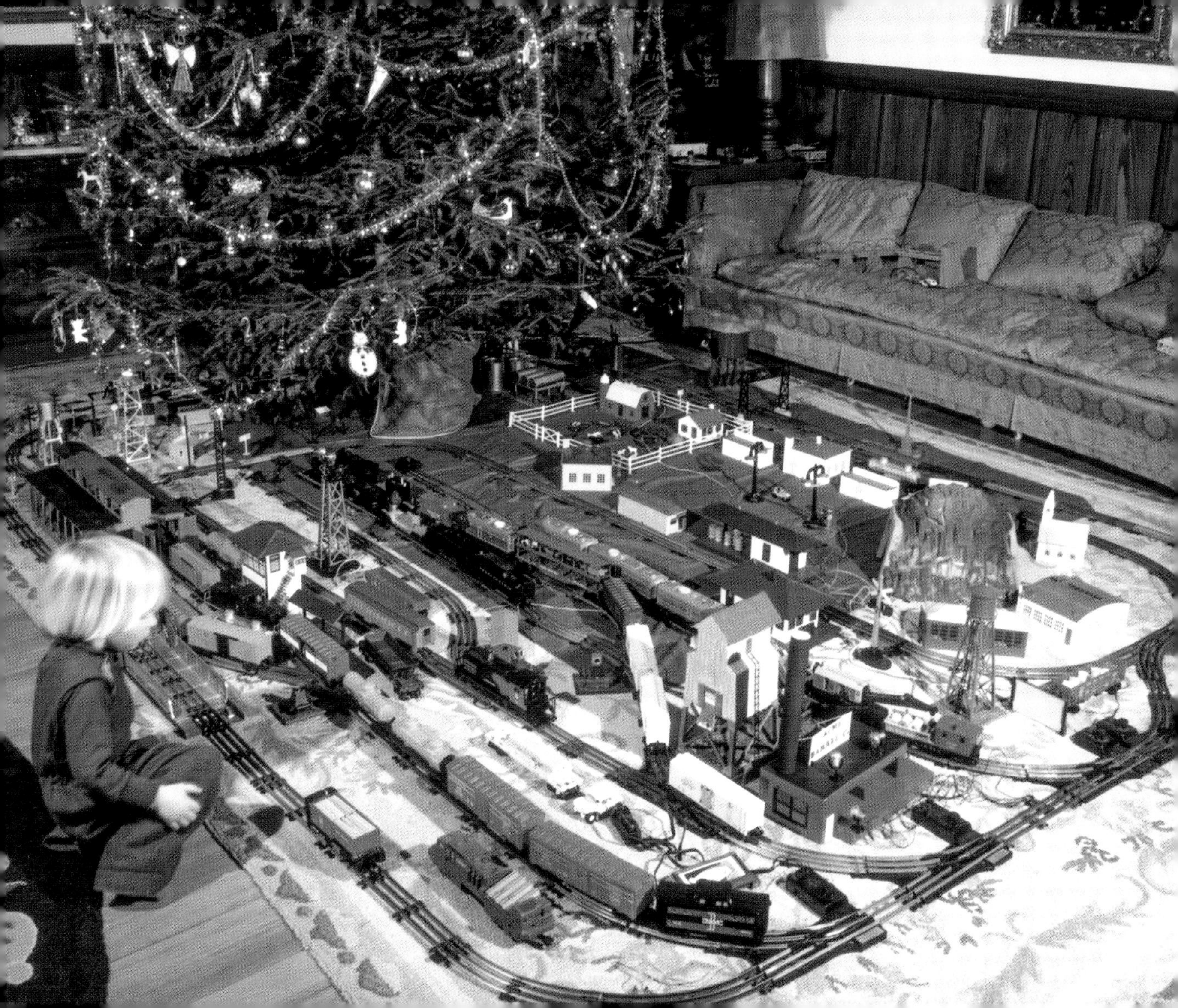

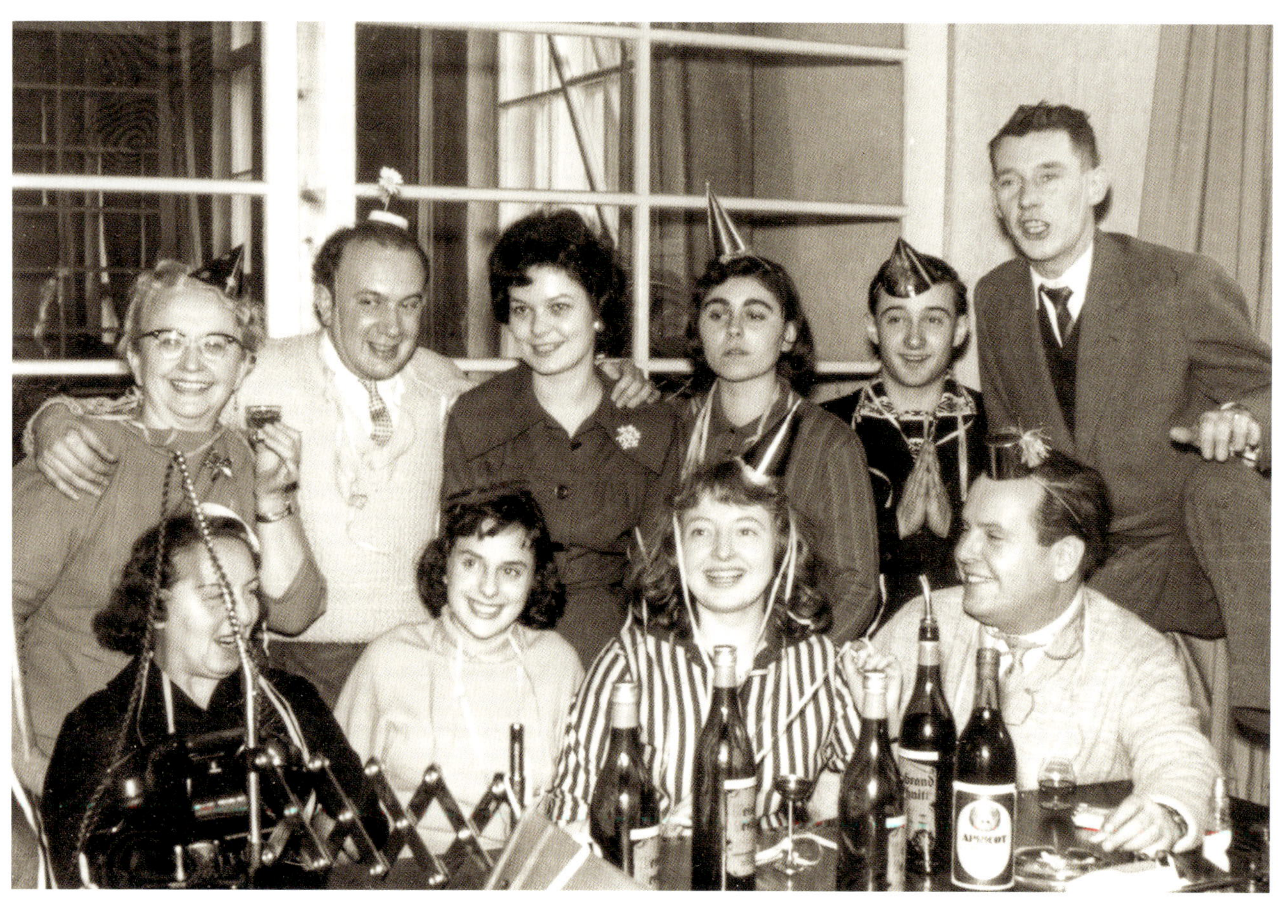

An office Christmas party,
Germany, 1950s

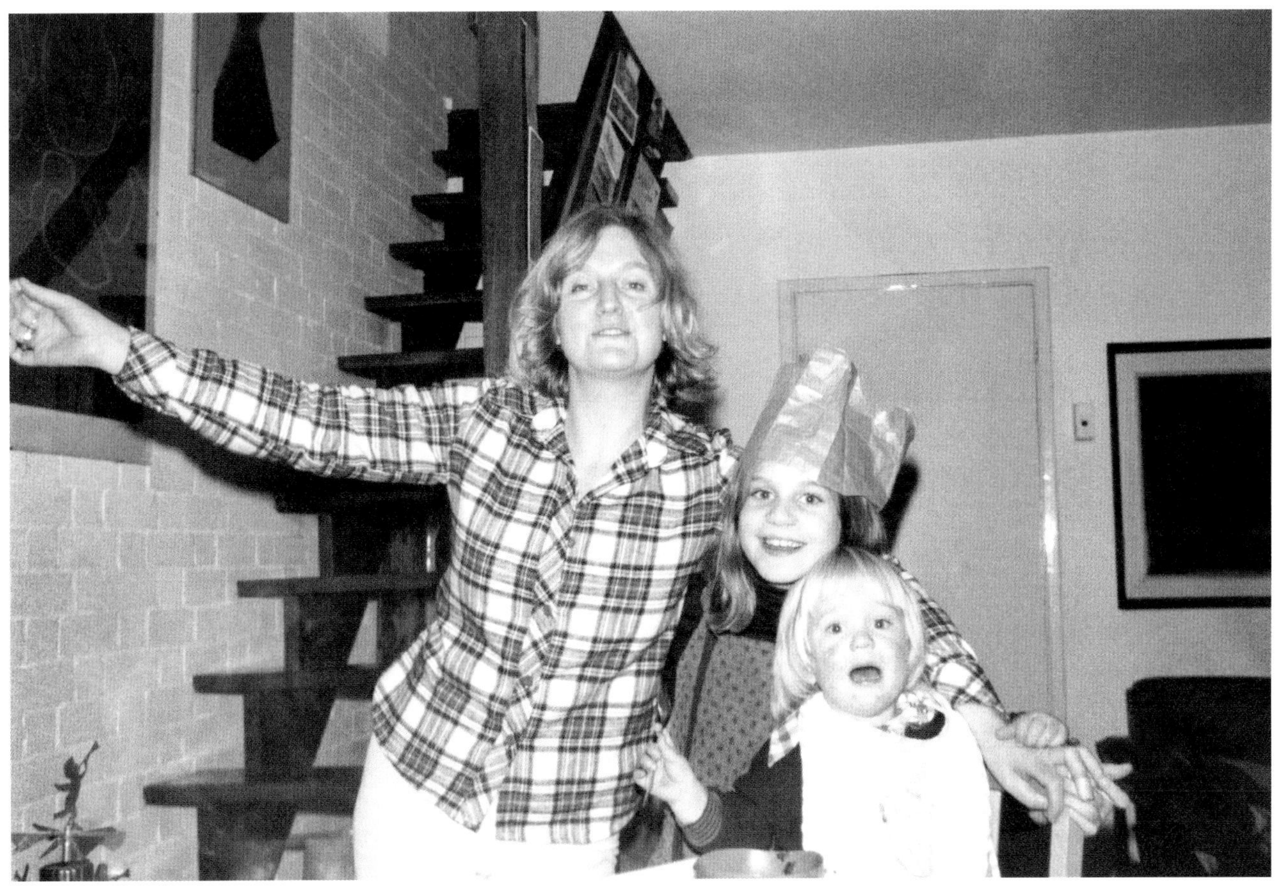

Family Christmas spirit

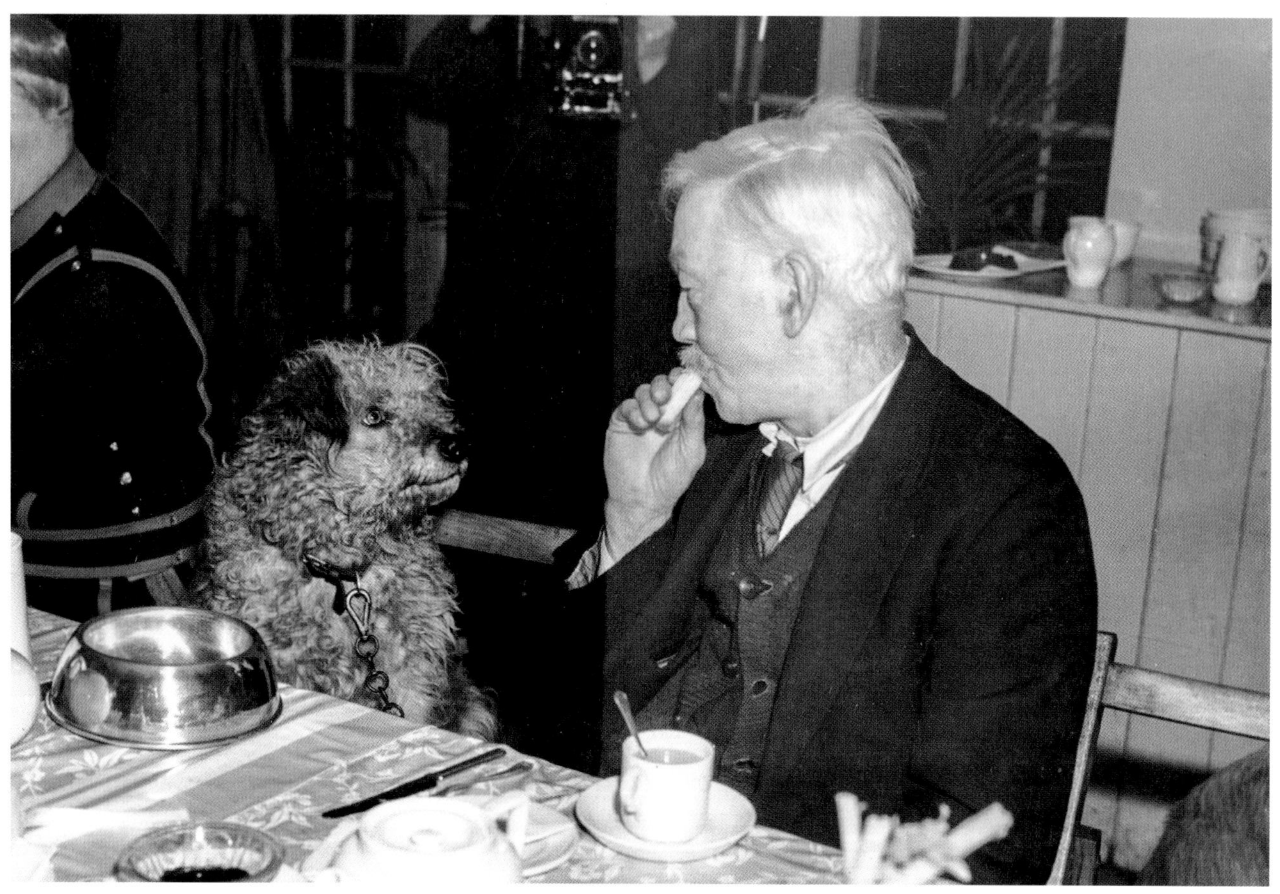

A dog patient from the People's Dispensary for Sick Animals, and its owner
being treated to Christmas dinner at the Tower of London, UK, 1950

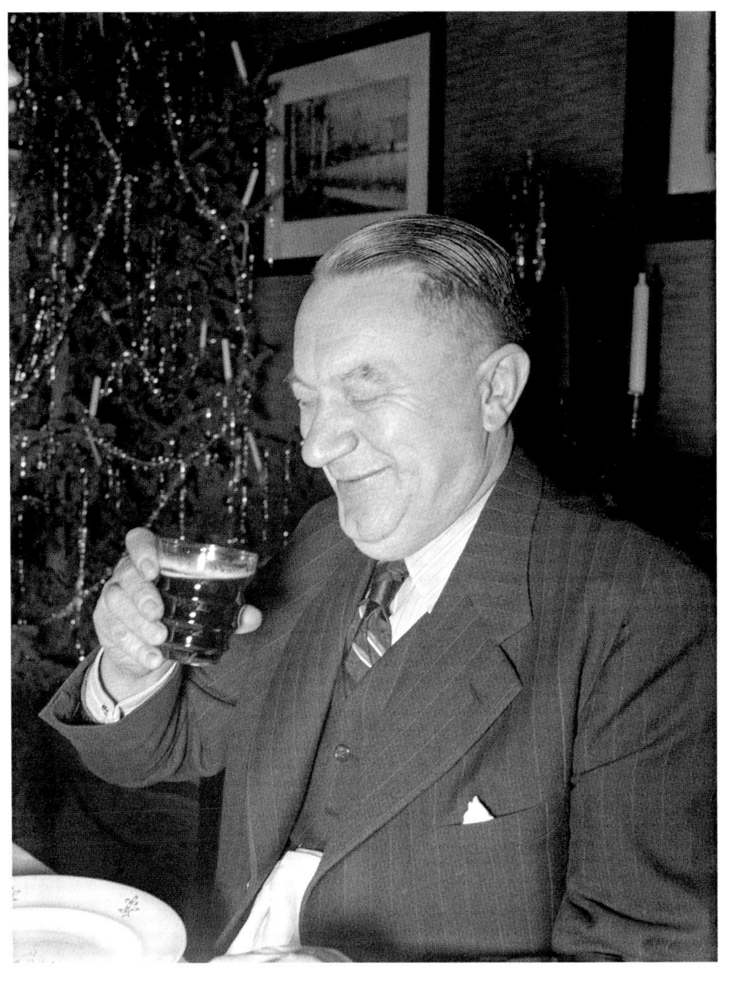

Enjoying a Christmas Eve tipple,
1940

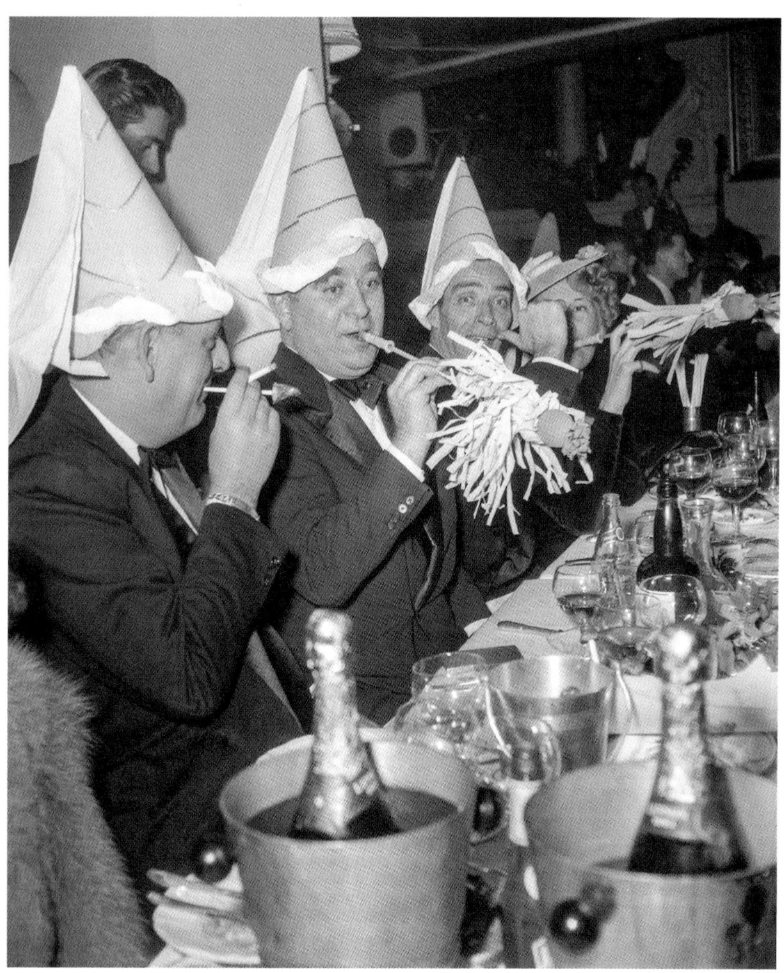

Christmas Eve party at Josephine Baker's home,
Paris, France, 1949

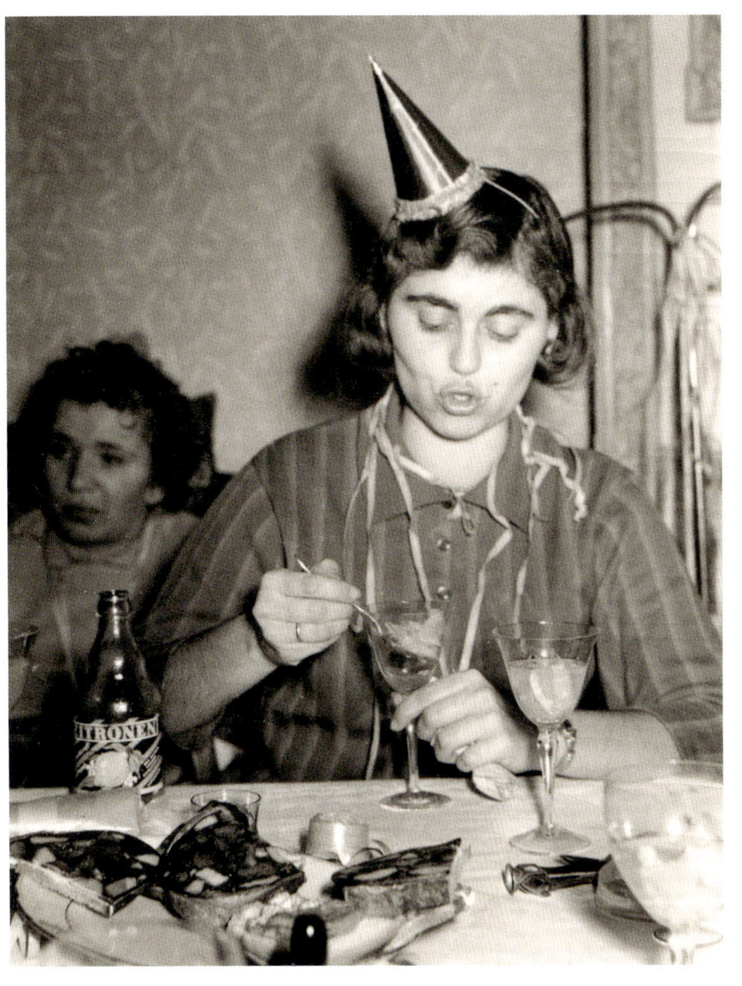

Enjoying some Christmas excess,
festooned with tinsel, Germany, 1950s

Christmas Eve in Montparnasse,
Paris, France, 1949

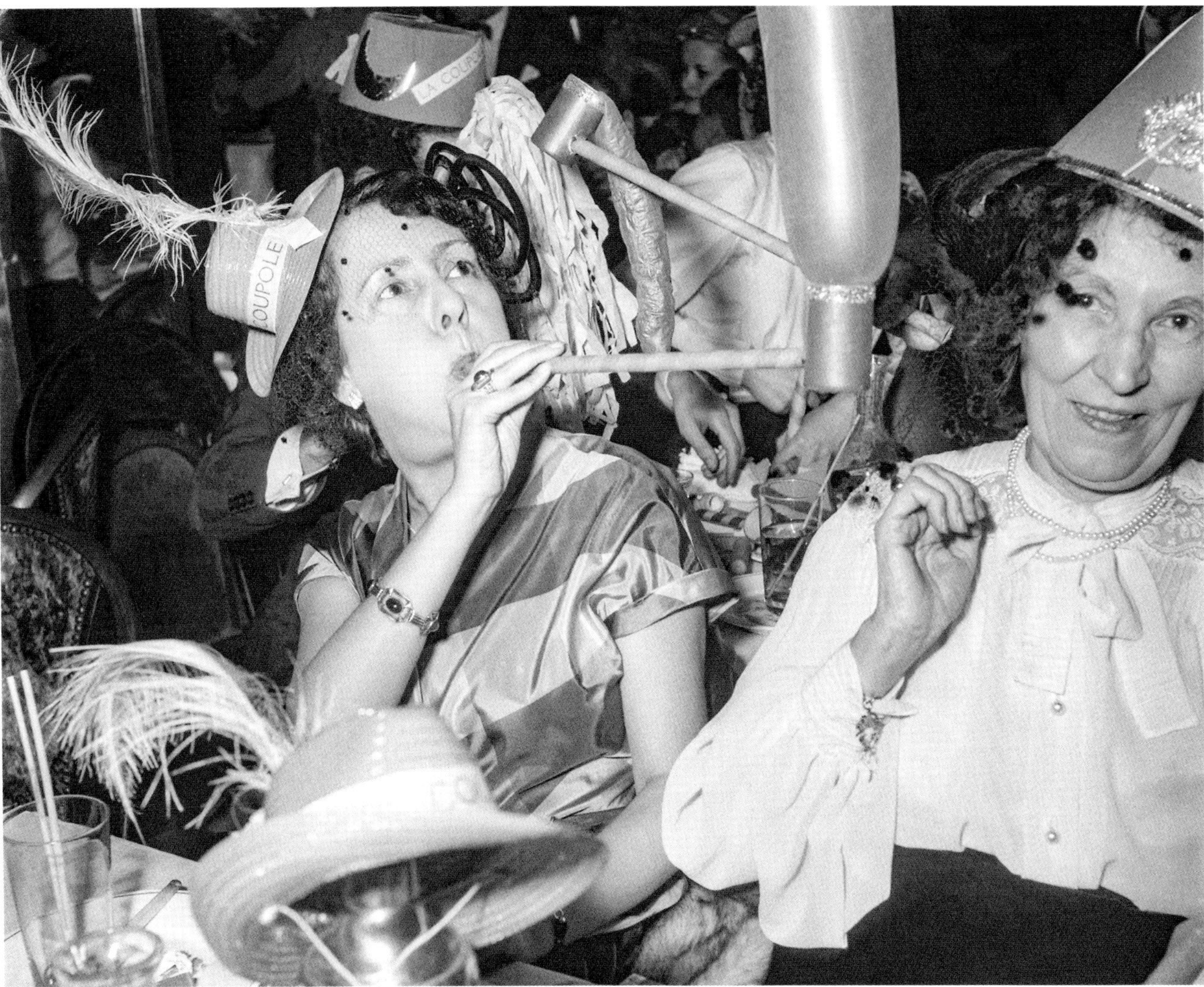

LA COUPOLE
COUPOLE

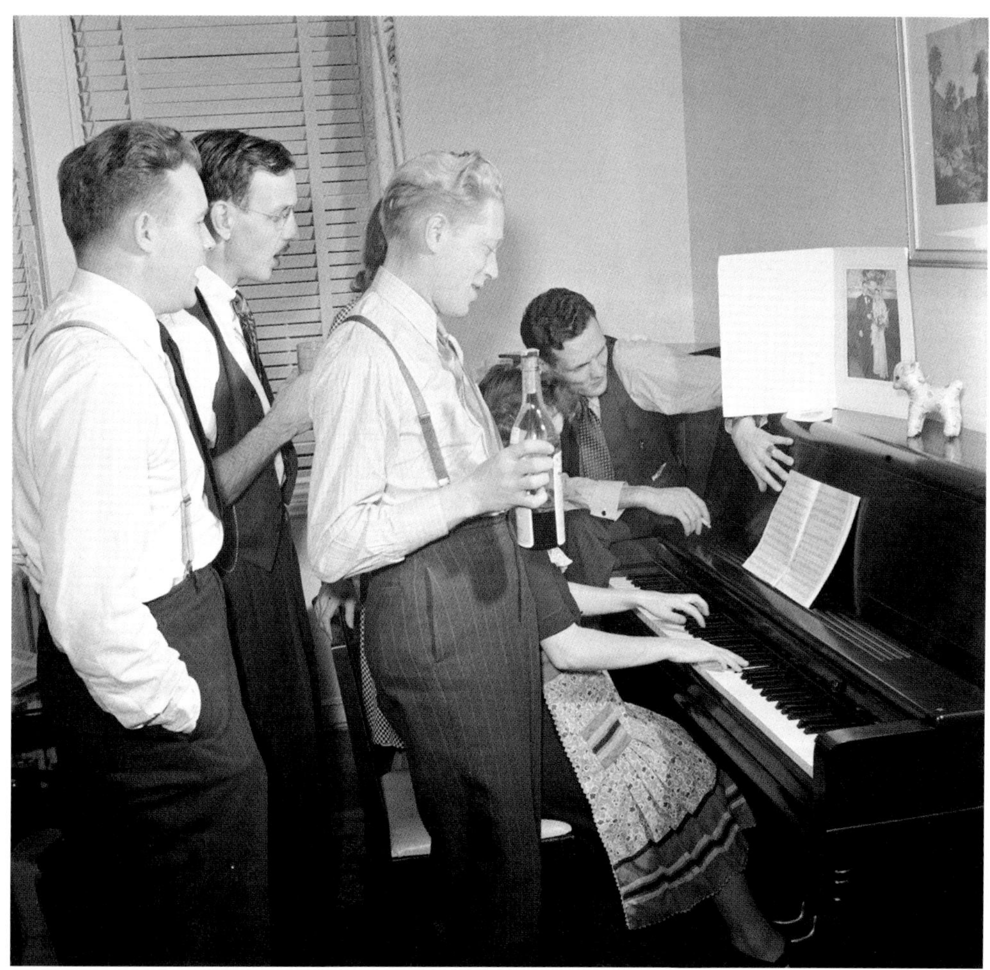

Singing carols,
Washington, D.C., USA, 1941

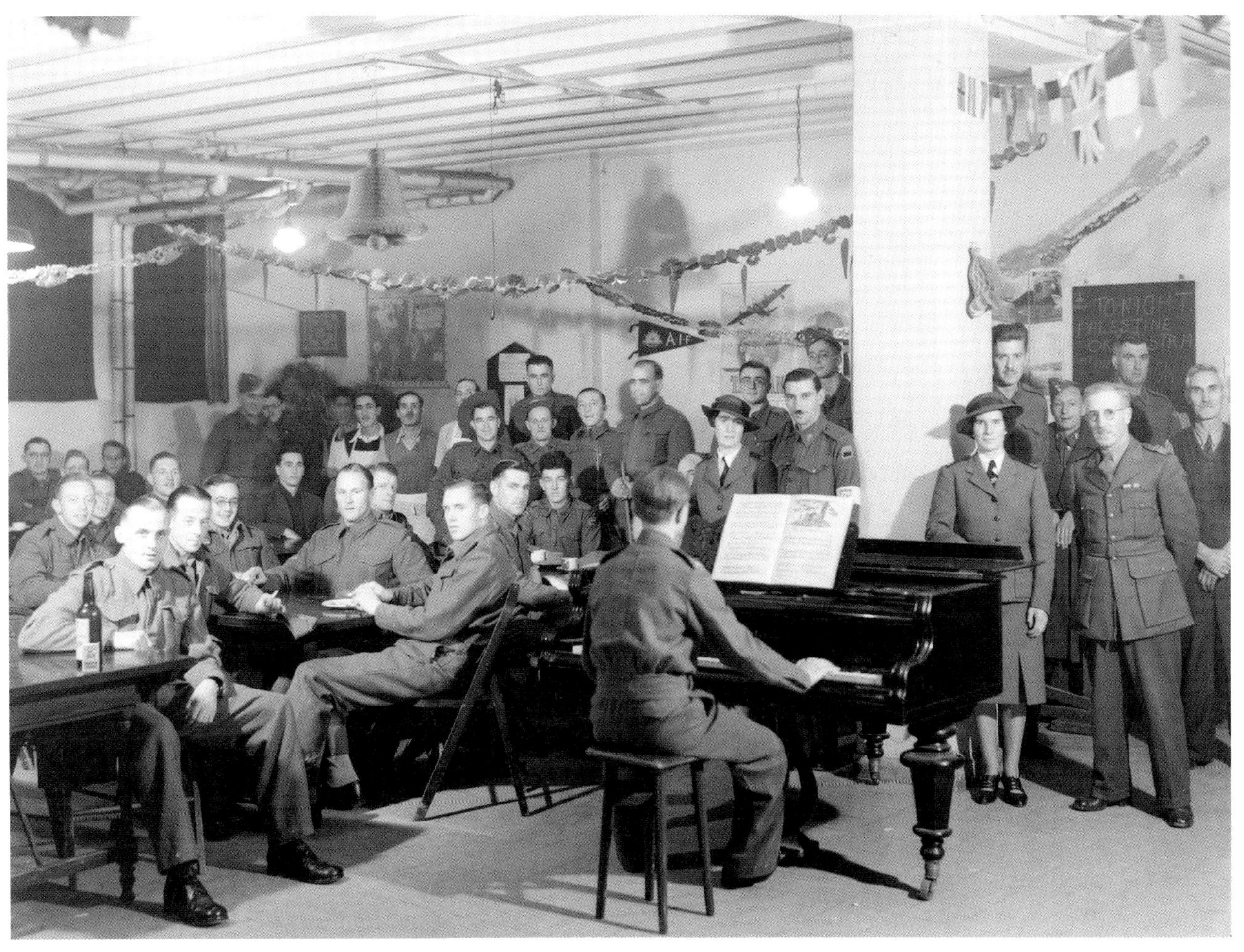

Military YMCA Christmas,
Jerusalem, Israel, 1940

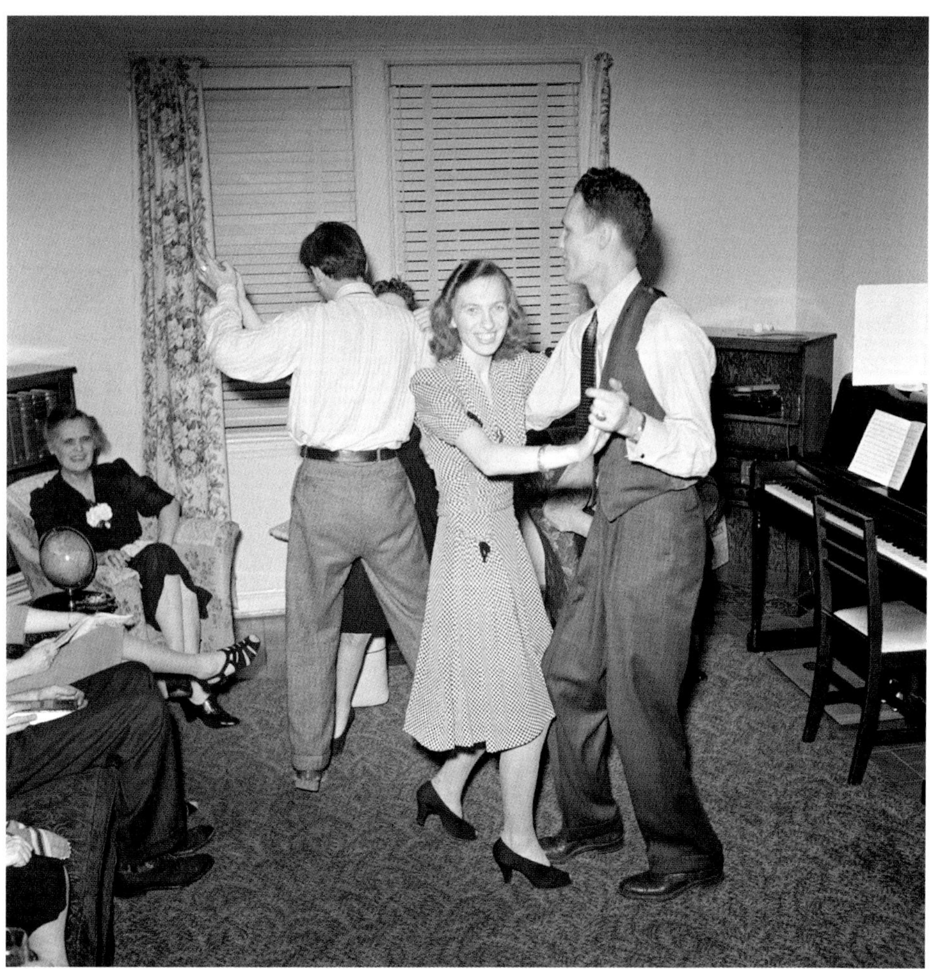

Christmas dance at home,
Washington, D.C., USA, 1941

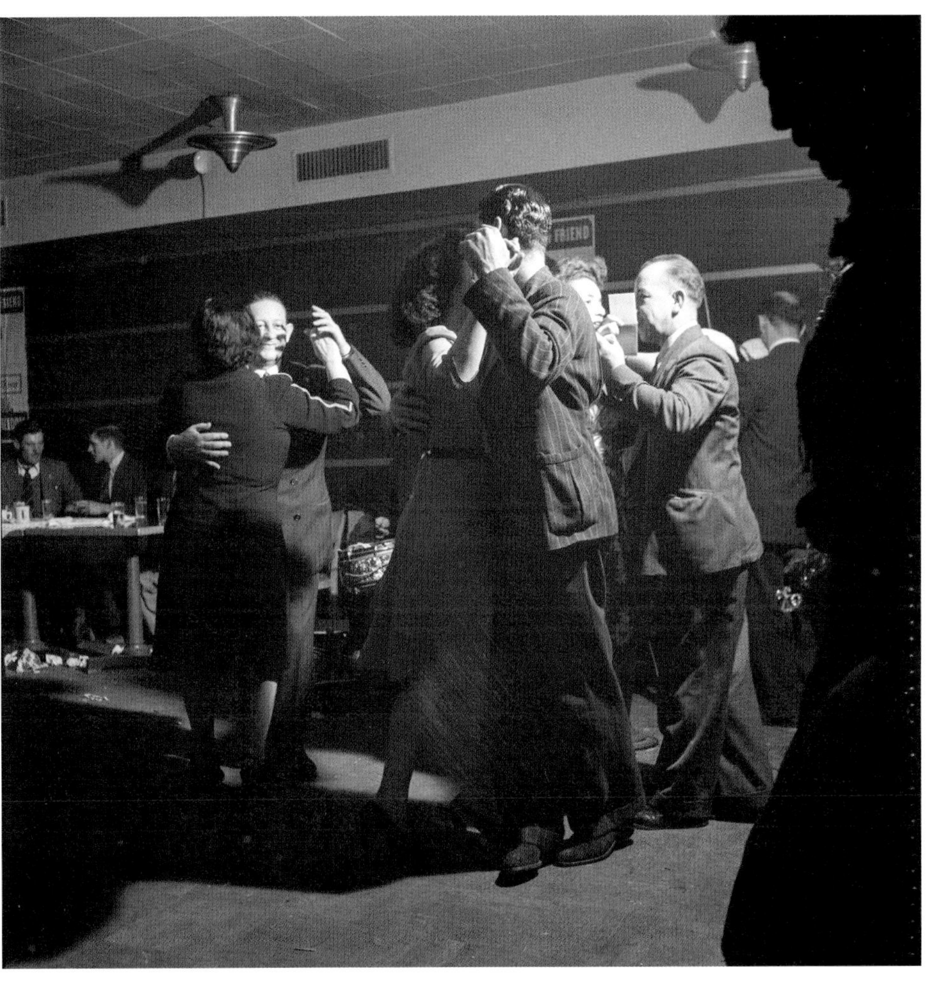

Merchant seamen's Christmas party at the
Andrew Feruseth club, New York, New York, USA, 1942

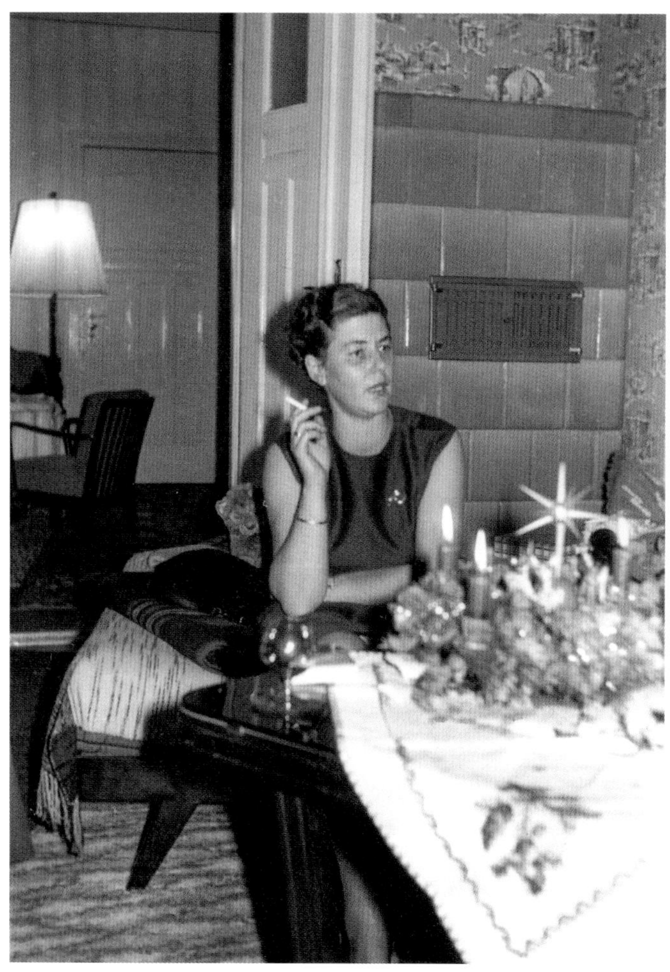

Smoking at the Christmas table,
Germany, 1960s

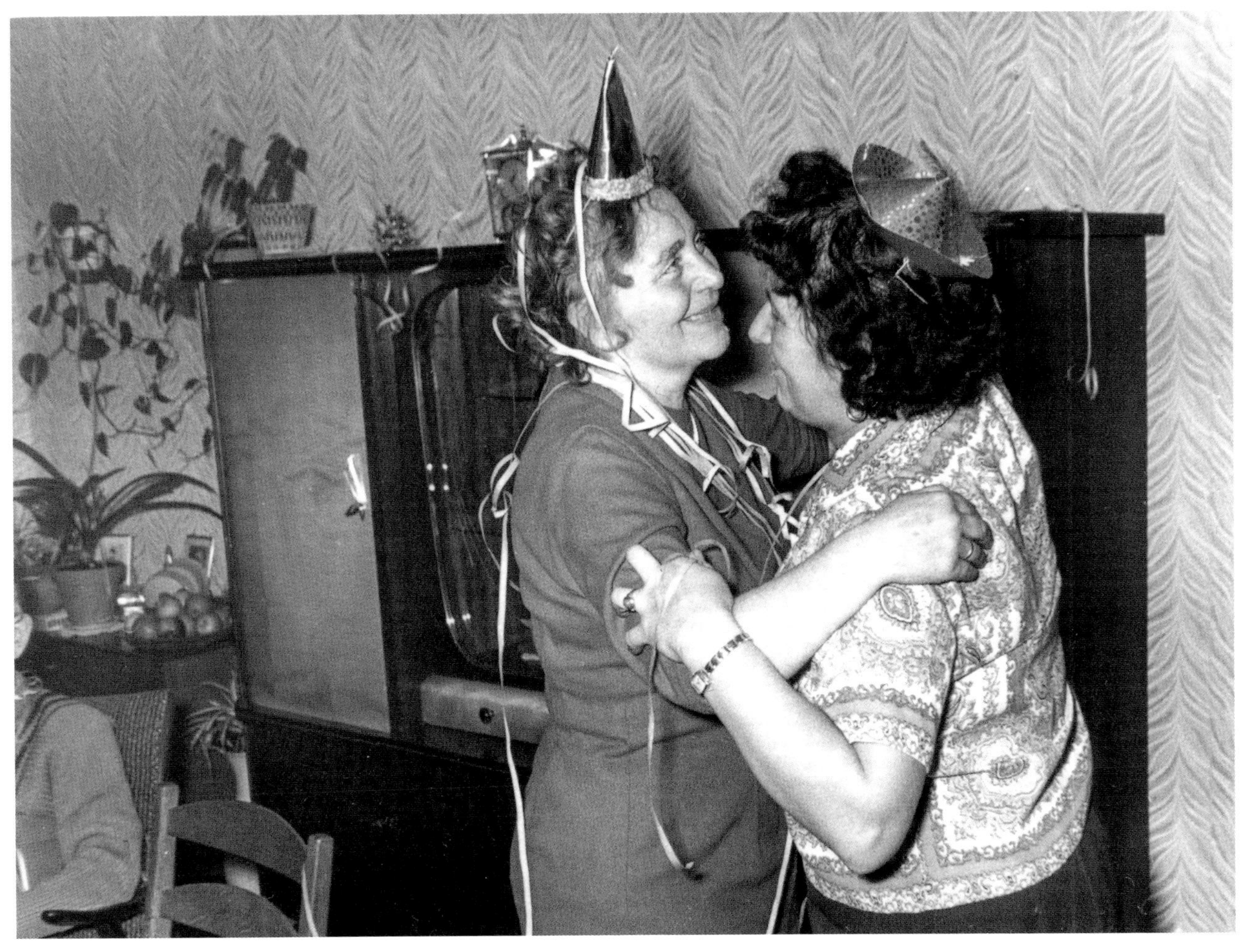

Sharing a Christmas day dance,
Germany 1960s

Young couple at the Christmas table,
Dresden, East Germany, 1950s

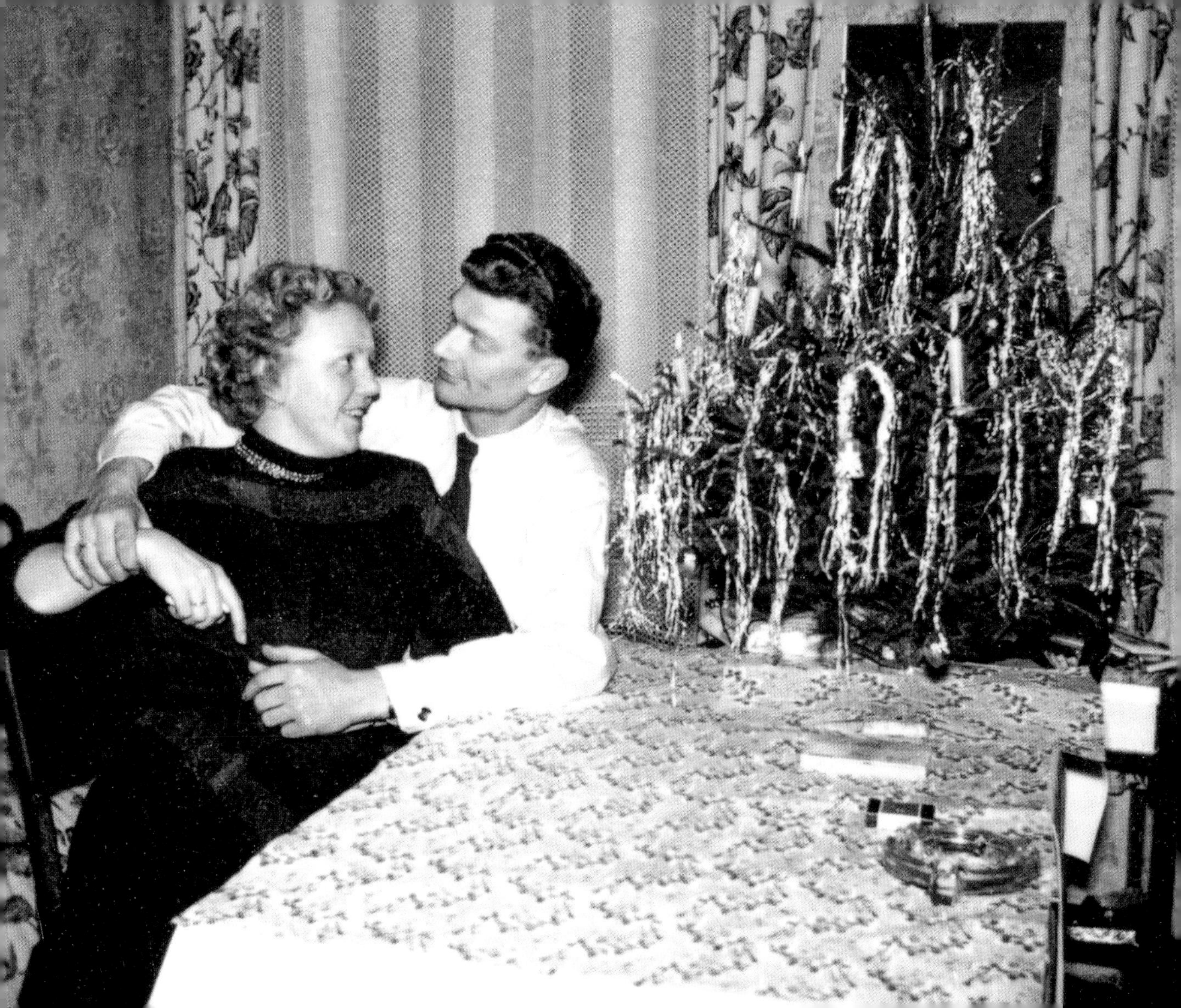

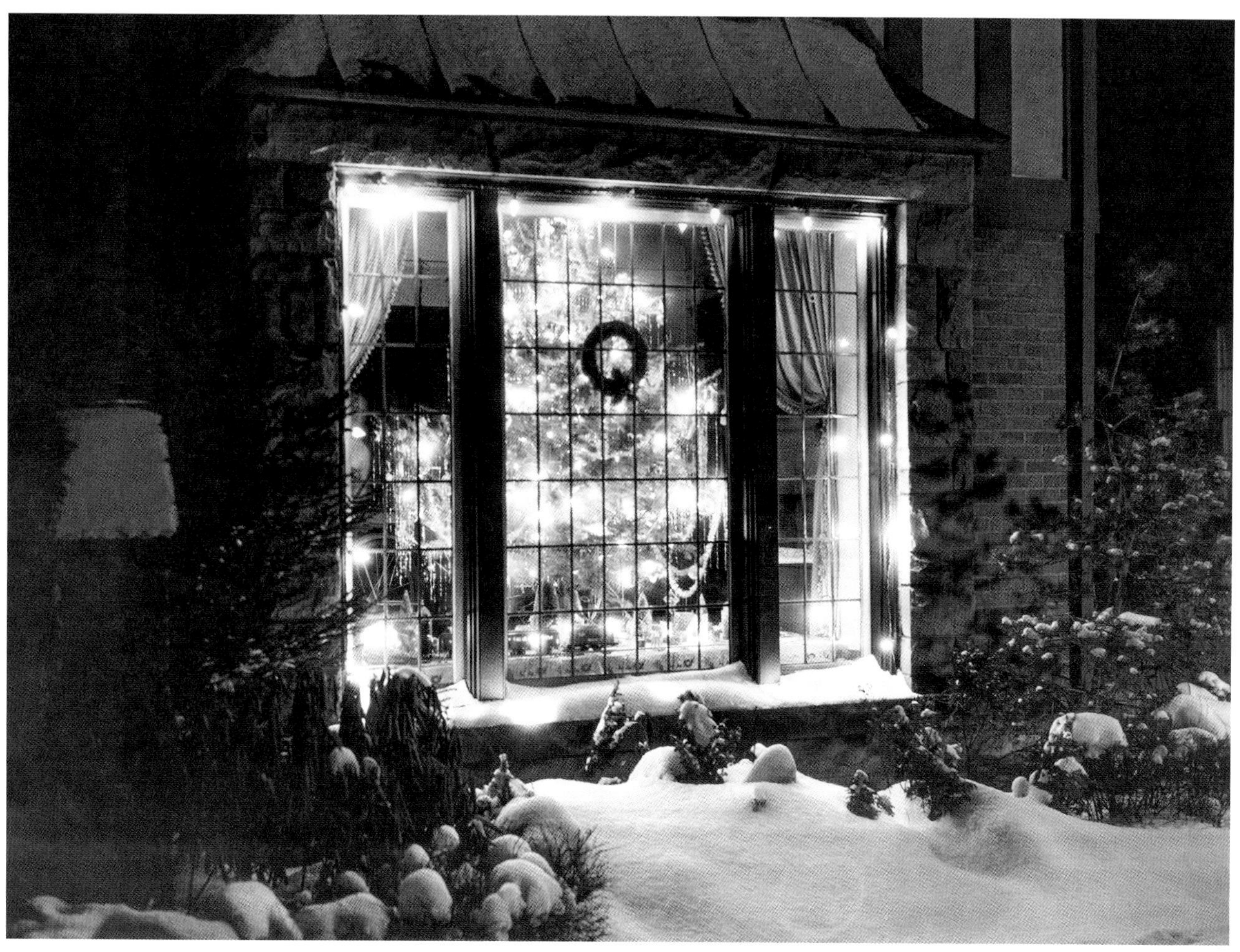

A lit Christmas tree gleaming
behind a window, 1940s

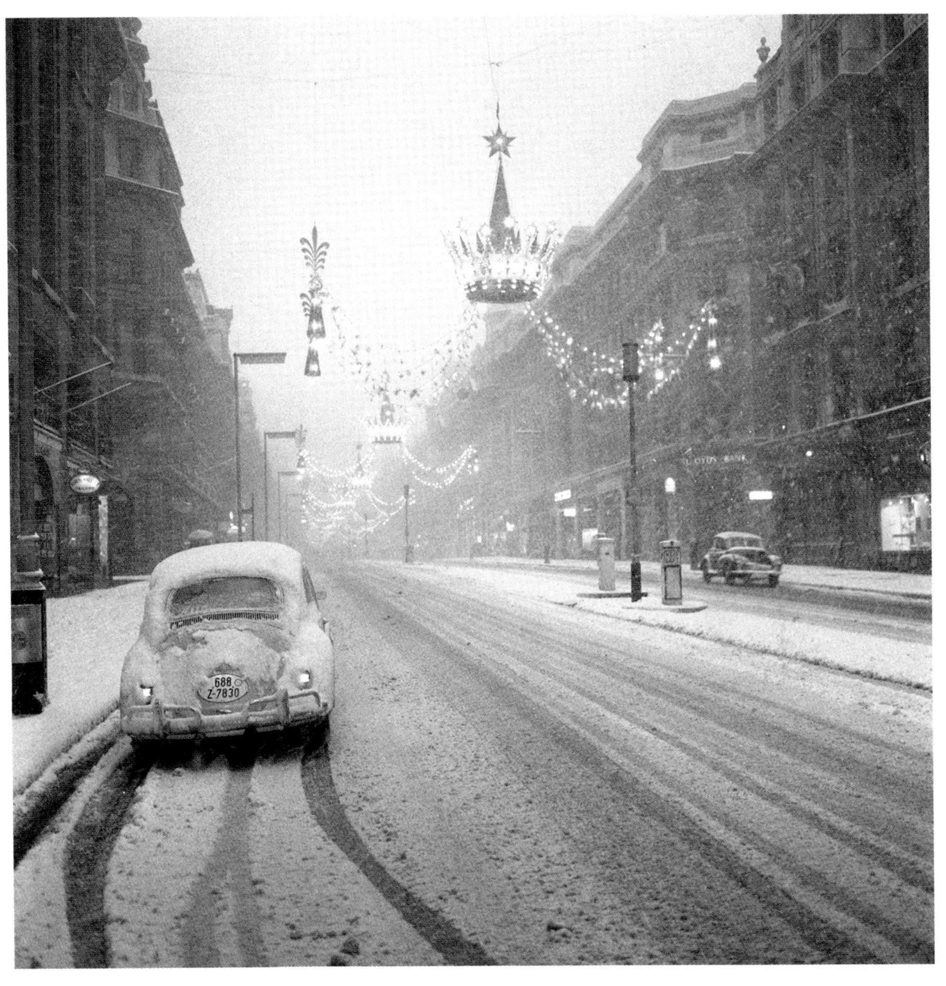

Snow on New Year's Eve,
Regent Street, London, UK, 1961

Fishing on a shingle beach with a rod propped
on a bare Christmas tree, Kent, UK, 1960s

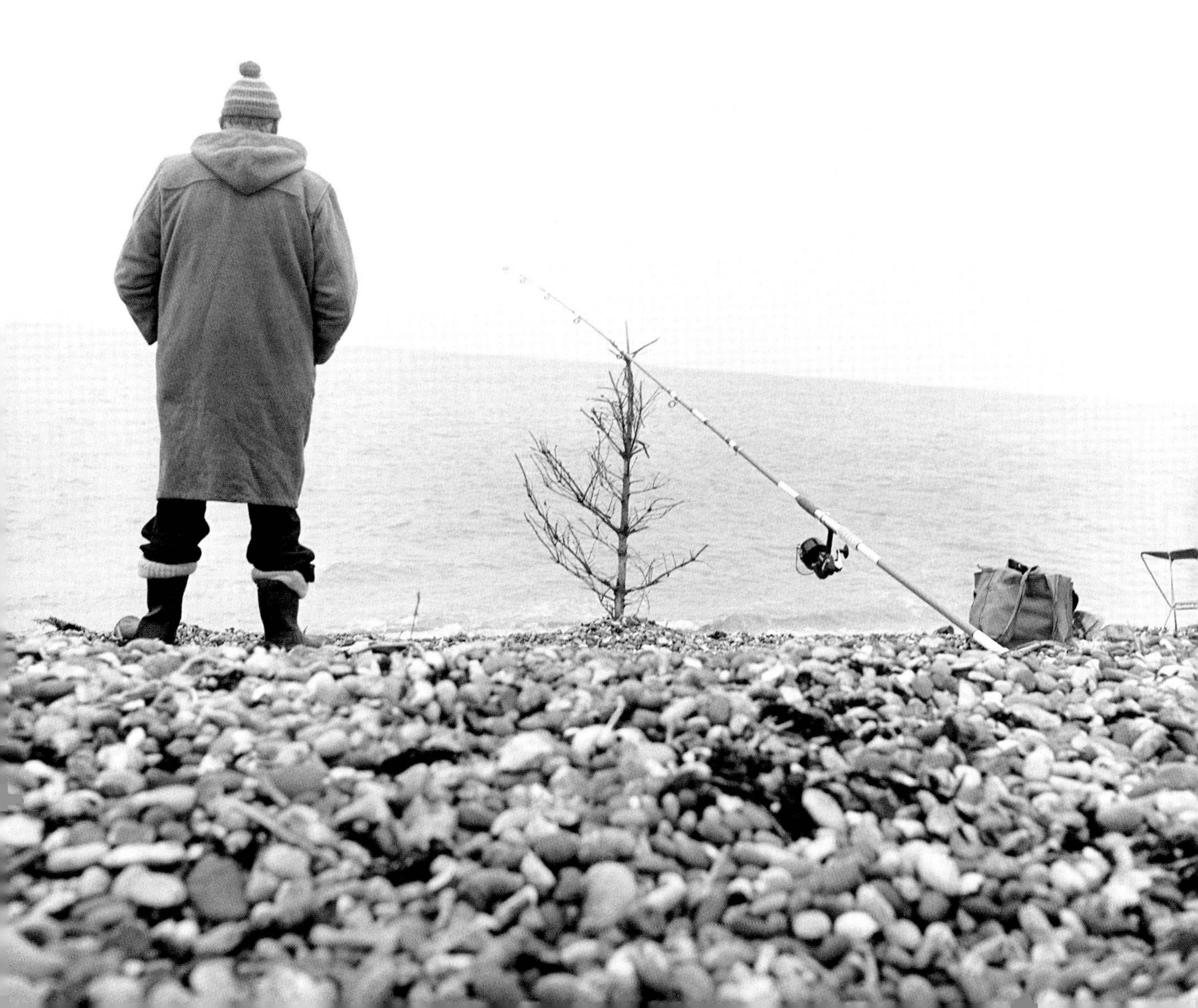

A Very Vintage Christmas, photographs 1900–1980

First edition, first printing, published 2024 by Hoxton Mini Press, London
Book design copyright © Hoxton Mini Press 2024
All rights reserved

Design and sequence by Friederike Huber
Introduction by Lucy Davies
Edited by Zoë Jellicoe
Proofreading by Florence Ward
Editorial support by Leona Crawford
Production by Richard Mason

A CIP catalogue record for this book is available from the British Library.
No part of this publication may be reproduced, stored in a retrieval system,
or transmitted in any form or by any means, electronic, mechanical,
photocopying, recording or otherwise, without the prior written permission
of the copyright owner.

ISBN: 978-1-914314-79-7

Printed and bound by Livonia Print

Hoxton Mini Press is an environmentally conscious publisher,
committed to offsetting our carbon footprint. The offset for this book was
purchased from from the printer's offsetting scheme.

Every time you order from our website, we plant a tree:
www.hoxtonminipress.com